THE ART OF

FLOURISHING

A New East-West Approach to Staying Sane and Finding Love in an Insane World

JEFFREY B. RUBIN, PHD

CROWN
ARCHETYPE
NEW YORK

Grateful acknowledgment is made to the following for permission to reprint
previously published material:
Erich Fromm Estate: Excerpts from Erich Fromm's portrait of D.T. Suzuki
from *The Eastern Buddhist* (New Series), pages 86–89, Vol. II (Kyoto: Kawakita
Printing Co., August, 1967). Reprinted by permission of the Erich Fromm Estate,
c/o Dr. Rainer Funk, Tuebingen.
Graywolf Press: Excerpt from "Once There Was Light" from "Having It Out
with Melancholy" from *Collected Poems* by Jane Kenyon, copyright © 2005 by The
Estate of Jane Kenyon. Reprinted by permission of Graywolf Press, Minneapolis,
Minnesota, www.graywolfpress.org.

Library of Congress Cataloging-in-Publication Data
Rubin, Jeffrey B.
The art of flourishing / Jeffrey B. Rubin.—1st ed.
p.   cm.
Includes bibliographical references
1. Mind and body.   2. Meditation—Therapeutic use.
3. Well-being.   4. Spiritual life.   I. Title.
BF161.R79   2010
158.1'2—dc22   2010034302

ISBN 978-0-307-71889-1
eISBN 978-0-307-71891-4

Printed in the United States of America

BOOK DESIGN BY BARBARA STURMAN
JACKET DESIGN BY JEAN TRAINA
JACKET PHOTOGRAPHY BY GYRO PHOTOGRAPHY/
AMANA IMAGES/GETTY IMAGES

2   4   6   8   10   9   7   5   3   1

First Edition

To my teachers,
Joel Kramer
George Atwood
T. K. V. Desikachar
Shinzen Young
Louis Mitsunen Nordstrom

And to my patients,
who have taught me more than they could ever know

Contents

THE ART OF

FLOURISHING

INTRODUCTION

In the spring of 2009, *The New York Times Magazine* published a story entitled "Enlightenment Therapy" about the psychoanalytic treatment of a Zen Buddhist master. The article generated great interest and controversy. Not only were psychoanalysis and Buddhism discussed together in a mainstream publication, but psychotherapy was written about from the point of view of the client—a highly esteemed Zen master—who had the courage and integrity to admit he had psychological conflicts and participated in psychotherapy, rather than adopt the mask of a spiritual teacher who had transcended emotional suffering.

The master had been abandoned and neglected in childhood, and Zen provided him with solace and insight, and more important, the only spiritual and emotional home he'd ever had. "Zen saved my life," he told Chip Brown, the author of the article. "Meditation put me back together again."

Decades of Zen training and meditation, however, never healed his core psychological wounds. In fact, Zen practice inadvertently led him to bury them, thus concealing his deepest conflicts from himself and ensuring that they would return in more destructive ways. "The Zen experience of forgetting the self was very natural to me," he said. "I had already been engaged in forgetting and abandoning the self in my childhood . . . that forgetting was pathological. I always had some deeper sense that I wasn't really there, that my life . . . didn't seem real. In therapy I began to realize this feeling of invisibility was maybe the central theme of my life."

His attempt at self-protection impeded truly caring for himself. "[W]ithout the therapy experience," claimed the Zen master, "I might have died without . . . having truly lived."

I was his therapist and what we did in those sessions was something I call *meditative psychotherapy*—a synthesis of the most powerful elements of Eastern and Western wisdom that I have developed over thirty years of professional practice and personal exploration. By combining meditation and yogic breathing to quiet and focus the mind with psychotherapy to illuminate the meaning of what arises during one's spiritual practice, the Zen master was able to reclaim his life and even to flourish. Meditative therapy also dramatically confirmed what I had realized through years of intense study and practice in Ivy League colleges and Buddhist monasteries: integrating the best aspects of therapy and meditation is profoundly more effective than practicing either alone.

Meditative therapy is central to the art of flourishing—engaging our life wholeheartedly and thriving; living well and completely; leading a meaningful and rewarding life. Flourishing—the most fulfilling way to live—is not a new topic. It was of central concern to Aristotle and ancient Greek ethical philosophers. In his *Nicomachean Ethics,* Aristotle defined flourishing as "living well and faring well."

Does flourishing come from outside of us? From "having it all," removing external constraints, and feeling good or happy? Or does it reside solely within—when we maximize our potential to achieve inner peace?

Neither.

Flourishing takes us in a new direction—toward a focus on internal emotional awareness, insight, and transformation, and on better relationships. We realize the best within ourselves and enrich the lives of those people we are close to. Because flourishing focuses both on changing ourselves *and* on getting along better with other people, it is richer than either endeavor by itself.

While flourishing may seem difficult to attain, it is eminently within our reach, once we understand what it is and how to achieve it.

We flourish when we cultivate clarity and equanimity in the face of the speed and confusion that surround us; when we access the untapped creativity within and appreciate beauty inside and out. Flourishing involves imaginatively addressing the challenges that confront us and discovering our passions and purposes.

Flourishing doesn't always feel good. Sometimes we must confront painful options or make difficult choices. On occasion, flourishing is just doing the best we can given imperfect and even undesirable circumstances such as familial, financial, or professional strains, illness, or the infirmities of aging.

We flourish when we take great care of ourselves, connect with spirituality, widen our moral imaginations, cultivate ethical accountability, and live authentically.

Once we have expanded our capacity to flourish we can create greater intimacy with those we care about and have infinitely healthier interactions and stronger bonds with partners, family, and friends. Flourishing is the most important goal we'll ever pursue.

My path to creating meditative therapy—my route to exploring flourishing—began in an unlikely place: the basketball court. Basketball was my first love. I played with passionate intensity. And it rewarded me by giving me the tools to understand the difference between mere happiness and thriving.

During my senior year of high school, my basketball team, the Woodmere Long Island Wolverines, was playing against The Fieldston School, a team we were favored to beat. In order to remain in contention for the league title, we *had* to win. And winning was next to godliness in my adolescent mind. It was a hotly contested, heart-throbbing, roller-coaster battle. When we scored with ten seconds left in the game, our one-point lead appeared to be invincible. But with six seconds to go, the other team scored. We were down by one.

Suddenly, a great calm descended upon me and I called time out. Five seconds remained on the clock. My teammates' faces showed panic as we huddled close together. I could see that they had given up. In their minds the game was over. I pushed through to my coach, Mr. Kastan, and put my hand on his shoulder. "Tell them not to panic and get me the ball."

We positioned ourselves underneath our own basket, ninety-four feet from our ultimate goal. A teammate rolled the ball to me near midcourt—the clock wouldn't start until I touched the ball.

There must have been noise, but when I dribbled up the left side of the court, the gym was as still as an empty cathedral. I didn't hear the crowd, the squeaking of sneakers, or the thumping of the basketball. I was in a cocoon of concentration—alert, focused, undistracted. My mind was Grand Canyon quiet. And clear like the open sky.

Time seemed to slow down and elongate. I floated up court with no sense of exertion. I felt no pressure, no fear. The hope of victory, the dread of losing, did not exist.

As I approached the top of the key, my defender picked me up. I sensed it was time to shoot. I squared my shoulders to the basket, bent my knees, and jumped into the air. My opponent leapt toward me. I scanned the basket like an archer measuring the target, and shot the ball. My defender's arms enveloped me and blocked my vision. I couldn't see the rim. My left arm was extended, right through my fingertips, straight and true. My left palm waved to the rim and then faced downward.

As my feet returned to the wooden gym floor, there was silence. I looked at the basket and saw the net rising skyward, the way it does when a high-arching shot drops cleanly through the hoop. I looked at the scoreboard. We had won. A teammate later told me my left hand punched the air downward as if I had beaten death. A deafening roar broke my spell as our fans mobbed the court.

The locker room was noisy—players, coaches, and parents shouted and pounded me on the back—but I was strangely still. I wasn't numb, and I wasn't indifferent to winning, but I was unemotional about our comeback because victory paled compared to what I had just experienced.

I stood alone, completely motionless in the locker room after my teammates had showered and dressed, and replayed my epiphany: the heightened attention, concentration, and clarity; the way time seemed to expand; the absence of thought, pressure, and fear; the ecstasy and serenity more joyous than victory. Before the last five seconds of that game, I would have called my childhood—which was devoid of religious training or spiritual experiences—nonreligious, but with that basket I had entered a realm I can only describe as sacred. While my teammates were celebrating our narrow victory, I was preoccupied with the tantalizing glimpse I'd had of another way of being: open to the moment without a sense of time; unself-conscious but acutely aware; performing under duress yet without worry.

This experience changed my life. After that game, something in me (call it Western male conditioning) died; something else was born.

The vicelike grip of ambition and competition—the divinities I had worshiped—was loosened. Now I saw them as false idols. Winning still felt better than losing, but the joy of just playing the game became as important as which team won. Although I couldn't articulate it until years later, this experience taught me that when I completely engaged the present—wholeheartedly immersed in what I was doing, without either anticipating the future or replaying the past—I could live more freely and fully than I ever imagined.

Seven years after that game-winning basket, I represented my class as the commencement speaker at the Columbia University School of Social Work, where I accepted my master's degree. My classmates probably expected a rousing pep talk designed to give them a running start on the working world. Still influenced by my epiphany on the basketball court, along with an intuition that a big bank account by itself wouldn't make us happy, I delivered a different message. "We will eventually retire from work," I said. "But while we're alive we will never retire from living. *The art of living well is the most important job we will ever have.*"

These remarks were an opening salvo, intuited, unseasoned by experience. I hadn't yet fallen in love or raised a child, and the only person close to me who had died was my beloved grandfather. But I had glimpsed a truth I could no longer ignore. And everything else—from having a career to fame and fortune—seemed less urgent.

After graduation I voraciously read the classics of Eastern and Western psychology and spirituality. Buddha and Freud, Lao Tzu and Krishnamurti guided my quest to answer those questions many young adults ask about who they are and their place in the universe.

As a consequence, I pursued a PhD in psychology and wrote a dissertation on psychoanalysis and Buddhism, studied psychoanalysis, attended meditation retreats and yoga workshops, and engaged in an intensive daily practice of meditation and yoga. At first, the principles and methods of psychoanalysis, Buddhism, and yoga seemed to be incompatible; they presented conflicting philosophies about what it meant to be a healthy and sane person. Psychoanalysis emphasized the development and cultivation of strong and cohesive individuals, Buddhism stressed seeing through the illusoriness—and the dangers—of our normal, taken-for-granted sense of ourselves as masterful, independent, and self-sufficient. I recognized that each tradition had valuable insights and crucial blind spots and could be made richer by being integrated.

Then a funny thing happened in my cross-cultural quest for how to flourish: I learned different yet complementary lessons from each discipline. Therapy, combined with meditation and yoga, helped me to relate to my clients, the universe, and myself in a fundamentally richer way.

The mind has a mind of its own. We can no more control our thoughts, feelings, and fantasies than we can control the weather. Even when we think we are seeing clearly, we are often observing our experience through a distorted lens. Meditation, the training of moment-to-moment attention, is a kind of microscope through which I could study my hidden conditioning. It slowed me down and opened me up. Meditation made me a better listener, which greatly enriched my therapeutic work.

I began to glimpse the motivations underlying my behavior. Through meditation practice, I was gradually able to open up a space between how I was conditioned to react and how I responded. Someone could behave provocatively, and I could feel his hostility without having to reply in kind. If I was angry or irritated, I became more able to identify hidden emotional hurt or deprivation. I felt more compassion for other people as I realized we were all imperfect creatures, striving to do the best we could. I also felt freer to respond creatively and spontaneously to the challenges I confronted.

The influence of yoga, the ancient Indian system of movement and breathing, ethics and meditation, was also profound. Before studying with my first teacher—Joel Kramer, an influential figure in the development of yoga in America—I thought yoga meant acquiring flexibility and performing physical postures (*asanas*) with agility and ease. I didn't realize that the heart of yoga was the *quality of awareness* we bring to doing the postures and living our lives.

The connection between breath, body, and mind is another aspect of yoga that is crucial to human flourishing, and too often neglected in our physically oriented American yoga. Yoga teaches that breath is the gateway between mind and body. An agitated mind leads to an agitated breath and a calm mind results in a calm breath, which brings about a radical possibility: if we change our breath we can change our state of mind. And if we can change our minds we can change our lives.

There are many moments each day when, although we are awake, we are not present. We are asleep to ourselves and to other people. We are eating the meal, but not tasting the food. We are listening to the music, but not hearing it. Yoga aided me in tuning into emotional and physical feedback and challenging self-imposed limits. Because of yoga, I gained the ability to be present and became more capable of experiencing whatever I was doing in a deeper way. Yoga, like meditation, showed me how greater intimacy—with myself as well as with others—is possible when we are more wholeheartedly engaged.

Psychoanalysis complemented my studies of meditation and yoga, and revealed buried aspects of myself—including self-protective strategies that can be self-sabotaging—that the Asian wisdom traditions seemed to miss. In our highly medicalized and quick-fix-oriented age, the word *psychoanalysis* often conjures up a range of negative associations that not only misrepresent it but neglect its inherent transformative potential. As a result, psychoanalysis is all too often maligned and viewed as a relic of another century. But psychoanalysis is one of the premier and unsung sources of wisdom in Western culture; it is a process by which terror and trauma, depression and despair can be explored with compassion and insight. Psychoanalysis provides the tools to reach the roots of what troubles us and to find constructive resolutions. In therapy clients can discover the strength and courage to face life's ordeals and sorrows, tap into the best within themselves, and access their highest values.

From my readings of the great theorists in psychoanalysis—from Freud and Jung to Winnicott and Kohut—I learned about the seemingly inexhaustible human capacity for self-deception and the elaborate strategies we all use to protect ourselves—what analysts call *resistance* and *defensive processes*. This knowledge enriched my ability to understand and resolve obstacles in my meditation and my life.

The practice of psychoanalysis at its best is not just an exploration of illness that reveals how human beings sabotage themselves and go astray; it is a testament to the incomparable power of human empathy. Participating in my own therapy, as well as practicing psychoanalysis, expanded my empathy, which allowed me to hear the depth of people's pain, thus giving me the tools to help them heal profound emotional wounds.

I charted a course using three compass points—psychoanalysis, meditation, and yoga—and began teaching psychoanalysis and Buddhism in colleges, psychoanalytic institutes, and meditation centers. I taught Buddhist meditation to yoga teachers and therapists; I taught the principles of psychoanalysis to students of yoga and Buddhism. Teaching not only broadened my integration of Eastern and Western theories and traditions, it illuminated blind spots in Eastern thought—especially the way meditation neglects *meaning*, which is why many meditators— students and teachers alike—often stay stuck in certain forms of conditioning for decades (not always treating themselves with the reverence they deserve, and sometimes fearing intimacy). This flaw in meditation is usually neglected; and easily remedied. Practicing a meditation of intimacy and engagement—a marriage of mindfulness and meaning— makes meditation infinitely more powerful than the way it is ordinarily practiced.

Teaching also helped me learn how to take Eastern practices off the cushion, out of the ashram, and into my students' lives.

Through this process I realized that no single psychotherapeutic or meditative tradition has the monopoly on truth. Each can enrich the other. Western psychology in general, and psychoanalysis in particular, sets the bar too low on human potential. The word *health* does not appear once in the twenty-four-volume Standard Edition of *The Complete Works of Freud* or the *Diagnostic Statistical Manual* that therapists use for assessing clients. Both books are maps of illness rather than of wellbeing. They also underestimate possibilities for health and happiness that are essential elements of most spiritual and meditative traditions. Although Eastern meditative disciplines value these capabilities for flourishing, they neglect the unconscious obstacles to achieving them.

Meditative therapy was the result of these explorations of Eastern and Western wisdom. When we lovingly examine the full range of human experience—which therapy and meditation and yoga by themselves often neglect—we access our untapped potential for self-healing.

Emotional wounds, thorny patterns in relationships, and destructive tendencies become fuel for awakening. The self-reflective relationship of therapist and client becomes the crucible for accessing and transforming old ways of relating to other people and treating oneself. Meditative psychotherapy not only reveals the ways we have drastically underestimated our potential, it provides concrete and accessible strategies for realizing our best selves, something that is vital in times of collective and personal crisis and malaise.

We are in an era of profound upheaval. Unprecedented economic uncertainty, a plague of amorality, and cultural earthquakes have left increasing numbers of people unsettled and adrift without meaning or direction.

Although no one courts misfortune, collective and personal crisis always affords opportunities for profound transformation. Calamity threatens the status quo and is often stressful and exhausting, but it is also the ripest time for change—potentially leading one to breaking through. When the existing coping strategies of either a person or an organization are not working they are more amenable to change. Efforts to reform the health-care system, for example, would not have been possible without its massive malfunctioning. Without suffering the loss of a parent, wrenching though it may be, many adults wouldn't take their rightful place in the world.

The first step in discovering the opportunities hidden beneath the turmoil, so we can use calamity constructively, is to name and confront what afflicts us.

Many of us, whatever our political or religious affiliations, sense that something is amiss in the world. We have difficulty putting it into words even though we experience it every day. It still eludes our grasp and troubles us; we feel powerless to remedy it.

Pundits highlight the economic depression, the threat of terrorism, and the destruction of the environment to name just three. So just imagine if, over the next few years, through wise leadership, discipline, and hard work, we were able to recover economically, mutually coexist with our antagonists, and reverse global warming.

Would we truly be happy?

Would we honestly feel that America was as healthy as it could be?

Would we flourish?

The answer, I suspect, is no.

The thousands of people I've worked with in therapy sessions and workshops over the past several decades tell a different tale than the pundits about what challenges us, and what helps us flourish. They describe having infinitely more choices than they used to have, yet feel increasingly powerless; and even when they have greater affluence, they still experience heightened spiritual impoverishment.

As I have reflected on what I heard, I realized that many of us struggle with shared challenges:

- **BOMBARDMENT OF INFORMATION.** We have trouble discovering and nurturing the best in ourselves while living at a merciless pace and drowning in an addictive stream of information, much of it trivial. This frenzied existence clutters our mind, exhausts us, and clouds our vision, making it impossible to think clearly and respond creatively.
- **CULTURAL POLLUTION.** We are inundated with unprecedented amounts of vulgarity and sleaze in media, entertainment, and politics, which often cause us to withdraw into private islands of solace and plea-sure or lower our standards for acceptable action. We are diminished when we focus on (or try to avoid) depravity instead of celebrating human possibility.
- **FEAR.** In the last decade we have faced numerous natural and man-made disasters and upheavals—pandemics and tsunamis, terrorism and economic uncertainty. When we're frightened and doubt our-selves, we look to authority figures—especially politicians and reli-gious leaders—to save us and tell us how to live, but this infantilizes us and undermines our self-trust. And when these authorities prove to be unreliable we feel cheated and even more vulnerable.
- **DEMORALIZATION.** In our world, the pursuit of personal gain often trumps principles and compassion. Every sector of modern life—from politics to professional sports—is a moral free-for-all in which getting what we want supersedes legal constraints and respect for each other. There is a nasty ethic afoot: *If I can get away with it, it's legal; and if you get exploited by me, then you are a chump who deserved it.* This epidemic of immorality disgusts, dispirits, and depresses many

of us—causing us to disengage from the world and attempt to protect ourselves.

- **ALIENATION**. When people are disillusioned, demoralized, and depleted they need one another. But working more hours just to stay afloat (or jobless and terrified about supporting our families) and overscheduled, we have less time for each other. Technology has been a mixed blessing—giving us unprecedented opportunities for bringing us closer—and simultaneously pushing us apart. Computers, cellphones, and iPods send more and more adults and kids into their own insular worlds. We can communicate with each other instantly, but all too often indirect, virtual experiences replace face-to-face, connected ones. Communication lacks nuance, and often, even humanity.

- **SPIRITUAL ANOREXIA**. Our response to the collapse of inner space, cultural pollution, fear, demoralization, and alienation perpetuates our unhappiness and makes us feel worse. We take lousy care of ourselves—engaging in cotton candy activities that seem appealing but leave us hungry for meaning, purpose, and intimacy. Anesthetizing ourselves through compulsive consumption, mindless media, and substance abuse leaves us devoid of vital spiritual nutrients and unequipped to handle what challenges us. (Of course, *I* never frittered away time surfing the Net or watching a *Law & Order* rerun.) When we deprive ourselves of spiritual nourishment we become spiritual anorectics who are starving and shrinking as we undermine our capacities to cope with the challenges we confront.

Part of what makes these struggles so pernicious is that their effects are difficult to measure. They have become fixtures in our existence that we take for granted and have yet to calculate their consequences. We tend to say, "That's just the way things are." What's harmful is believed to be normal and natural. And then one day we wake up and realize the trains that are our daily lives switched tracks a while ago and we don't like where we are headed.

Society's solutions to these challenges amount to putting out a collection of pots and pails to catch the water from a leaky roof with shoddily repaired holes; they don't stop the damage or fix the roof. And as everyone knows, patchwork jobs eventually fail, damages reoccur, and we pay more in the long run.

"I hope you are going to give them some hope," my mother said to me before I spoke on the art of flourishing at the Longboat Key Educational Center in Florida a few years ago.

"Things are worse than we believe," I told her, "and there's more hope than we know."

In this book I'll show you how to access hope by using some of the principles of meditative therapy so you can flourish.

In my three decades as a psychotherapist and a student and teacher of Eastern meditative practices, I have helped people access their most profound potential and witnessed extraordinary acts of wisdom and courage, compassion and moral bravery. These experiences have taught me how to cultivate twelve qualities that can help everyone flourish:

1. **EXPAND INNER SPACE** to access untapped creativity and increase the ability to see with fresh eyes and respond in ingenious ways.
2. **CULTIVATE CLARITY** so we can experience our feelings and determine our needs.
3. **DEEPEN EQUANIMITY** so we can respond to the challenges that we face.
4. **APPRECIATE BEAUTY**, and in so doing, truly cherish the world in its infinite splendor.
5. **LEARN TO READ FEEDBACK** so we can continually grow and evolve.
6. **CREATE HARMONY** between our mind and body and achieve peak health.
7. **COMPOST FEAR TO DEVELOP COURAGE**, enhance self-trust, and foster self-reliance.
8. **CULTIVATE INTEGRITY AND MORAL ACCOUNTABILITY** so we can embody our ethics and enrich our relationships.
9. **DISCOVER OUR PASSIONS** and find direction and purpose.
10. **PRACTICE GENUINE SELF-CARE** by learning what our authentic needs are.
11. **CONNECT WITH OUR SPIRITUAL SELVES** to grow in compassion and wisdom and feel greater meaning and hope.
12. **NOURISH OUR CAPACITY FOR INTIMACY** and enrich our closest

relationships, which validates our perceptions, deepens self-trust, and supports making the world a better place.

The *Art of Flourishing* is divided into two sections: "Planting the Seeds of Self-Care" and "Cultivating the Garden of Love." Self-care is the foundation of intimacy, and intimacy is the final stage and culmination of self-care. In the first half of the book, we'll explore how to cultivate many of the capacities and skills that comprise the foundation of wonderful intimacy. In the second part of the book, we'll discover how to build on genuine self-care and create that intimacy.

While I shall be writing about romantic relationships in Part II of this book, the advice and techniques can be applied to all relationships including friendships. And if you are single, and wish you weren't, don't lose heart. Improving your capacity to flourish will enhance your ability to create a healthy relationship.

It would give me great joy if the view of flourishing I present not only offers realistic hope in challenging times, but opens your mind, touches your heart, and enriches your life.

PART

I

Planting the Seeds of Self-Care

1

What lies behind us and what lies before us are tiny
matters compared to what lies within us.

—RALPH WALDO EMERSON

EXPANDING INNER SPACE

When you are having a really hard day, it's nearly impossible to think about flourishing. Take my recent Monday of many trials. It was nine o'clock at night and I had been bombarded by emails, phone calls, and text messages since I had arrived at my office twelve hours earlier and first checked my answering machine and BlackBerry. I felt both drained and edgy. There was a message from a lawyer informing me that he needed a report and letter about a patient of mine "yesterday." As I listened to this message, the phone rang—it was a man whose father was headed toward jail for embezzlement. He asked if I could see him at lunchtime, so I had to fit in lunch between sessions. During my hasty lunch a teenager's mother called asking if I could possibly see her daughter immediately because she intentionally cut herself in school after an actress she idolized was hospitalized for similar behavior. Later, after I packed up to leave work, the phone rang and a patient told me she had just discovered that her husband was having a cybersex affair and wanted to know if I could see them first thing in the morning.

As I left my office, my mind raced and was so cluttered that I had no perspective. I felt overwhelmed and disoriented, unable to get any traction. I had so much to do and think about that I had no idea where to begin.

On the way home, I was impatient with everything: the slow elevator, the friendly and sports-loving doorman who wanted to chat about the misfortunes of the New York Knicks, and the heavy rain that meant I would probably not get a cab. Having forgotten an umbrella, I was soaked by the time I reached the subway. I got off at Grand Central Station, wet and chilled, and had to run for my train. It was packed, maybe a couple of cars too short for the late commuter crowd.

I finally found a seat between a large man who spread his legs into my space without hesitation or any apparent consciousness that I was next to him, and a young woman listening to an iPod. I squeezed into the middle seat, apologizing for my dampness. There was tinny music coming from the woman's ear buds. I wondered if it would eventually make her deaf, since *I* could hear it, loud and clear. I carefully reached into my briefcase, which was between my feet, and rooted around for a journal, which contained an article I wanted to read for a class I was teaching the next day. As I started to flip through the pages, the train emerged from the underground tunnel into the rainy night. The man next to me pulled out his cellphone, punched in a number, and began a very loud conversation about how he was excited about the possibility of making a killing buying foreclosed homes. I tapped him on the shoulder and asked if he could lower his voice a bit. I was surprised by the hostility in the look he gave me. He raised his voice.

I had fantasies of yanking the guy's phone out of his hands and breaking it. I resisted the impulse. Desperate, I closed my eyes and mouth and began breathing through my nose. I tried to breathe slowly and quietly. After I realized that I had lost track of how many breaths I took, I breathed twelve more times. The desire to crush the cellphone still had not disappeared. I shifted focus and concentrated on the sounds of rap music and loud, obnoxious conversation. At first I heard them more clearly and became more agitated. I continued to focus on noise around me. Eventually the irritation faded and all I heard were sounds that no longer disturbed me. By the time we pulled into my station, an hour later, I felt very different—renewed and centered, ready to begin my evening. I slowly walked up the steps from the train platform, and my head was clear for the first time in hours. I was not thinking about all I had to do. I was thinking that I was happy to be home; I was at peace. In this relaxed state of mind, I was able to get perspective on what was pressuring me during the workday. And I was able to stop lugging the enormous weight of too much to do. Yogic breathing and Buddhist meditation, two of the foundations of *meditative therapy,* helped me let go of the stress of the day and center me for the rest of the evening. And I was also able to live my life again on my own terms, without getting sidetracked by the demands and snares of the world.

What I had created on my train ride was *inner space*. It is the part of us that is independent from our surroundings and not affected by external noises, intrusions, and pressures. It's not a physical place, but the capacity we all have to sit with and reflect on thoughts and feelings at our own pace. It's what you are exercising as you are reading this. And in this personal quiet zone, we can examine and empathize with different points of view, access creativity, and play with new ways of doing things.

Have you ever been gripped by a problem whose answer not only eluded you but disturbed you, consumed you, kept you awake?

The more you tried to solve it, the more the solution slipped out of reach.

Then, all of a sudden, seemingly out of nowhere, while your mind was taking a rest from the problem—as you were walking, showering, working out—you saw the answer clearly.

Where did clarification come from?

From within you, when there was inner space.

There is a creative source within each of us that is more accessible and powerful than we ordinarily realize.

Humans have a remarkable, and often relatively untapped, capacity for inventiveness, which is indispensable for coping with the unanticipated problems of our frenzied and rapidly changing lives. Since the world of the future will demand talents and abilities that we might not have yet developed, those individuals and societies that nurture imagination and ingenious solutions to nagging problems—such as global warming, fossil fuel depletion, and terrorism—are more likely to survive and flourish than those that don't. Many of us feel pressure to devise novel solutions to vexing personal and social problems, and need to reach more deeply within ourselves for answers. We can do an infinitely better job if we have an inner space to go to.

Social scientists in recent years have recognized that there are many types of creative activity—from solving a previously complex problem (like the structure of DNA) to developing a seminal way of organizing people (like a kibbutz) to fashioning an original work of art.

Skill in one area does not always translate into another. A visionary leader might be lousy at math and an artist hasn't necessarily mastered interpersonal communication. While there are a variety of relatively independent creative endeavors—as Howard Gardner suggests in *Five Minds for the Future*—in my view creators all share one characteristic: the ability to expand and maintain inner space.

Inner space is the place within each of us that can't be touched by anyone else and is ours alone. It's the birthplace of empathy, intuition, and innovation. When we are in it we are clearheaded and centered, with room to think, imagine, and dream.

Nurturing inner space increases productivity. Not only do we have greater freedom from external impingements, we have heightened capacity to be creative and compassionate.

When we access inner space, we have an enhanced ability to notice ideas "out of the blue" and achieve greater insights, and that enables us to trust ourselves and increases our ability to take wise risks.

Inner space is essential to healthy mental functioning.

You can be in a place where you have no privacy—even in a hospital or a prison—and access inner space. Or you can live in a secluded cabin yet have no inner space. We can experience inner space on a meditation cushion or a yoga mat, while chopping vegetables, at work or stuck in a traffic jam. Anywhere.

There are many ways of reaching this place. Meditation and yogic breathing, reading and music are my favorites, but you can get there by walking in nature or writing in a journal, cooking or running. I con-sider inner space one of the most important human capacities, and a cornerstone of a sane and psychologically healthy life.

The more we understand what erodes inner space, the easier it is to expand it.

The Assault on Inner Space

The primary challenge is that our inner space is under attack. The pace of modern life is so frenetic that we're lucky to get two free moments in a row, and email and texting, Facebook and Twitter offer further distractions. There are dramatic changes in our society because of instant connectivity with each other and the world that alter how our lives are structured and what we expect from them. Plus, we don't always realize how harmful these transformations are to us.

The digital revolution and new technologies have miraculously narrowed the universe and made the faraway immediately available, linking us to an ever-expanding network of people, places, and products. In addition, they have exponentially increased productivity. Unfortunately, these advances have resulted in consequences we have yet to fully calculate. We are forced to be like hypervigilant off-duty cops—always alert to potential threats in the form of incoming messages received on any number of devices. We are overwhelmed, distracted, and depleted. The inhuman demands on our time and attention impair memory and sleep and leave us feeling exhausted and deprived; consequently we function at subpar levels and our deepest potentials remain dormant.

From the moment the alarm shocks us out of sleep, to the time we fall asleep lulled by the chatter of late-night television, we are bombarded with more information than we could possibly process. Our inner space is under constant attack. We often feel as if we are drowning in demands on our attention. We are flooded, yet we blame ourselves if all we can do is tread water instead of somehow effortlessly handle the immensely deeper challenges.

CULTURAL POLLUTION

When the surrounding culture—radio shock jocks and sleazy political campaigns, salacious TV programs and misogynist song lyrics—pollutes our minds with unprecedented images of crassness and debasement, that's an assault on inner space.

The alluring array of diversions that are available around the clock—from instant messaging, Facebook, Twitter, online pornography, and gambling, to blogs and video games—are *weapons of mass distraction.*

We are being polluted every day. And it's not just our air and water. It's the trivial, vulgar, and degrading news scandals and unseemly behavior of politicians, entertainers, athletes, and even religious leaders that pervades the media and the Internet and trumps serious news.

We are being exposed to unprecedented images of crassness and debasement. I call this epidemic of decadence and sleaze *cultural pollution.*

Too many people seem indifferent to the cost of cultural pollution because they are either titillated by it, accept that it is the price we have to pay to be more prosperous, or are profiting from it. But littering the airwaves and the billboards with lurid communications and crude distractions ultimately causes us to shut down and withdraw from life in order to protect ourselves. Several students in a graduate course I taught at Union Theological Seminary told me that they don't watch TV or the news because they don't want to grow inured to the vulgarity passing as current events. While this can be a way of checking out—which I am not recommending—sometimes it's the only way to avoid cultural pollution.

THE EXPECTATION OF IMMEDIATE GRATIFICATION

The movies-on-demand function on my TV was malfunctioning. I had to wait longer than usual. I began to get disproportionately impatient and irritated. What exactly had happened? I'm a long-term meditator who values equanimity, but I was upset because I couldn't watch a movie at the exact moment I wanted to—I had developed the habit of wanting instant results.

Our expectation of immediate gratification threatens inner space. Technological advancements bring instantaneous communication into every aspect of our lives from shopping to connecting with loved ones, altering our consciousness and ratcheting up our expectations. Most of us demand our wishes be granted *now*.

A patient told me that he felt homesick in his first weeks of college forty years ago. He was so upset that he wrote home three times a day, by hand, on paper. He anticipated a response from his parents, via "snail mail," within a week. He handled his pain by talking with his roommates, sitting with his feelings, and trying to keep busy so he wouldn't be excruciatingly lonely.

Today a lonely freshman would immediately text message or email his parents or close friends or post on Facebook until contact was made and his pain was instantly relieved.

The technological advances that make this possible seem, at first glance, like a godsend. If my homesick patient were a college student today, he would have received a reply in hours, if not minutes—rather than waiting days for a response.

But there are hidden costs to this nearly instantaneous communication. It radically alters our consciousness and our expectations.

Nowadays, when someone desires something, he or she says, "I *need* it." Years ago people tended to say, "I *want* it." When technology can deliver what we desire the moment we want it, and wishes become entitlements, we are trained in the expectation of immediate gratification. This not only lessens our tolerance of frustration, it actually teaches us to be impatient. We have instant pacifiers to shut off what we are feeling, but gain no self-knowledge or new skills. Our culture weakens our capacity to handle frustration.

My homesick client gained crucial capacities, such as learning how to comfort himself and relieve his distress without the benefit of contemporary technology. He had to handle his feelings, sit with them, and soothe himself. None of that damaged him. Far from it. It taught him that he could survive bad patches by himself. The next time he was in an emotionally demanding situation it wasn't as scary because he had better tools to handle adversity.

The instantaneous communication we now take for granted would have prevented him from developing these kinds of healthy coping skills.

THE INVASION OF PUBLIC PLACES

While public waiting rooms, lobbies, and trains were never calm oases (remember boom boxes?), they seem noisier than ever before, which makes it even more difficult to recover from the impingements in other aspects of our lives. When we are sitting in an airport or in the waiting room of our doctor's office, hoping to relax, and we are rudely interrupted by the blaring of a television, we try to ignore it, but the volume overwhelms our capacity to focus or tune it out, so it feels impossible to react peacefully or wisely. As we seethe, we are further assaulted by cellphone conversations, often only a foot or two away.

It's no wonder that so many people complain of feeling overwhelmed, exhausted, and foggy. The barrage of noise and stimulation that threatens to drown us is constantly undermining our capacity to recover.

We know we are being assaulted—it's the troubling reality we struggle with every day. What we don't fully appreciate is its impact or how to respond.

The ability to concentrate, to keep focused on what we are doing, is one of life's most important skills. The wise employment of attention—when we are completely absorbed, engrossed, and wholeheartedly engaged—is indispensable to human flourishing. When we are aware of our genuine needs and our goals and dreams, we can pursue a life of meaning and purpose with passion and discipline. When we are constantly distracted, we are lost—unable to focus on what we cherish—so it becomes easy to remain scattered and lose our way.

The frenzied pace of life, the sensory overload, the cultural pollution, the expectation of immediate gratification, and the invasion of public spaces distracts us and impairs and atrophies clarity of perception, attention span, and short-term memory.

This growing distractibility—and the other assaults on inner space—cloud our judgment, impair sleep, and undermine mental and physical health. We then strive to anesthetize ourselves and escape these impingements, making us more insular and disconnected from more crucial concerns—like how we might flourish.

We are so accustomed to drowning in information, operating at a destructive pace, expecting instantaneous fulfillment, and having inner space crushed that we no longer believe anything saner is possible.

Albert Brock, the protagonist of Ray Bradbury's 1953 short story "The Murderer," became increasingly sick of the noise and distractions of technology. He destroyed his radio, phone, TV, and the interoffice communication system.

Imagine Albert Brock today trying to destroy his links to the vast communication networks we take for granted. From the perspective of nearly everyone who lives a wired life, Albert Brock might be viewed as crazy, but "The Murderer" raises the questions: Are we the prisoners of technology? Are we being murdered by it?

If you think this is exaggerated, imagine you have a close friend or family member who regularly turns off his or her cellphone, only answers email at certain designated times of the day, and only sends text messages in an emergency. You might wonder if there was something wrong with the person, when in reality, perhaps the expectation of instant communication is what's really harmful.

We obviously can't turn back the clock and live in a pretechnological world, and we would not want to. But unless we combat the collapse of inner space we will all become more overwhelmed and disoriented and less creative.

Peace Begins Inside

There are two ways to expand inner space: protect it and enlarge it.

MINDFULNESS OF WHAT WE INGEST

We are what we consume. This includes data and stimulation; the influences of people, food, water, and air; and an excess of information and demands on our time—all of which can harm us.

A talented artist who is disturbed by the state of the world complains about sleeping poorly and feeling foggy and disoriented when she awakes. She compulsively listens to late-night talk radio before she tries to go to bed in order to inform herself about, and "arm" herself against, the problems in the world. She does this even though it agitates her. "Knowledge feels like it helps me protect myself," she says. As she begins to realize that her "armor" is keeping her up half the night, she turns off provocative programs before trying to fall asleep and listens to soothing classical music instead. Her sleep improves and she awakes rested and eager to greet the day.

The yogic tradition counsels selectivity in what we ingest. *Pratyahara*, restraint of the senses, is one of the eight limbs of the yogic path. The senses usually exert a magnetic grip over us. They cause us to become like puppets on a string, pulled to and fro by our desires and aversions. We habitually gravitate toward pleasant sights, sounds, tastes, smells, and we avoid unpleasant ones. The process of desire and aversion is usually mechanical and instantaneous. The goal of *pratyahara* is to use our senses wisely and selectively, which involves careful consideration of what we expose ourselves to. This allows us to remain focused on what we are doing, freeing our minds from the involuntary intrusions and enslavement caused by our highly conditioned reactions to sensory activity.

Instead of always searching for Wi-Fi and complaining about slow connectivity, some people feel held hostage by the myriad distractions of a wired world. In "Stop the Internet, I want to get off!" Rebecca Traister, a staff writer for Salon.com, wrote about installing "Freedom," a program that disables online access on a Mac computer for one minute to eight hours, so she was protected against her own impulses to check emails, professional list serves, blogs, word games, and fantasy vacations.

We each have to find our own ways to protect ourselves from being held hostage by technology. I usually turn my cellphone off when spending time with friends and family, or when I am reading, meditating, writing, exercising, or doing yoga.

A friend of mine turns her cellphone off when she is with her husband and her daughter, saying, "The most important people are here with me. Everyone else can wait."

In the organizational expert Julie Morgenstern's book, *Never Check E-Mail in the Morning,* she recommends several strategies for handling the onslaught of email, including not checking it for the first hour of the day, only looking at it during designated times (rather than indiscriminately), and creating standard responses to routine requests.

LISTEN TO THE RUMBLE STRIP

My paternal grandmother lived until she was ninety-four. I think one of her secrets was that she listened to her body and responded accordingly. Whenever she began feeling slightly "under the weather," for example, she went to sleep earlier and often prevented incipient illness. Humans have a remarkable capacity to pay attention to and read feedback. We have our own version of rumble strips, those safety features on the shoulders of many highways that alert sleepy drivers to potential danger by causing a loud vibration when their cars veer off the road. Our personal rumble strips are sometimes subtle, but often loud and clear. Emotional resentment in a relationship often indicates that we feel deprived and are being self-neglectful. Feeling impatient and irritable may signal that we are overburdened and need to set better boundaries and lessen our emotional load. Jealousy often informs us about what we want more of. Eating when we are full or shopping when money is tight may signal that we feel emotionally deprived.

When we feel cranky and overwhelmed it may be feedback about the harmful impact of what we are exposing ourselves to. We need to set limits to protect ourselves. Turn off the radio in your car on your way home from work. Let your mind soak in the quiet and the scenery so that you can rest and recover from the grueling day.

When we dread answering the phone it may signal that we need to turn the sound off and let our voice mail pick up calls because we are either engrossed in a meaningful activity that nourishes us or too depleted to talk. In either case, pay attention to your need and do not let outside forces interfere with self-care.

Parents can also set limits with their children, thereby protecting inner space. "Give MySpace some space," a father said to his eleven-year-old daughter after finding her online at two in the morning. And when she returned from summer camp—a place that did not allow computers—he noticed that she was much happier and more engaged with her mother and him.

CHANGING CHANNELS

Every moment of experience, according to the classical Buddhist model of the mind, takes place in one of six areas—the five senses (seeing, hearing, tasting, touching, smelling) plus thinking. If we add *feeling*, we have seven potential kinds of experience.

The old TV sets consisted of seven stations. Imagine each of the seven kinds of experience—seeing, hearing, tasting, touching, smelling, thinking, and feeling—taking place on one of those seven channels. Changing channels is another powerful way of protecting inner space.

Imagine driving home from work stewing about an offhand remark a coworker made about your appearance. The more you think about it, the more disturbed and tired you get. Change the channel by listening to beautiful music on your iPod or car radio, or appreciating the exquisite sunset through the window.

One crucial way we can all change channels is to focus on what is uplifting, meaningful, and moves us, rather than on what titillates or depletes us. Make it a daily practice to pay attention to both kinds of experiences and their respective impact on your body and moods.

Humor is another powerful means of changing channels. Whether it is your favorite comic, or bantering with your spouse or friends, lev-ity loosens the grip of how we feel about a situation and protects inner space.

A client who struggled with self-loathing told me about a fantasy he had about saying something that would shake up the staid, boring, and uptight Sunday-evening dinners with his parents and siblings. We had spent a good deal of time exploring the sources and current impact of his self-critical attitudes. I detected his guilt and embarrassment after he shared what he imagined doing. I slowly reached for my phone while maintaining eye contact with him.

"What are you doing?" he asked nervously.

"I'm making a call," I replied.

"Who are you calling?" he asked.

"I'm reporting you to the Thought Police for your fantasy," I said.

For an instant he stared at me.

After we both burst out laughing, I knew that his inner space was less constricted. Humor loosens the grip of what we are rigidly attached to—an idea, an image of a person, or an emotional state. It gives us more breathing room; we can take a step back from the immediacy of what is looming and gain perspective on what we are seeing too narrowly.

DECLUTTERING

"In difficult times," Alice Walker said to her daughter Rebecca, your house "must suggest a sparkling future. Room must be made for your ship to come." Decluttering is another way of resisting the forces that close down inner space. Many people discover that getting rid of excess and creating more physical space immediately opens up more inner space.

When my personal space is organized and my papers are in a logical order, and I can access what I need very quickly, I feel infinitely more clearheaded than when my desk is cluttered and chaotic.

For some people, inner space is frightening. Many years ago a begin-ning student of meditation told me that she felt threatened when she got quiet and clearheaded while meditating. Her avoidance of medita-tion was designed to keep silence and clarity at bay so she would not be fearful. As we explored the underlying danger of intimacy with herself—especially the specific threats she associated with quietude and clarity—she slowly became more comfortable with inner space.

Once we have removed some of the forces that compress inner space, we need to focus on enlarging it.

EXPANDING YOUR INNER SPACE: YOGIC BREATHING

Yogic breathing and meditation are two powerful ways of cultivating clarity and equanimity, thereby expanding inner space. Conscious breathing—awareness of the quality and texture of our inhalations and exhalations—is a foundation of yoga. Normal breathing is an automatic process that we take for granted. The yogic tradition has systematically studied and mapped the breathing process. When we are agitated our breathing is constricted and irregular. When we are calm our breathing is relaxed and even. The yogic tradition offers the radical teaching that changing our breathing—especially finding ease in our breathing and lengthening our exhale—can transform how we feel and see the world.

Try this experiment: write down how you are feeling emotionally and physically.

Sit in a quiet place, turn off your cellphone, close your eyes and your mouth, and breathe through your nose. Place all of your attention on inhaling and exhaling. Breathe without straining. Begin with a long exhalation, gently pressing your abdomen toward your spine. Take twelve quiet and easeful breaths.

Now take a long exhale, gently pressing your abdomen toward your spine and try, as best as you can, to make each exhale slightly longer than each inhale without straining. Take twelve breaths.

Write down how you feel emotionally and physically.

Do you notice any difference? Do you feel any clearer or more centered? If you do, you have expanded inner space. If you don't, don't panic; perhaps another approach will be helpful.

MEDITATION

Meditation, paying careful, nonjudgmental attention to what you are experiencing, is another simple yet powerful technique that anyone can learn to do. We can practice meditation either by sitting quietly and noting, without judgment, whatever we are experiencing, or by engaging in everyday activities—such as washing the dishes or taking a bath or listening to sounds—with wholehearted attention. That is what I was trying to do on the train after my demanding day, and it helped me feel more inner spaciousness and centeredness. We can focus on any aspect of our experience—from hearing a melodious bird, to tasting what we are eating, or feeling our joy or sadness—and use this process of uniting with what we encounter to expand inner space.

Here's another experiment:

Write down how you feel emotionally and physically.

Close your eyes again. Notice any places of restfulness in your body. Feel and appreciate them. Do this for several minutes.

Again, write down how you feel emotionally and physically.

Note any changes. Whatever is troubling you may still be present, although perhaps it is less perturbing.

Cultivating equanimity—learning to accept our present reality—is another indispensable way of enlarging inner space. Meditation, like yogic breathing, is a potent tool for doing this. Later we'll explore meditation in greater detail. For now, let me describe an experience I had that illustrates the way meditation can be used to develop equanimity. I had been writing for several hours on a Saturday morning. Suddenly the quiet was invaded by the buzz of a neighbor's chainsaw, which threw off my concentration. I lost focus and momentum and had trouble returning to writing. Instead of wallowing in frustration, I decided to change channels and meditate. When I began, I was still assaulted by the whine of the saw and the shouts from the guys working. I felt irritated and annoyed by the intrusion. *Do they think they are the only people in the universe?* I realized that I could resist the noise, which would increase my frustration, or I could open to it, immerse myself in it without fighting, and become one with it. I concentrated on the sounds, rather than on the contents of the conversations. As the gap between the noise and me shrank, I heard more clearly. At first it was louder and cacophonous. Eventually there was the particular sonic intensity of the saw and the voices, without any judgment attached to it. My meditation deepened and the noise no longer bothered me at all. After about ten minutes I felt refreshed and clearheaded and effortlessly returned to writing.

MEDITATING IN DAILY LIFE

You can try this yourself anytime during the day. Start with something that only slightly bothers you, say the noise of the washing machine or traffic. Make the sound the object of your focus. Join it completely. If your mind wanders, try to return without judgment to whatever you were listening to. Watch what happens. Once you get the knack of it, you can transfer this to other, more frustrating situations such as police sirens or jackhammers. When a friend of mine could merge with the disturbing and distracting noises outside her office, for example, her faith in this form of meditation grew and she was eager to apply it to even more challenging situations. Later she was able to merge with slight physical discomfort and then low-level pain. Eventually she tackled challenging emotions. All of this expands inner space.

MUSIC

It was a nightmare day. My alarm never went off, there was a leak in the roof, traffic was horrific, the train was incredibly noisy, I was drowning in emails, a friend was in a car accident, and several people I knew felt life was meaningless and intimacy was impossible.

When I got home I was emotionally beaten up and foggy-headed. Instead of staying miserable, I listened to some Coltrane and then to Tchaikovsky's *Nutcracker*. After a few moments I was borne aloft on a wave of joyous delight—happy to be alive. I not only experienced an encompassing peace, I was transported to a realm of boundless possibilities.

Whether you are moved by Mozart or Motown, Beyoncé or the B-52s, music—like movies or plays, reading or art—is a powerful way to change channels and open up inner space as well as your heart.

TIMELESS TIME

Another wonderful means of expanding inner space in daily life is to tap into what Joel Kramer and Diana Alstad in *The Passionate Mind Revisited* call "timeless time," the mental time zone of children and vacationers. Most adults live in a universe that is goal- and future-oriented; dominated by watches and plans. Filling up time and being productive is a virtue. Minutes feel as if they speed up, but inner space gets impinged upon and possibilities shrink. "Clocks slay time," wrote William Faulkner in *The Sound and the Fury*, and "...only when the clock stops does time come to life."

While timeless time is accessible to anyone, we can't live in it constantly. Although we all have responsibilities and appointments, we can experience timeless time more often than we might think. David Levin, cofounder of the KIPP charter school network and superintendent of KIPP's New York City schools, works seventy-five to ninety hours a week. "I don't wear a watch on Sundays," he said. "It's nice not to look at the time every minute."

Don't fill all of your leisure time. Let it unfold, organically and spontaneously. When you can, treat your days as if you are a tourist in a foreign city without agendas, not a tour guide who is already an expert and won't learn anything new. Tourists of everyday life are open to adventures; they are drawn into what moves them and flow with unexpected opportunities that may arise. Try it today. Don't check the time or consult lists or agendas. Continue that interesting conversation with a parent at your child's athletic event, rather than stopping it prematurely because of the force of habit or the belief that you should be elsewhere.

FREE ASSOCIATION

Psychoanalysis teaches us that there is another way to take a vacation from our ordinary means of experiencing daily life and open up inner space. Freud called it "free association." He instructed patients to say whatever came to mind without concern for social propriety or self-censorship. Freud was tapping into a state of mind that we all have access to, which sometimes fosters both unexpected thoughts and images, as well as cross-pollination between two seemingly unrelated ideas or topics. This cross-fertilization often spurs creativity. As you read this book pay attention to any seemingly stray realizations, feelings, or visual images that arise. Explore them with a nonjudgmental spirit, instead of dismissing them, and see if they move you in a new direction.

FREER ASSOCIATIONS

One of my Zen teachers is fond of saying, "There are very few real human beings."

There is something exhilarating and expansive about friendship and authentic human connections and conversations. While conserving inner space sometimes requires protecting ourselves against people who are demanding or draining, after an inspiring talk with a friend— someone who knows and values us—we feel "more ourselves" and are inevitably rejuvenated. We have much greater self-trust and faith in our creative resources, and our perspective on our lives and ourselves is immeasurably enriched.

E xpanding inner space is one of the foundations of flourishing. When we cultivate clarity, equanimity, and centeredness we can both resist those cultural forces that threaten to cloud our minds and sabotage our well-being, and access our enormous capacity for creative living.

Inner space is central to flourishing. It fosters more openness and clarity, and ingenuity grows and flowers. We can more readily access our dreams and passions and begin to craft a life of meaning and passion.

Creating and appreciating beauty is another crucial way of expanding inner space.

2

It is crazy not to celebrate whatever reconciles us to life.

—PETER SCHJELDAHL

THEY CAN'T STEAL THE MOON

The renowned yoga teacher T. K. V. Desikachar once told an illuminating story during a seminar on the therapeutic aspects of yoga. A depressed and suicidal man in his twenties, who saw the world as empty and devoid of meaning, consulted Mr. Desikachar. The student informed him that he believed in "nothing" and if their work together failed he was going to kill himself.

"Will you teach me asanas?" the student asked.

"No," Mr. Desikachar replied.

"Yogic breathing?"

"No."

"Chanting then?"

"No," Mr. Desikachar said. "Instead, I propose an experiment. Would you be willing to buy an inexpensive camera and black-and-white film and take pictures of symmetry in nature?"

The student, who had the financial resources and flexibility to travel, agreed. For the next six months he visited Tibet and Mongolia and other ordinary and exotic locales and took countless pictures of symmetry in nature. His debilitating headaches slowly disappeared and his depression lifted. Discovering beauty gave him something to believe in. It provided tangible evidence—that he couldn't deny—that the world had meaning.

Human beings are "hungry for beauty; we seek it everywhere—in landscape, music, art, clothes, furniture, gardening, companionship, love, religion and in ourselves," wrote John O'Donohue in *Beauty: The Invisible Embrace.* Beauty is not only an antidote to cultural pollution, it is one of the cornerstones of a life lived well. Beauty is often mistaken for glamour and reduced to physical attractiveness. Once we broaden its definition and scope to also include those experiences that galvanize our attention, elicit our appreciation, and remind us of the world's magnificence—from the splendor of a mountain's peak to the radiance of a virtuous person—beauty's indispensability to flourishing becomes more evident. Nothing else affects our soul and buoys it, or transports us to new realms in quite the same way.

When we are in the presence of beauty—flowers and sunsets, the language of Shakespeare and the music of Mozart—we feel elated and uplifted, alive and engaged.

Matisse aspired to make paintings so beautiful that when people encountered them all their problems would subside. The novelist and philosopher Iris Murdoch eloquently illustrates how beauty can be an emotional salve:

> I am looking out of my window, in an anxious and resentful state of mind, oblivious of my surroundings, brooding perhaps on some damage done to my prestige. Then suddenly I observe a hovering kestrel. In a moment everything is altered. The brooding self with its hurt vanity has disappeared. There is nothing now but Kestrel. And when I return to thinking of the other matter it seems less important.

Beauty is not a single thing. Psychoanalyst Hans Loewald conveys its range:

> We get lost in the contemplation of a beautiful scene, or face, or painting, in listening to music, or poetry, or the music of a human voice. We are carried away in the vortex of sexual passion. We become absorbed in the proportions of a building, the plastic force or harmony of a sculpture, in a stirring play or film, in the beauty of a scientific theory or experiment, or of an animal, in the intimate closeness of a personal encounter.

In an evocative cross-cultural study, *Six Names of Beauty,* Crispin Sartwell explored the meaning of the terms for beauty in six languages—ancient Greek's *to kalon,* the Japanese idea of *wabi-sabi,* Hebrew's *yapha,* the Navaho *hozo,* Sanskrit *sundara,* and our own *beauty*. He examined how the words referred to the ideal and the flawed, the earthy no less than the exalted. High art, the perfected human form, physical spaces, sounds, aromas, literal and metaphoric illumination, the "exalted archi-tecture of the Parthenon and the humble pottery of the Kizaemon tea bowl" all illustrate beauty.

No matter how we define beauty, it is neither an accessory nor a luxury—it is indispensable to our emotional health and peace of mind. One of the most powerful insights I've had studying yoga is that we take on the attributes of what we are connected to. When we see a stun-ning landscape or painting, for example, we are fortified and enlivened. When we encounter vulgarity and trash—that which is course and vile, degrading, and mediocre—we are repulsed and depressed and that can be deadly. The doctor in Abbas Kiarostami's film *The Wind Will Carry Us* defined death as what happens when you "close your eyes on the beauty of the world." While decadence and crassness stifle our senses, dampen our spirits, and cause us to withdraw from life, beauty in all its myriad forms makes life worth living.

A friend told me a story that illustrates this. She awoke early on a summer day. Not only was she caught in the grip of an allergy attack and hardly able to breathe, she was tired and crabby. Carrying her edgy and constricted self like a heavy backpack, she walked outside her home in the country. At first she ignored the way the wet grass welcomed the soles of her bare feet. But then she noticed light emerging through a small space between the trees, illuminating the early morning mist. A door opened between her and nature. She entered.

A bee landed on a nearby pot of pristine white daisies creating a black and yellow ripple in the quiet air. She felt cradled in a rich and lavish silence. One of her cats ran by and suddenly reversed direction, exuberant. She savored the deliciously fragrant heliotrope in a pot near the back door.

Beauty took her by surprise, transported her away from her agitated state. The world began to seem hopeful. Feeling connected to something limitless, yet within reach, she suddenly realized that life was right; life was good. Not only did she experience radiance, beauty melted away everything that was weighing her down. It gave her perspective. She took a deep breath, filling herself with all that she was experiencing.

Without the invitation beauty offers—to engage the world and be enlivened—life feels grim, dominated by ugliness and degradation. It helps to know that there are two ways to cope with cultural pollution: lessen our exposure to it, and create or appreciate beauty.

Because cultural pollution can be paradoxically so enticing—think of our addictive fascination with the private lives of public figures—we may need a counterforce in order to resist it. In Homer's *Odyssey,* Odysseus asked his compatriots to tie him to the mast of their ship so that he could hear the intoxicating song of the sirens without being lured to his death. We lessen our exposure to cultural pollution—as we decrease the impingements on inner space—by being selective about what we take in, and that involves discipline, will, and mindful consumption. We can protect ourselves by exercising judgment.

I know a couple that recently endured a long, protracted family tragedy. It was, by turns, soul-wrenching, sad, and exhausting. For weeks they didn't turn on the TV because each felt it was too harsh and that the sounds alone were depleting. Instead, they sat with each other in the evening, lights low, sometimes listening to gentle, soothing music, but also really talking with each other. When they went to sleep one of them remarked that he did not miss watching TV.

It is not enough to lessen cultural pollution; we also need to appreciate beauty.

There are at least two ways we can bring beauty into our lives: we can create it or we can simply appreciate it. We can create beauty through whatever moves us—gardening, singing, painting, dancing, sewing, decorating, or writing.

Appreciation refers to the capacity to recognize, value, and derive satisfaction from the existence of beauty and goodness in the world. We can cherish beauty in seven realms—the five senses plus thinking and feeling. Beautiful sights, sounds, smells, tastes, sensations, thoughts, and feelings are ever-present, as Walt Whitman powerfully illustrated. In *Varieties of Religious Experience,* William James distinguished between the "healthy-minded" and "sick souled." The former are open to the world, feel it is worthwhile, and see it with gladness, even though they acknowledge that there is immorality and suffering. Those with sick souls view the world as a snake pit to be shunned. Whitman epitomized for James the healthy-minded. Whitman savored the sights, sounds, and people he encountered. His "favorite activity," according to his disciple Dr. R. M. Bucke, "seemed to be strolling or sauntering about outdoors by himself, looking at the grass, the trees, the flowers, the vistas of light, the varying aspects of the sky, and listening to the birds, the crickets, the tree frogs, and all the hundreds of natural sounds. . . . He appeared to like . . . all the men, women, and children he saw. . . . It was evident that these things gave him a pleasure far beyond what they give to ordinary people."

A person with an abundance of appreciation takes little for granted and savors everything—walking in a city or hiking in nature, talking with a friend or listening to the laughter of an infant. In my clinical experience he or she is more likely to feel awe and wonder, joy and gratitude. Such individuals not only experience greater meaning and purpose, they connect more richly with other people.

We can cultivate appreciation of three areas: physical beauty; the talent and virtuosity of artists, athletes, and performers; and character, by which I mean admirable deeds and moral beauty, a topic I'll return to at the end of this chapter.

In our fast-paced world, in which many of us operate in perpetual overdrive, multitasking and impatient, appreciation of beauty isn't always easy. Why do we often neglect it, and what prevents us from cherishing it?

Beauty may not always seem practical. It doesn't necessarily add to our bottom line. Or maybe we subconsciously believe that we aren't entitled to it. After the trauma of 9/11, I observed many people— including clients and friends—who felt guilty about pursuing activities that gave them gratification and fulfillment because they believed it was self-indulgent, even shameful, to enjoy themselves while so many people suffered.

Perhaps we are so disturbed that beauty is "fated to extinction," as Freud said, that we devalue it because it is transient. Maybe we have experienced too much disappointment and pain and have detached ourselves from life. Or our ordinary existence may be so comfortable—and we are so anesthetized to the pain that it causes—that beauty seems unnecessary. Perhaps our commitment to social justice or taking care of a developmentally challenged child seems more urgent.

Make discovering beauty a high priority in your life. A dean at a prestigious college—with a great deal of competing demands and pressures—religiously takes a few minutes out of her busy schedule each afternoon to look at her favorite paintings or listen to a few minutes of beloved music in her office. She can't imagine a day without exposure to beauty. Incorporating beauty into our lives helps us to expand internal spaciousness and flourish.

A friend of mine hates paperwork and has great anxiety over bills and other mail. She is an artist and loves color, so she found a small wooden table, which she carefully refurbished in white and used beautiful baskets and pretty file folders to organize her papers. She filled the drawer with colorful Post-it pads and paper clips. She now has an office area that is visually appealing to her and she tries harder to keep current with paperwork so the beauty she created shines through.

Since beauty is all around us—in the shaft of light coming through a bedroom window or in the butterflies cavorting in the garden or the symmetrical presentation of sushi on a plate—we don't so much have to discover it as be receptive to its presence. "The real voyage of discovery," noted Marcel Proust, "consists not in seeking new landscapes but in having new eyes."

The eighteenth-century Zen master Ryōkan saw with fresh eyes, which opened him to realms of beauty that are right in front of us and easy to miss. Ryōkan lived in a very humble hut in Japan with no possessions. One day he returned home to discover that he was being robbed. "You may have come a long way to visit me," he said to the startled thief, "and you should not return empty-handed. Please take my clothes as a gift." The thief was astonished, but he took the teacher's clothes and ran away. Later that evening Ryōkan sat naked, watching the moon. Poor fellow, he thought, he can't steal the moon.

One way to not miss the moon—or any other splendors the world continually bestows on us—is, as Ralph Waldo Emerson knew, to pay attention to, instead of look past, the familiar. "I ask not for the great, the remote, the romantic; what is doing in Italy or Arabia; what is Greek art, or Provençal minstrelsy; I embrace the common, I explore and sit at the feet of the familiar, the low," Emerson wrote. Learn to cherish beauty by cultivating an appreciation of the ordinary. Enjoy the tiny rainbows flashing on your walls from the prism you hung in a sunny window. Relish the loving and good-hearted people you encounter. Be grateful for the moon.

"Boredom is lack of attention," according to the gestalt therapist Fritz Perls. We can try to enjoy what we are doing—looking out the window, making a meal, washing the dishes—instead of rushing to do something else. By wholeheartedly engaging and appreciating the ordinary, we are more receptive to the beauty of everyday life.

I have found that a powerful way to appreciate what might seem commonplace is to make the distinction between our *aesthetic* and our *cognitive* relationships to the world. In a cognitive stance, we see a traffic light—which has a particular shape and three colors—not as a potential aesthetic object but as a sign signaling whether to stop or go. When we treat something aesthetically we put aside practical concerns and appreciate the artistic properties of what we are viewing, rather than focusing on how it can be used for a pragmatic purpose. Treating things aesthetically rather than cognitively—as potential sources of beauty rather than means to an end—helps us be receptive to the beauty of daily life.

So does reconnecting with our childlike amazement and curiosity and noticing the charm of the ordinary—the light gracing a building, puppies unself-consciously playing, the sound of fluttering flags. Growing up—moving from childhood to adulthood and reaching maturity—is an education in learning to take the world for granted. Children exult in the mystery and wonder of the particularities of whatever they encounter. The price of maturity is greater dullness. Adults don't lose the capacity to rejoice—it can be nurtured and emerge with practice—but we grown-ups often overlook a great deal of life. Being mature, responsible, and serious does not mean we have to forsake joy, excitement, and astonishment. We can be adults and still notice the yellow frame of the light against the blue sky or the sudden, intense, rich sound of a thunderclap.

Beauty, like flourishing, also includes living with dignity amid adversity and suffering, another way of elevating the ordinary. Antonioni's 1962 film, *The Eclipse,* illustrates this. After a man loses fifty million lire in the Italian stock exchange, a woman named Vittoria follows him to a bar. He orders a drink, which he barely touches. Then he goes to a café and hardly drinks his *acqua minerale*. He writes something on a piece of paper and leaves it on the table. The audience imagines it is something melancholic or hostile. Vittoria approaches the table and discovers a drawing of a flower. The financial victim responds to catastrophe by affirming the human capacity to create something of value and substance that brings joy and meaning.

When I recently saw the following statement on a plaque in an aquarium in Florida, I was reminded that beautiful characters or souls, who have sometimes weathered much adversity, are part of the beauty of ordinary life:

IN LOVING MEMORY OF GEORGE PETER STELLAS
WHO FOUND BEAUTY IN THE WONDERS OF NATURE
AND GOODNESS IN THE HEARTS OF PEOPLE

Appreciating excellence of character—a beautiful soul—is the final aspect of bringing splendor into our lives and flourishing. When people are devoted solely to their own pleasure and gain, qualities of enlightened personality such as honor, virtue, and accountability may seem quaint and dated, but that makes them even more important.

We encounter splendor of character in literature and philosophy, religion and the arts, as well as in daily life. When a family member, friend, or mentor embodies it, we can be inspired to be our better selves. Joe Temeczko, a Polish immigrant and former prisoner of war, illustrated this. Joe was a handyman who did odd jobs and lived very modestly in a small house in Minneapolis. He roamed his neighborhood looking for junk to fix up and sell or give away. His home was filled with the things he scavenged from the street. Joe took the news of the 9/11 attacks in New York City hard. He rewrote his will, leaving $1.4 million to the City of New York, which helped fund a park renovation, as well as the "Daffodil Project," in which thousands of volunteers planted more than two million flower bulbs across New York City as a living memorial to 9/11. We access beauty when we allow the Joe Temeczkos we meet or hear about to inspire us to reach for the best within ourselves and appreciate and support it in other people.

When we observe a beautiful action or soul, we feel that life is benevolent and we are inspired to contribute to the enrichment of the world. One of my patients, a therapist in her eighties and a dedicated social activist, spoke of a woman who had just died: "She created beauty wherever she went. Her death was a loss to life." We have all felt this about people whose example of cherishing life or embodying character and integrity inspired us and made the world feel like a better place.

Beauty speaks in a different language than practical concerns or goal-oriented behavior, but it's accessible if we slow down and listen to its song, which is always available to us in nature, people, and excellence of character, but not always heard. When we open to beauty, the world becomes again what it always has been—a miraculous splendor of possibility that will expand inner space and make us feel infinitely more grateful to be alive.

When we appreciate beauty, which both expands inner space and helps us flourish, we are more willing to take good care of ourselves, which is the subject of the next chapter.

What Bruce Lee and Carl Jung Can Teach Us about Training for Intimacy

Physical health is a crucial element of self-care and ultimately flourishing. It leads to improved mood and self-image, and to enhanced self-confidence. The key to physical flourishing is a harmonious relationship between mind and body. If we get too little sleep, for example, we will feel mentally and physically exhausted and perhaps even depressed the following day. On the other hand, as research on the psychological factors that strengthen immune functioning demonstrates, if we have meaningful relationships with other people and feel fulfilled, our immune systems will actually be stronger and more effective.

While increasing numbers of people know that mind and body are not separate—they are the intimately connected facets of one energy system—most of us do not live as if we believe it. The chief reason, I suspect, is because few of us understand the *emotional* obstacles to mind-body harmony such as ambition and self-coercion, deprivation and false nurturing.

When mind and body are allies, mental and physical health is enhanced. We experience more vitality, clarity, and well-being. We face life's challenges and possibilities eagerly. Not only do we have the confidence to tackle what we might have been avoiding, our efforts to change and grow are exponentially increased. Our relationships and sexual lives are enhanced. We feel more deeply, work more productively, and love more passionately.

Despite the potential rewards, many of us ignore our physical selves. While the body seems to take on paramount importance in a culture that worships appearance, the opposite is all too often true. The shadow side of our vastly increased productivity and instant access to products, services, and people via the Internet and PDAs, as I suggested in chapter 1, is that we are in a constant state of overdrive—multitasking our way to exhaustion. We're too tired to exercise or make consistently good food choices, and we're overeating out of emotional deprivation and fatigue. This pattern of physical self-neglect leaves us prone to heart disease, cancer, diabetes, high blood pressure, obesity, ulcers, stress headaches, and back injuries—conditions that are preventable, but escalate dramatically with an unhealthy lifestyle.

It is no surprise that we live in a greatly diminished manner when we are chronically stressed, out of touch with our bodies, and worn down. This interferes with deeper intimacy, as well as self-care, for we are not as willing and able to be close to somebody else when we are physically depleted or unhappy about how we look and feel.

The good news is that we can make a U-turn and move in a more positive direction. But this takes knowledge of what helps us flourish and an awareness of what motivates negative behavior, as well as what can—with concerted effort—effect a change in attitude. We know what to do to be healthy, but aren't doing it. The chief reason is often that our minds neglect or are antagonistic toward our bodies. There are many causes for this—cultural bias, blind spots, habit, fear, and embarrassment. Our culture places great emphasis on accomplishments, but not on the *quality of our lives*. In addition, many of us are trained to overvalue our conscious, rational thoughts over the feedback we receive from our bodies. And many of us have a submissive relationship to the medical profession, treating doctors as experts on our physical states—not always trusting our instincts and capacities for self-healing. The body is an organ of perception and judgment and a vessel of pleasure and fulfillment that can fuel pride and self-worth. It is also a site of pain, a reminder of aging and mortality, and, for some, the seat of the soul's corruption, and thus a source of guilt and shame.

The spiritual teacher Ram Dass speaks for many when he describes his own neglect of his body in his book *Still Here*:

The relationship I had with my own body has been checkered at best. As a young man enduring the usual struggles with identity, emotions, and sexuality, I made an unconscious decision to subordinate my body. For many years, I was able to justify this denial by telling myself that I aspired to be a holy man, transcending the passions and pains of the flesh (though of course I never fully did). As I began to age, this denial seemed all the more justified; why in the world would I want to attach myself to a physical body that was obviously declining? . . . Now was the chance to leave my body even further behind and dwell in "higher consciousness."

After a debilitating stroke, accompanied by horrific fear, Ram Dass "called on spiritual practices of several decades—Vipassana meditation, jnana yoga, bhakti, guru kripa." What he turned to most often was "Ramana Maharshi's practice of 'I am not this body,'" where he would note each part of his body and say, "I am not my arm. I am not my leg. I am not my brain." Dass realized, "That helped me avoid getting caught in the mind's fears and the body's sensations." But over the next several months, he recognized that "however wonderful it is as a practice, 'I am not this body,' is only half the truth. The stroke brought me squarely in touch with the fact that, although I am certainly *more* than my body, I also *am* my body."

"The stroke happened to me for many different reasons," he realized. "I had spent most of my life keeping my awareness 'free of my body' . . . I can see now that I was also ignoring my body; pushing it away. . . . no matter what my body was telling me, I was disregarding it. So then came the stroke."

Anyone, from a professional athlete to a cubicle-bound office worker to a weekend warrior, can fall into this trap. It can take various forms, from ignoring feedback we receive about injuries or stress, to not paying attention to physical feelings telling us that we need to turn off our laptops and go out and get some fresh air.

The relationship between the mind and the body can be antagonistic as well as distant. Many of us are oblivious to feedback and coercive toward our bodies. We do not forget that we have a body—far from it; we actually allow our minds to dominate and control it. When the mind coerces the body, then what we *think* we should do or accomplish becomes more important than what our body really needs. We override or neglect the messages about what it feels and push ourselves to go beyond what we can safely physically handle, or we don't give ourselves the physical activity we need. Either way we effectively interrupt the balance and wisdom of the body known as homeostasis—our self-regulating and self-correcting mechanism. This is the internal system that provides feedback so we can maintain a healthy state of functioning. Take thirst, for example. If we ignore it, we will become dehydrated. If we don't take our dehydration seriously, we will experience more severe consequences.

Cecil did not recognize the connection between his mind and his body. It gradually became apparent to me that there was a problem between his mental and physical self-regulation. Cecil was a bright, hardworking, and talented artist who seldom went to the doctor. He did not need to, for he rarely got sick. But Cecil and I gradually began to recognize that something was amiss in his body-mind relationship. Cecil valued achievement and loved his work. He taught art during the day and painted far into the night. He frequently stayed up late—even when he was tired—so he could have more time for creative pursuits. Cecil was addicted to not sleeping. He would override his physical needs and remain up beyond the point at which he was tired despite how he felt physically. When he tried to go to bed earlier he inevitably lay there, wide awake. He allowed his feeling of deprivation and excitement about his own work to take over and artificially stimulate him. When he sacrificed sleep, he was physically depleted although creatively inspired. He did not heed the feedback of fatigue and diminished energy. He was often tired and foggy-headed in the morning and had difficulty getting up, but the next evening he would continue to override the feedback that he was exhausted and push himself to stay awake.

Cecil was afflicted by a *dictatorship* in which his mind ruled his body without concern for the latter's welfare. Cecil's physical self was a slave to the wishes and demands of his mind and emotional needs.

For Cecil to resolve his struggles he needed to understand what he gained by overvaluing his mind, as well as ways he could develop a more creative partnership between body and mind. In exploring his sleep deprivation we came up with several possible reasons why he was ignoring physical signals, including the realization that staying up late was his way of cheating and stretching time and accomplishing more, which made him feel that he was a good person because he had attained his goals. Despite this realization, nothing changed for Cecil until we uncovered the deeper reason for his behavior—a consequence of how he had attempted to heal himself during his childhood.

Cecil's parents emotionally neglected him. Excessively involved in projects and commitments outside the home, his mother and father often left him to his own devices as a child. He felt alone and lost, without guidance. His mind and its capacity to help him manage his life was the only compass he had to give him direction. It served as his guide for living when he was a child, becoming a kind of foster parent; a substitute for an absent mother and father.

As a result of feeling heard and understood in therapy, as well as acknowledging the implications of his behavior, Cecil began to trust himself and realized that he was staying up late to extend his day, accomplish more, and attempt to justify his life. He increasingly recognized that when he pushed himself in this way, his physical health and the quality of his work ultimately suffered. As the need to justify his worth through measuring how much he accomplished each day lessened, it grew easier for him to let physical feedback regulate his rhythms of sleep and work. He gradually relinquished his rigid control over his life. He stopped parenting himself with his mind. He began to give his body its due. Gradually his self-regulation became smarter and more balanced and he was able to have a more harmonious relationship between his mind and his body by listening to feedback. He began going to sleep when he was tired rather than overriding messages from his body. He avoided adversely programming his mind with bizarre or violent images from television, the Internet, or movies before he went to bed—thus expanding inner space—because he realized that such memories affected the quality of sleep and rest. Cecil also engaged in more calming activities, which promoted restful sleep. He practiced winding down with something relaxing—a hot bath, an art magazine, soothing music, or meditation. Needless to say his health improved and he felt greater energy and clarity. And his work took on more vibrancy.

Separating Reality from Myth

L ike Cecil, we can enjoy a better relationship between our minds and bodies and greatly improve our physical health. The first step in doing this is to separate myths from realities.

Body Myths/Body Realities

MYTH: *Health is an absence of symptoms.*
REALITY: Despite the rising popularity of holistic and alternative medicine in the West during the last several decades, there is still a predominant belief in Western medicine and among patients that health is the *absence* of symptoms. But one can be devoid of illnesses or injuries and not be healthy. Cecil, for example, had no overt symptoms or medical complaints, yet he was not as vital and clearheaded as he might have been. Optimal physical and emotional functioning involves a state of balance and harmony between our minds and our bodies. We need to work at being healthy, not merely prevent ourselves from getting sick.

MYTH: *There is one path to health.*
REALITY: Everyone is unique. Health plans need to be individualized and adaptable.

Some people, for example, need to exercise less vigorously, while others must challenge themselves. Dietary plans, like exercise prescriptions, also need to be completely geared to each person, rather than standardized. You may need more carbohydrates than I do, and we each may thrive by eating completely differently from one another.

MYTH: *If I can't do a good workout, there's no point in doing anything.*
REALITY: A little exercise is usually better than no exercise. Regular exercise for a brief period of time brings more benefit than being inactive—from improving the functioning of the immune system and lessening stress, anxiety, and depression, to boosting creativity, enhancing the quality of sleep, and enriching sexual fulfillment.

MYTH: *Other people, with greater willpower than mine, always feel like exercising.*
REALITY: Few people feel like exercising all the time. Those who exercise regularly just don't take their feelings of not wanting to exercise so seriously—they listen to their bodies as well as their minds. (More on this a little later.) As a result they often experience the energizing and rejuvenating effects of exercise or movement, which encourages them to do it more regularly.

MYTH: *You have to constantly maintain a healthy diet.*
REALITY: Few people eat perfectly. I think it is healthier to think of a Buddhist middle path between asceticism and indulgence, rather than perfection. Deprivation triggers indulgence and overeating, literally weighs us down and depletes our energy and clarity. When we slip—which most of us do—we need to learn from our struggles and begin again with as much patience and curiosity about what happened as we can muster.

The Hidden Wisdom of the Body

The second step in creating a harmonious relationship between mind and body is a shift in our attitudes toward their relationship. We have been taught to believe that the mind and body are separate and that our corporal selves are inferior to our intellectual selves. This is the unfortunate legacy of the French philosopher René Descartes. "I think, therefore I am" not only disconnects what is intimately connected but overvalues the mind and marginalizes the body.

Contrary to Descartes' dictum, the body is a source of creativity and wisdom, and it often reveals more than our conscious, rational minds. I was reminded of this in a locker room after playing basketball a few years ago. I couldn't remember the combination for my lock. The more I thought about it and tried to open the lock, the more it seemed to elude me. I only succeeded when I drew on body memory and "let my fingers do the walking" without thinking about the combination.

"Artists are the antennae of the race," claimed Ezra Pound, grasping cultural trends before the rest of us. The body tells the unvarnished truth about how we are doing and is our early warning system, signaling stress, illness, and breakdown before we are conscious of them.

We need to become friends with our bodies and treat them as allies and sources of wisdom rather than opponents whose needs must be vanquished. Instead of dominating, or neglecting, our bodies, we must try to listen to them and take responsibility for what we hear—a method I call *inner fine-tuning.*

Inner Fine-Tuning

S truggling with his meditation practice, an earnest and agitated man went to the Buddha for advice. The Buddha listened to the man's description of the tension created as he strove for spiritual advancement. Knowing that he was a musician, the Buddha said that to play beautiful music an instrument must be properly tuned—the strings should be neither too loose nor too tight. The man suddenly realized that he needed to loosen the strings—to strive less hard. By easing up and going more with the flow he was able to fine-tune his life.

Inner fine-tuning not only helps mind and body become allies—it is the crucial ingredient in deepening self-care. The Olympic hurdler Edwin Moses had a unique system of training, which exemplifies inner fine-tuning. He decreased his strenuous workouts when he did well *and* when he was struggling. At first this approach seems counterintuitive; success encourages most of us to continue doing what we excel at. It feels wonderful, even ecstatic, to be in a physical flow or zone and performing at the highest athletic level with little conscious effort or striving. Most people become addicted to that experience and sense of achievement and crave more of it. Moses realized that no one performs at an optimal physical level over an extended period of time. Because the other side of such "peaking" is breakdown, he would scale back his workouts ever so slightly when he was performing extremely well to avoid burnout and injury.

Most of us get upset and push harder—if we don't quit—when we are doing poorly in a physical activity. When we try to get out of a slump we tend to pressure ourselves and therefore do even worse, which perpetuates a negative cycle of frustration, stress, and further impaired performance. Moses understood that when he was not performing at a peak level it usually meant that he was stressed out. He had the wisdom and self-trust to back off, which allowed him to recover, and led to rejuvenation, improved health, and optimal performance.

Moses perfected the art of inner fine-tuning. He was like a musical instrument that was strung neither too loose nor too tight. His original and balanced training philosophy contributed to his being a two-time Olympic champion in the four-hundred-meter hurdles, and remaining the finest hurdler in the world and undefeated for nine years—a super-human level of performance.

While few people are Olympic or professional athletes, any of us can learn the art of inner fine-tuning. Here are three questions we might ask ourselves to cultivate inner fine-tuning:

WHAT IS MY ENERGY LEVEL?

When you wake up in the morning, do you feel renewed and energetic? Or do you drag yourself out of bed and need a shower and a cup of coffee to get going? Many of us use stimulants to make it through our days. If we regularly crave coffee, tea, or caffeine-laden soft drinks to wake up and stay up, we are not getting enough sleep or are taking on too much work, and in the process, we are wearing our bodies down. Any self-care evaluation must include how much sleep we really need, and how much we are actually getting. When TV public service announcements start telling us we need more sleep, this should indicate the enormity of the problem. All the latest sleep research shows that the effects of sleep deprivation are disastrous. There's a reason sleep deprivation is a form of torture.

HOW IS MY MOOD?

Are you calm and relaxed, focused and clear-thinking, eager to face challenges? Or are you overwhelmed and anxious, harried and complaining that everything is too much? If so, your body may be telling you that something is amiss that you haven't yet consciously realized.

DO I IMPOSE A WORKOUT ON MY BODY? OR DO I LISTEN TO HOW I FEEL?

An astonishingly large number of injuries occur in yoga class. Surprised? One reason may be that the participants blindly twist themselves into positions that someone else insists on—rather than paying attention to how their own bodies are feeling moment to moment, which is actually the correct way to do yoga. For instance, if we bend to touch our toes and feel a tug in our hamstrings, that is feedback that we need to listen to or we may get injured. We have to pull back a bit until we feel the stretch but not the pain. Even if we only get halfway down, we are actually in greater harmony with our bodies and will do yoga longer with fewer injuries.

For people who work out or walk on a regular basis, there will be days when we can do more because it feels right—and days when we must do less or nothing, because we have determined that although we want to be physically active, we have to rest. The right amount of exercise for the fitness level and current state of the person is more beneficial than a longer routine that causes the person to have soreness that lasts for a few days.

Meditating and Dreaming Your Way to Health

Meditation and dreaming are excellent tools for the cultivation of inner fine-tuning. Engaging in body-based awareness disciplines such as tai chi or yoga—which are, of course, meditative practices—can foster awareness of our bodies. This is most likely to happen when we focus on the process—the specific postures or movements—rather than attempt to achieve some ideal result. Such bodily attunement helps us in at least two crucial ways: illness and injury prevention, as well as inner fine-tuning.

Whether we are Olympic athletes or occasionally practice yoga, we need to cooperate with our body before crisis. It is much easier to prevent an illness than to cure one. Try to notice physical imbalances and subclinical problems as soon as they arise. Pay attention to your body—to its actual inner needs—before it breaks down or gets injured. To do this we must give ourselves space to gain more awareness of the actual relationship between our minds and our bodies. Sensations—tightening in the throat, a creaky lower back, an opening in the heart—are doorways into our physical and emotional states. Are you feeling sluggish or depleted? Vitalized or energized? Do you crave movement or stretching? When you are run down or getting sick, listen to this feedback.

Meditation can enhance our awareness of our bodies. A good beginning practice is something that I call *opening to the body meditation*:

- Close your eyes.
- Relax your eyelids and jaw.

- Let your shoulders drop.
- Let the chair or cushion or couch hold you.
- Close your mouth.
- Breathe through your nose and pull the air to the back of your throat.
- Relax your shoulders and chest.
- Let your breath be gentle and easeful.
- Do this for twelve complete breaths.
- Now, keep your eyes closed and bring your attention to your body.
- Notice any active physical sensations—itches, twitches, energy— and attend to them with curiosity, as if you are encountering them for the first time.
- If your mind wanders, as soon as you notice that you have drifted away, gently return without any judgment to the experience of appreciating physical sensations.
- Do this practice for a few minutes.
- Spend a moment noticing any restful places in your body. Attend to them with a welcoming spirit.
- Four of our senses—eyes, ears, tongue, and nose—connect us to the world. Focus on them for a few minutes and listen to what they are communicating as you continue meditating.
- Gently and slowly open your eyes and return your attention to the room. Write down anything you discovered. If there are any images or metaphors that arose during meditation, ask yourself what they reveal to you.
- Record anything that comes to mind.

Dreams, like meditation, can offer unexpected insight into the needs of the body. Dreams are often early warning systems that signal the onset or the existence of physical symptoms or illness. I once threw up after teaching a class on integrative psychotherapy with a colleague. The class had been very frustrating and nonproductive and the students looked bored and irritated. When I woke up the next morning I remembered the following dream: I was driving a car that was pushing an empty truck with no cargo. The truck went off the road and into someone's backyard. I got out of my car and wondered if the owners of the house would mind that I was on their property.

When I reflected on the dream my thoughts drifted toward the previous evening. The other instructor and I were each supposed to lecture for half of the three-hour class. She wanted to speak first. Since she had invited me to join her in this project I felt that this was her decision. She lectured for nearly the whole time and I had only ten minutes to teach. The glazed looks in the students' eyes while she was speaking confirmed my own feeling that she hadn't said much of substance. The empty cargo in the dream symbolized that her presentation was superficial and lightweight, and that I should take charge and not worry about what others—the teacher/house owners—thought. Through a dream I learned that my vomiting might have been communicating that her one-sided teaching arrangement nauseated me; that it was more than I could swallow.

Mental Reflection and Physical Health

Along with separating myth from reality, shifting our attitudes by using inner fine-tuning, meditation, and dreaming, another way to increase awareness about the physical aspect of our lives is by keeping a journal and reflecting on what facilitates and hinders physical health. As I observed what helped me take the best possible care of myself and other people do the same, as well as the kinds of pitfalls we are all prone to, the following ten questions arose:

1. How do I feel about my body?
2. What is the relationship between my mind and body?
3. What were the attitudes toward my body in my family of origin?
4. What tone of voice do I speak to my body in?
5. Do I boss or belittle my body?
6. Do I nourish my body?
7. Who is in charge of my life? My mind or body? What type of power does it wield?
8. What is the benefit each part of me derives from the current relationship between my mind and body?
9. What would I like to change about this relationship?

10. What do I visualize as the obstacles to creating change? What do I need to do to address these potential obstructions?

Now that we are trying to create harmony between mind and body, discover myths about health, and use meditation and our dreams to fine-tune our relationship to our bodies, it is time to explore ten indispensable ingredients of self-care.

The Ten Pillars of Physical Health

Conventional wisdom emphasizes that there are four pillars to physical health: cardiovascular or endurance, strength training, flexibility, and repose. Developing each is essential for optimal well-being. Advice about each is readily available from coaches and trainers, nutritionists and yoga teachers, as well as magazines, local newspapers, and TV talk shows. I'd like to explore ten *other* pillars that I have gleaned from the psychotherapeutic, yogic, meditative, and martial arts traditions. While these principles haven't received as much attention from the mainstream, they are indispensable. As a lifelong athlete, I've found these principles to be invaluable in my own efforts to flourish and successfully compete against much bigger and more physically talented athletes. They have also enabled me to continue to play basketball with players three and four decades younger than me. I am confident that these strategies can help everyone flourish physically, and that is crucial to genuine self-care.

1. Individualize rather than standardize your approach to fitness.
2. Challenge your limits—what Joel Kramer calls "playing the edge."
3. Be flexible (and I don't mean limbering up before a workout).
4. Be willing to experiment.
5. Absorb what is useful.
6. Integrate opposites, which leads to the best results.
7. Modify whatever you do based upon feedback from your body.
8. Build into your life whatever aids your physical self-care—rather than fitting it in.

9. Adhere to the yogic principle of *vinyāsa krama*—goals are more readily (and safely) achieved when they are done in an orderly progression.

10. When you slip, don't panic.

INDIVIDUALIZE

Since everyone is physically, as well as psychologically, unique, our styles of physical self-care need to be individualized—tailor-made for our situations—rather than standardized. One-size-fits-all approaches to exercise, diet, and rest that neglect our unique needs, capabilities, and challenges, for example, will inevitably miss the mark, inhibit progress, and lead to injury.

Healthy eating is a central element in the well-being of the body. Few people would disagree that cutting down on sweets, processed food, food additives and colorings, and caffeine diminishes illness and increases physical health and vitality; but there is no one diet for everyone. "The popular saying that one man's food may be another's poison," wrote Mahatma Gandhi in 1921, "is based on vast experience which finds daily verification." Each of us needs a plan that is geared to who we are. Some people need more or less of a particular food group than the next person depending on genetic makeup, gender, age, climate, and the amount of physical expenditure of energy. While higher protein and lower carbohydrates are the preferred diet of many high-level athletes I know, other people need less protein and more carbohydrates. Whatever balance works for us, however, increasing our consumption of healthy foods and lessening our intake of unhealthy ones improves physical health and the health of the planet.

PLAYING THE EDGE

The problem with workouts is that they tend to become routinized. We do what feels good and avoid what doesn't. A crucial part of enriching one's exercise regime is something that Joel Kramer calls "playing the edge." The edge is the physical limit in our bodies, the place we can't stretch beyond, the point after we are challenged but before we feel pain. It is where we can confront physical (or emotional) limits without injuring ourselves. Pain and injury reveal that we were insensitive to feedback, perhaps overly ambitious, and overrode our edge. Playing our edge means challenging our physical limits, which are often mental rather than physical. There are numerous ways that we can do this, from going against the grain of what is familiar, to facing what we normally avoid, to backing off physical activity when we are injured. We can hold a yoga posture longer than we normally do or skip our workout if we feel tired or stale. We might swim at a slower and more relaxed pace until we feel physically ready to go faster, play tennis for several minutes longer than usual, or jog more slowly (or quickly) than we ordinarily do.

If we feel rushed in terms of time for our workouts—as increasing numbers of people do—it is tempting to have an all-or-nothing attitude toward exercise. We may tell ourselves that because our schedule is too jam-packed for a quality workout, we won't do anything at all, but it is often better to do something rather than nothing. A ten-minute jog or brisk walk is healthier for us than sitting all day. It is helpful to improvise if we don't have enough time for our normal workouts. We might, for example, bike or run or swim harder or treat the shorter workout as a break from more strenuous activity. All are ways of playing the edge.

FLEXIBILITY

Because everyone is unique, *flexibility* is crucial. And deepening your capacity for reading feedback and inner fine-tuning are immensely helpful. Any rules we follow may need to change, so it's best if they are held lightly rather than tightly. Like individualizing, flexibility is crucial for physical self-care. Not only should we start with a set plan for cardiovascular and strength training, but we need to give ourselves the complete freedom to improvise in the moment based on how we feel. Having a flexible schedule aids in greater attunement to what we really need, as opposed to what we think we should do. We can try to ascertain at the beginning of each day exactly what our bodies require. Are we tight and need to stretch? While we might want to jog, would yoga be a better choice? Will vigorous activity such as running or dancing get the circulation going? Are we stressed and needing rest or recovery?

Flexibility allows us to take a brisk walk one day and jog or go to the gym the next. We can notice how we feel right after each activity we engage in, and throughout the day. Were we energized or depleted, clearheaded or more sluggish?

EXPERIMENTATION

Those who take risks more readily make discoveries. When Bruce Lee used music for martial arts classes in the 1960s, he was forging an original path and couldn't have known that this would later be a staple of workouts in exercise classes decades later.

Experimentation with diet, movement, rest, or any other aspect of physical self-care allows us to exercise our creativity and be more responsive to our goals and challenges. I discovered the joys of swimming when I hurt my Achilles tendon many years ago and needed a vigorous form of exercise that would not exacerbate my injury. When we give ourselves permission to try something new we may also potentially reinvigorate our physical self-care.

Cecil experimented by going to bed earlier and at a regular time, and painting in the morning before work. After a while, he began to feel that his painting was actually becoming more inventive and vibrant.

ABSORB WHAT IS USEFUL

Some years ago I participated in a workshop with Dan Inosanto, one of the leading martial artists in the world and the best friend and training partner of Bruce Lee. The name Bruce Lee conjures up images of martial arts movies and extraordinary physical prowess, but Lee was also a visionary thinker who critiqued the limitations of existing martial arts schools and styles in a way that had far-reaching implications. Allegiance to a set style of martial arts, Lee realized, was ultimately imprisoning, trapping the practitioner in the system he or she had been devoted to. Together with Inosanto, Lee integrated twenty-six different physical disciplines ranging from Western boxing to Filipino weapons systems that combined the best aspects of each into an ever-evolving approach geared toward self-liberation rather than simply physical prowess. He called it Jeet Kune Do, "the way of the intercepting fist."

I approached Inosanto before the workshop began and told him that I was trying to practice as a therapist what he and Lee had done in the martial arts, and that I was curious about what the glue was that held Jeet Kune Do together so that it wasn't simply wild eclecticism, a mishmash of different schools, styles, and techniques. "Absorb what is useful, reject what is useless, and add what is specifically your own," was

Inosanto's response. I found his respect for innovation, as well as tradi-tion, liberating.

We can experiment by drawing on whatever works for us, and by borrowing widely and wisely from different traditions and methods. "The history of science is rich in the example of the fruitfulness of bringing two sets of techniques, two sets of ideas, developed in separate contexts for the pursuit of new truth, into touch with one another," wrote the scientist Robert Oppenheimer. Such juxtaposition often yields something greater than the sum of the individual parts. Medita-tion and yoga, for example, helped my basketball game and vice versa.

What often happens when we are receptive to a cross-pollinating dialogue is that we become exposed to a better way of reaching our goals or we approach a stubborn obstacle in a more skillful manner. The activities I began doing when an injury prevented me from running became staples of my exercise routine when I was healthy, affording me a chance to still get quality exercise the day after a challenging workout.

INTEGRATE OPPOSITES

The Tao Te Ching, a foundational text of Taoism, tells us:

> *When people see some things as beautiful,*
> *other things become ugly.*
> *When people see some things as good,*
> *other things become bad.*

Ancient Greek philosophers emphasized the mutual entailment of the virtues—*antakolouthia*. Courage without moderation, for example, often leads to rashness. Awareness without action is insufficient for change.

The integration of opposites—male and female, rationality and emo-tion, introversion and extroversion—was also central to the psychoana-lyst Carl Jung's work. "Neurosis is self-division," Jung wrote, and health entails reuniting opposites such as masculine and feminine, thinking and feeling, conscious and unconscious, so that we are unique and whole.

Integrating challenge and recovery, two apparent opposites, is also central to physical self-care and flourishing. Stress leads to illness, or so goes the conventional wisdom. Thus avoiding stress is essential for health. But stress doesn't *have* to lead to illness. How we respond to stress—emotionally and behaviorally—is crucial in determining whether it makes us ill. One person's stress is another person's constructive challenge.

Reducing stress and having a positive attitude are not sufficient for mind-body health. Health involves a balance between energy expenditure and recovery, notes Irv Dardik, a former surgeon who served for seven years as chairman of the U.S. Olympic Committee's Sports Medicine Council. What he observed in his work with world-class athletes and patients with chronic illnesses (multiple sclerosis to anorexia, cancer to chronic fatigue syndrome) was that too much stress, or stress without recovery—think of a driven type A executive—compromised performance and was physically harmful. But too little expenditure or effort—think of a depressed or sedentary person—can be unhealthy as well, resulting in stagnation or even illness. "Health," Dardik wrote, "depends on a balanced relationship between stress and recovery, a recurrent, rhythmic wave of energy expenditure and energy recovery."

The challenge is not to avoid stress—which is impossible—but to respond to it with strength, hardiness, and flexibility. Stress can lead to growth if it is not too intense or severe or if there is sufficient recovery and rest.

Balancing stress and recovery can both rejuvenate our bodies and avert breakdown. Vacations from work, daily responsibilities, and routine are essential for mental and physical health. To achieve a balanced cycle of stress and recovery we need to take mini vacations throughout the day, not simply get periodic respites at night, on the weekends, or during our allotted two weeks off from work. Consider, for example, taking small breaks every hour and a half or so at the office and move, drink some water, and change your focus. Even when I have back-to-back patients throughout the day, I try to take a break after each session and meditate for several minutes and do at least a few yoga postures. By the end of the day I have sometimes completed a whole yoga routine.

MODIFY BASED ON FEEDBACK

In 1975, years ago, my body taught me that doing yoga before playing basketball made me physically uncomfortable and hindered my performance. If your workouts have an adverse effect, physically or emotionally, adjust accordingly.

Injuries are inevitable. The causes are numerous and range from sudden stress on muscles or joints to emotional conflicts such as excessive ambition or buried anger. We need to treat injuries as our teachers, because just like pain, they may be feedback indicating any number of things including that we are striving too hard because of either greed or inattention.

Meditation and hatha yoga have helped me tune into and read feedback. This has allowed me to respect and more regularly avoid injuries, rather than try to override them—which almost always leads to pain and/or incapacitation.

We need to modify what we do based on feedback from our bodies, and work within the limitations imposed by injuries. Patience and flexibility are essential. Don't overwork or underwork. Play the edge of the affliction. In the case of pulled muscles, for example, the temptation might be to remain sedentary. We will certainly prevent further damage if we are inactive, but we may also prolong the healing process, for the affected area will not get enough circulation. What if we did a yoga posture that involved the damaged muscle and stopped the stretch right before the place where we felt pain and held it for an extended period of time, say a minute or two longer than usual? We might improve circulation without risking worsening the injury.

An arena where this really comes into play is our attitude toward food. Have you ever asked yourself why you do not do things that are physically good for you, like eating the right amount? There are probably many reasons ranging from physical hunger, to painful feelings we wish to anesthetize, to emotional deprivation, but a crucial factor, I suspect, is that we are eating for our *minds* and not for our bodies. Immediate gratification, pleasure, and short-term wishes overwhelm our awareness of longer-term consequences—what we need to flourish.

We need to eat for our bodies not for our minds, which is another aspect of modifying our efforts at self-care based on feedback. When we are tempted to overeat—or when we do—we can try to reflect on our emotional states. Are you feeling bored, angry, or emotionally deprived? Trying to deaden emotional pain?

Eating is ordinarily a relatively unconscious process. We gulp down food with hardly any awareness. The emphasis on moment-to-moment attentiveness in Eastern meditative practices can be applied to how we eat, and is a wonderful antidote to the problem of mindless and careless consumption of food, which is, with inactivity and poor nutritional choices, a central culprit in the epidemic of obesity in the United States.

When we slow down and eat more mindfully, we taste the food and are tuned into how we feel. We can be clearer and more aware, and it is easier to read feedback and modify our behavior accordingly. When we deal with our feelings more consciously and directly—especially the urge for emotional consolation and meaning—we also can more readily eat for our bodies instead of for our minds.

When clients who are struggling with weight issues experiment by eating more mindfully—thoroughly chewing, tasting, and savoring each bite—they inevitably report that it enhances the experience, they eat in a more balanced way, and they lose weight.

Similarly, some people find it helpful to reflect upon a period of good health and energy in their lives. What did we eat? How often did we exercise? Think about what you can learn from an especially healthy time in your life. During that period did you have more sustaining relationships and fulfilling work? Were you in a better sleep routine? Did you handle emotional conflict more skillfully?

Another way that we can hone our ability to modify our behavior based on feedback is to notice the impact of what (and when) we eat on how we feel by noticing which foods energize or deplete us. Detecting patterns of increased energy or sluggishness alerts us to foods that agree with us or that we are allergic to. Increased lethargy may signal that we are allergic to certain foods even though we like them.

BUILD IT IN

When I first studied tai chi, I noticed a disturbing pattern. Since I was a beginner, and only knew a limited number of poses, I could practice everything I learned in class numerous times and it would take only ten or twenty minutes. I still practiced irregularly. During the same period in my life I participated in a three-times-a-week basketball game with my best friend that took up significantly more time, but I never missed it. I began wondering why the basketball game happened without a hitch but the tai chi didn't.

The basketball game was *built into* my schedule; the tai chi was *fitted in*. Whatever is built in—like your morning routine before work or walking the dog—happens almost all the time (except for emergencies). Whatever is fitted in—*maybe I'll meditate at some point tonight or tomorrow morning*—only happens some of the time because it is crowded out by pressing deadlines, other commitments, and feelings of "not wanting to" in the moment.

No one always wants to exercise. At one time or another everyone lacks motivation or confronts physical injuries. Job or family stresses, anxiety, and depression sap our will. You may be "under the weather" or emotionally stressed out. You "just don't feel like it." You believe that you don't "have the energy" to work out. Without a structure, most people have trouble with self-discipline and mindlessly drift.

Sometimes "not-wanting to" exercise can be feedback that we are mentally or physically tired and need a break; just as often it can be a sign of a rebellion against what we perceive as an external, critical command—from an authority figure with the power to control us—but that is actually our own wish. Refusing to do what we want to do and what is good for us may be a way of thumbing our noses at the inner tyrant. But at other times we need to be wary of taking the feeling of not wanting to do something too seriously. We need to make whatever supports our physical health an unquestioned part of our routine.

VINYĀSA KRAMA

The best way to attain even lofty objectives is through an orderly progression, called *vinyāsa krama* in yoga. "Vinyāsa krama is a correctly organized course of *āsanas* progressing appropriately towards a desired goal," according to T. K. V. Desikachar in *The Heart of Yoga*. *Krama* is the step, *nyāsa* means "to place," and the prefix *vi* translates as "in a special way." He continues, "The concept of vinyāsa krama tells us that it is not enough to simply take a step; that step needs to take us in the right direction and be made in the right way." While *vinyāsa krama* is usually treated in the yogic tradition as a wisely organized sequence of yogic postures, it is also a wonderful asset for physical health. For whatever we do, from cardiovascular training to changes in eating, goals that are broken down into their component parts and approached slowly and methodically are much more easily achieved.

An inactive person can't, and shouldn't, suddenly participate in a 10K race without proper preparation. Instead begin with gentle walking with rest in between, proceed to light jogging, and gradually increase the duration and intensity, letting your body acclimate to changes before proceeding to a higher level. And a person who wishes to drastically change his diet should also do so in carefully calibrated stages including identifying what he would like to subtract and add to his diet and then slowly doing each. A wise sequencing increases the likelihood that change is realistic, not sabotaged by discouragement or injury, and that we can integrate it into our lives so that it will not be harmful.

DON'T PANIC WHEN YOU SLIP

We are all "human, all-too-human," as Nietzsche said. Most people go off the rails in their physical self-care at some point. More often than not, some (if not all) of our plans for physical health will be momentarily disrupted because of life circumstances, self-doubt, or impulsivity. It's hard to always avoid sleeping too little, drinking too much, pushing too hard, getting injured, canceling exercise because we are drowning at work, or binging because we are especially anxious or depressed.

Mindfulness, which is essentially awareness without judgment, is indispensable in both compassionately responding to slips and increasing the likelihood that we can catch ourselves before we actually revert to old, bad habits. When we greet such lapses with a kind heart, it makes it much easier to treat imperfection as a sign of our humanness, not proof of our badness. Self-acceptance and patience help us learn from what happened, begin again, and not stay stuck in a vicious cycle of shame and denial.

Many years ago a friend of mine who knew an enormous amount about physical health kept getting respiratory ailments. Once she realized what Freud called the "secondary gain," or the "gain from illness"—that she smoked to avoid gaining weight—she felt freed up to address her concerns about excess poundage more directly. As she ate more mindfully and exercised more regularly, she stopped smoking and maintained a comfortable weight.

When we slip, it is helpful to study the triggers and what benefit we derive from going off course. What caused you to deviate from a healthy self-care plan? What is the hidden payoff for what you did that you otherwise feel guilty about?

Concepts and techniques from the *Yoga Sutra*, the core text of the yogic tradition, may be enormously helpful when neither meditation nor reflection prevents slipping. When we are in an agitated or disturbed state of mind, we have little clarity, our perception is foggy, and we make mistakes that lead us astray. The compiler of the *Yoga Sutra*, Patanjali, mentions the power of the out-breath in sutra 1:34: "The mind also attains serenity through prolonged exhalation." This is something you may have experienced while trying the meditation I recommended in chapter 1. Quiet, easeful breathing with an extended exhale before we eat is a way of calming the mind and creating expanded inner space so that we can reflect more fully on the longer-term impact of the short-term choice we are tempted by. I have used this when I am eating a meal after a challenging psychotherapy session and feel either perturbed or dull. Inevitably I feel more relaxed and alert after doing the yogic breathing; ready to eat based on what my body needs, rather than on what my feelings might dictate.

"When harassed by doubt, cultivate the opposite mental attitude," says sutra 11:33. Reversing one's state of mind—one suggestive commentary writes of seeing with opposite eyes—is presented as a way of gaining some perspective on what we are tempted to do. I eat a careful diet, filled with small amounts of fish or chicken and large portions of vegetables and fruits. One of my "vices" is to get buttered popcorn once in a while when I go to the movies. I have recently noticed that I am congested the next day. Shifting perspective—imagining how I will feel the morning after consuming popcorn before I order it—is an effective way for me to reflect on the consequences of eating what I may be allergic to.

The prevailing wisdom in more progressive Western medicine and alternative or complementary schools of thought is that exercise, healthy diets, and holistic practices balance and strengthen the immune system, the body's network and system of self-protection and healing. This is true. All of these factors can improve our immune systems.

Yet there is another crucial source for enhancing our physical health—the healing potential of particular psychological traits and qualities such as self-awareness and the ability to express what we are experiencing, psychological hardiness (the capacity to overcome adversity and find meaning in life through being committed to work, creative pursuits, or relationships), healthy assertiveness, close relationships, and altruism. Significant research suggests that the presence of these personality traits improves immune functioning, protects us against the negative effects on the body of stress, and nurtures a strong body and a strong mind. What I have seen in my practice and my life, for example, is that lives of meaning, fulfillment, and connectedness have more resilience and joy, creativity and vitality, than lives of wealth and power that lack purpose and intimacy.

Befriending Our Bodies

When we are in harmony with our bodies we feel better about ourselves and are more capable of and eager to open ourselves to other people and share ourselves physically, as well as emotionally. Physical vitality is a great attractor not only because fit people look good, but also because they exude a healthy self-love that suggests that they have the potential to love others. For all of these reasons, befriending our bodies and cultivating physical health is a crucial preparation for and way to enrich intimacy.

Now that we are more at home with—and in—our bodies, we are ready to connect to and take sustenance from the wonders of spirituality, which moves through and within us, even when it comes from outside us. It's time to examine what spirituality is and how we can bring it into our lives.

BRINGING SPIRITUALITY
DOWN TO EARTH

The question prospective patients most frequently ask when they are deciding if they will work with me is: "Do you have a spiritual orientation?"

Surprising? Not really. I've noticed in my practice that more and more people are interested in spirituality and hoping to integrate it into their lives.

Erosion of trust in established authorities of government and organized religion has created a vacuum for many of us. As faith in institutions that once gave us a sense of meaning and belonging declines among individuals, many people feel adrift. For example, I've noticed in my work that increasing numbers of clients feel betrayed by their religion—and spiritually homeless—after their highest ideals are violated by religious leaders. My clients also feel that core beliefs within faith communities don't always offer completely convincing explanations or sufficient solace for some of the challenges confronted in this new millennium, including genuine threats to planetary and personal survival.

There is a yearning among many of us for sustaining sources of guidance, meaning, and solace. Increasing numbers of people are dissatisfied with the dominant ethos of materialism and egocentricity and feel that there is more to life than wealth or power.

Spirituality is one crucial source of that "something more." Intense and compelling, moments of spirituality—when the barriers between the world and ourselves decrease and we feel at one with the universe—teach us that reality is more vast and wondrous than we conceived and there are potentials of the human spirit that we never imagined.

Spiritual experiences give life to life.

No longer the stepchild of religion, spirituality is idealized and exalted—perhaps as an antidote to the greed and corruption that permeates our culture. Authors proclaim its transformative powers; polls, books, magazine articles, movies, and television talk shows attest to its central role in our collective consciousness; and workshop leaders profess to teach us how to access it.

There is also great confusion about what spirituality is, and how to bring it down to earth and into our lives. When we hear the word *spirituality* it may conjure up images of saffron-robed monks in Buddhist monasteries or men in ceremonial outfits in houses of worship—either of which might appear to inhabit radically different worlds from our own.

Writers don't even know that they disagree about what the term *spirituality* means because it is never defined and is used differently by each person. One reason spirituality may be so popular is that we know very little about what it is, which provides huge leeway in fashioning it in our own image and using it to pursue a way of life that feels very distant from values such as materialism that disturb us.

Is spirituality divorced from daily life and can we only experience it by self-denial or ascetic behavior—renouncing everyday pleasures and passions? Is spirituality a feeling of being connected to something larger than us? Or does it involve appreciating the small miracles? If spirituality is connected with and expressed in compassion for others, then why are so many spiritual seekers focused on themselves and their own progress?

"I'm afraid and confused about spirituality," a client of mine, a thoughtful woman in her early thirties, recently said to me. "I want to find a spiritual home, but it's not working. I worry that I'm not a deep person."

She is not alone. Many of us want to be more spiritual and are not quite sure how to get there. Can we find spirituality in the midst of daily activities—working or dating, parenting or playing—or is it necessary to attend religious services or meditation or yoga retreats? Can we still be spiritual even if we can't live up to the lofty ideals that the great religious traditions espouse? Do we have to follow a set of prescribed rituals dictated by an organized religion or religious leader to experience spirituality? And can we lead a spiritual life in the midst of the stress and speed of everyday life?

When a word like *spirituality* has many vague definitions and is used profligately, confusion follows. Several years ago I asked every client, colleague, and friend who used the word how he or she defined it. What I discovered was that while people tend to think of spirituality in terms of their own particular experience of it, spirituality has many facets. While this may seem on the surface to be obvious, in practice few people ever clarify what they mean when they use this word. Spirituality cannot be restricted to a single person's interpretation, any more than love or sadness can.

Six Kinds of Spirituality

There are at least six types of spirituality: a state of natural wakefulness in which we feel deep clarity and openheartedness; union with something greater than ourselves; cultivation of character; living our lives based on a larger meaning and purpose; developing our highest self; and following a systematic path to fundamental transformation.

Sometimes spiritual experiences arise out of pain. Other times, from silence or beauty. Whatever the source, the spiritual is all around us. Spirituality is definitely not something we have to go somewhere special to access; rather it lives in the ordinary world of responsibilities and pressures, joys and sorrows. It can touch us anytime, anywhere: in our daily activities, at work, in our homes, and in our relationships. When we stop seeing it as separate from daily life, its power touches us more often. We can see the sacred in every moment and thereby make every moment sacred. We can, in fact, encounter the spiritual in everything— parenting a child, participating in an intimate relationship, communing with nature, creating and viewing art, or playing sports.

NATURAL WAKEFULNESS

Natural wakefulness is the first kind of spirituality. It's a state of luminous clarity, heightened presence, and expanded kindheartedness that we can always awaken to.

A patient describes hurrying to the subway, lost in thought, feeling irritated and down. She's late for work and tired of rushing. "Look at the quality of the light," she hears someone say. When she looks up she sees a middle-aged woman on crutches gazing intently at the sunrise. The patient looks too. Suddenly her constriction and moodiness vanish and her mind feels peaceful and spacious, unclouded like a clear sky. She also feels immensely kindhearted and grateful; awakened to the beauty of the world—natural wakefulness.

Natural wakefulness is like a channel that is always on but that we are not always tuned to. We don't own it and we can't hold it in our hands, but it's a simple, profound, natural dimension of being that is hidden until we experience it, eminently real and accessible to us all in every moment. There are many doorways into it, from meditation, prayer, and yoga to playing and intimacy—anybody can enter. And when we do—which is an ever-present possibility—we relate with less constriction and more love, and have greater reverence for the people and world we encounter.

THE SPIRITUALITY OF UNION

"Once, in my early thirties," the poet Jane Kenyon wrote in "Having It Out with Melancholy," her poem about depression, "I saw / that I was a speck of light in the great / river of light that undulates through time. / I was floating with the whole / human family. We were all colors—those / who are living now, those who have died, / those who are not yet born."

The experience of oneness with the larger world is another facet of spirituality. We can feel this when we are intimate with another person, linked on a deep level; when we are connected to the natural world; when we are engaged in a physical activity in which our bodies and minds are in harmony; or when we are doing work in which we are wholeheartedly immersed.

The spirituality of union is important because it makes us feel connected to something beyond our isolated selves and can thus lessen self-alienation and foster greater compassion and care toward others. Moral accountability expands when there is a deep sense of interconnectedness between people, something that is illustrated by the mercy of the Amish toward the family of Charles Roberts. On October 2, 2006, Charles Roberts IV killed five Amish schoolgirls and then himself in Nickel Mines, Pennsylvania. The Amish community responded to the massacre not by seeking vengeance, but by establishing a charitable fund for Roberts' widow, Marie, and their children. Marie Roberts wrote an open letter to her Amish neighbors thanking them for their forgiveness, grace, and mercy: "Your love for our family has helped to provide the healing we so desperately need. Gifts you've given have touched our hearts in a way no words can describe. Your compassion has reached beyond our family, beyond our community, and is changing our world, and for this we sincerely thank you."

The response of the Amish deeply touches our hearts, profoundly challenges our preconceptions about human nature, and illustrates the moral dimension of spirituality.

THE SPIRITUALITY OF CHARACTER

A few years ago at the Seattle Special Olympics, nine contestants, all physically or mentally disabled, assembled at the starting line for the hundred-yard dash. At the gun, they all took off—not exactly in a dash—with pure enthusiasm for the race. One boy stumbled on the asphalt, tumbled over a few times, and began to cry. He seemed devastated. The other eight children heard him. They all slowed down and looked back and then returned to the boy on the ground. One girl with Down's syndrome bent down and kissed him and said, "This will make it better." The eight children picked the boy up. All nine children linked arms and walked across the finish line together. Everyone in the stadium stood, and the cheering went on for several minutes. The audience at the Seattle Special Olympics had witnessed the power of compassion and the spirituality of character.

Spirituality of character is the development of particular virtues and attributes that are often neglected in daily life; qualities such as wonder and tolerance, tenderness and generosity, reverence and wisdom. Just as we are what we eat, we are what we *do*. We can cultivate certain qualities within us that, when practiced on a daily basis, will change our characters. We can teach ourselves to feel gratitude for what we have; to be more empathetic and compassionate; to look inside for wisdom and resilience. Our attention to these virtues will allow them to grow within us and we will become what we value.

We are practicing spirituality of character when we respect life in all forms; are grateful for our health and that of our family; appreciate the way our spouses show their love, even when it is in a different "language" than what we would prefer; and have sensitivity to and rise above another person's behavior even when it disturbs us.

Cultivating the spirituality of character could change the ethical climate of relationships and politics, business and international affairs, ultimately fostering more compassion and generosity. When we cultivate respect and empathy toward people with very different viewpoints—including individuals from whom we were formerly estranged—we often decrease mistrust, lessen a sense of betrayal, and collaborate more effectively.

THE SPIRITUALITY OF MEANING AND PURPOSE

A woman from California who lost all of her possessions in a fire—every family photograph, a grandfather clock built by her husband, a treasured quilt, and all the hand-knit sweaters that kept her warm—says the tragedy forced her to "look at *what really matters*," wrote Sue Bender in *Everyday Sacred*. The tragedy "fine-tunes my attitude about the remainder of my life," she said. She now possesses deeper gratitude for what she has and she no longer wastes time being unhappy about decisions she's already made.

When we live our lives based on meaning and purpose greater than personal gain, we can work for something bigger than merely ourselves. There are two ways we can embody the spirituality of meaning and purpose. We can wholeheartedly take care of the responsibilities that make up our lives—as a parent, spouse, business leader, or employee—and we can try to improve our community. Working toward peace and social justice and lessening pollution, increasing literacy and carrying a stroller up the subway steps for a besieged mother, are all ways to do this. Cultivating spirituality of purpose and meaning would encourage individuals, elected officials, and business leaders to focus on the collective good as well as the financial bottom line. Groups such as the World

Business Academy, for example, encourage businesses to "include social progress in their bottom line." The joint efforts of Bill Gates and Warren Buffett to give billions back to society illustrate how you can focus on the collective good as well as financial success.

THE SACRED SPIRITUAL SELF

Whenever we respond to life from a clear, balanced, and caring place— rather than from a constricted, narrow, and reactive one—and connect to a deeper, holier sense of ourselves, we are manifesting the sacred spiritual self. When we live in a more spacious, generous, and truthful way we act from the best within us—treating others and ourselves kindly and patiently, with care and affection. Expansive and connected, we experience self-acceptance and greater intimacy. We can be open to the unique qualities and needs of the other while respecting ourselves.

While obviously not all of us have the capacity for compassion and forgiveness that the Amish demonstrated, we can still access the sacred spiritual self in our own ways when we respond to life's challenges and injuries by reaching for the best within us instead of reacting based on pride or revenge. Take Aba Gayle, a silver-haired grandmother of five. Gayle has visited Douglas Mickey in San Quentin Prison a couple of times a year since she moved from California to Oregon. She also regularly exchanges letters and phone calls with Mickey—the man who stabbed her daughter to death. As Vince Beiser wrote in "The Ultimate Forgiveness: To Err Is Human, to Forgive Divine—to Befriend Someone Who Took the Life of a Loved One Is Another Matter" in the *Los Angeles Times Magazine* in April 2004, "Gayle was submerged in a miasma of depression and rage. Then one night, in an epiphany, she decided to forgive Mickey. She wrote him a letter saying so. From his cell on death row, where he has been since 1982, Mickey wrote back, full of remorse, and invited her to visit." The two kept corresponding, which led to more visits, until Gayle reached the point where she could say, "'I consider Douglas a good friend. He's such a wonderful man.'" Certainly, Gayle's story is extraordinary, but as Beiser notes, it is not unique:

> She is one of a small but resolute society of individuals who have had a beloved relative murdered—and gone on to befriend the murderer. . . . There's the San Diego investment banker who wants to see the man

who gunned down his son released from Pelican Bay State Prison. The Connecticut reverend that helped get his son's murderer out of the penitentiary and later officiated at his wedding. The Kansas housewife who sent birthday gifts to her stepfather's slayer and tearfully witnessed his execution last year. The retired steelworker in Alaska who helped get the girl who butchered his grandmother off of death row and regularly writes her letters. The Texas machinist who visited his sister's killer, Karla Faye Tucker, in prison, spoke out on her behalf and went to her execution as a friend. It's not even an exclusively domestic phenomenon: After Newport Beach native Amy Biehl was beaten and stabbed to death by a mob in South Africa in 1993, her parents hired two of the convicted murderers to work for the foundation they had started in her name.

While these are remarkable acts of compassion—and may, at times, involve denial and rationalizing away tragedy—every smaller gesture we make, no matter how seemingly insignificant, can have ramifications that we cannot predict, but that may contribute to creating a more humane world.

"I pride myself on being spiritual," a client said to me recently. "But I regret that I don't have a practice." Many people find it helpful to have a systematic way to cultivate and refine their spirituality. A spiritual path is the sixth aspect of spirituality.

THE SPIRITUAL PATH

The great spiritual traditions recognize that direct experience of the sacred—that which is of ultimate concern and worth cherishing—as opposed to mere knowledge about it, is indispensable. Spiritual practices are based on what facilitated the enlightenment or realization of the founder of the particular tradition. The ethical commandments and contemplations of a spiritual path are all designed to foster such realizations in those that follow them. The spiritual path—which may include rituals and practices like prayer and meditation, confession and the following of specific ethical guidelines such as the Ten Commandments in Abrahamic faiths or the Eight-Fold Path in Buddhism—also aids the seeker in experiencing other kinds of spirituality.

In recent years an increasing number of people have created spiritual paths that combine features from one or more traditions. I know one person who, while born a Jew, considers herself a Buddhist; another who is a student of yoga and a devout Christian; and yet another who is an observant Catholic who practices tai chi. While there is a danger of superficiality when pursuing two traditions simultaneously, there can be advantages as well. Blind spots and limitations within one tradition become more readily apparent when theories and methods are viewed in light of another. Judiciously combining insights and practices from different paths can make each richer than if pursued alone, as I experienced with meditative psychotherapy.

Another advantage is that we are all different. Our paths and practices must reflect our individualities, as T. K. V. Desikachar writes in *Health, Healing and Beyond*. Whether we follow a traditional way of life or an eclectic and nonsectarian one, the road we take should be geared to the person rather than the other way around. We also need to seek a practice that goes against the grain of, and challenges, our conditioning, habits and patterns. Type A people might be drawn to vigorous yoga practice with a lot of sweating, but might do better with a more soothing and calming practice. Those of us who are shy and uncomfortable with our assertiveness could be attracted to a meditation practice that allows us to hide and isolate, but what might be more helpful is something that is physically and emotionally empowering such as the martial arts.

Five Pitfalls on the Spiritual Path

Spirituality is usually presented in idyllic terms, as a wonderful and completely positive experience. During a recent lecture on psychotherapy and the spirituality quest, I discussed with the audience the positive features of spirituality. I then asked them—doctors, psychotherapists, psychology students, and spiritual seekers—if there was anything we had left out. They were silent. No one said a word about the negative aspects of spirituality.

But as with any experience, spirituality has pitfalls, which interfere with flourishing. Let's consider five.

ETHICAL DANGERS OF THE SPIRITUALITY OF UNION

There is no guarantee that the experience of union with someone or something beyond us is positive. Many spiritual seekers blindly follow charismatic teachers. In its most extreme versions such surrender can unfortunately take the form of masochistic submission in which one becomes pathologically deferential toward a leader. Initially the uncritical devotion may offer relief as it seems to promise connectedness and even direction about how to live. But over a longer period of time the seeker no longer thinks for him- or herself, denying signs of group-think, and rationalizes disturbing behavior on the part of either the teacher or members of the community. The consequence is that individuality is obliterated, not enriched. When the teacher is immune to feedback and the student has no impact, then authoritarianism rules the day. Questions that cannot be asked about the teacher, and doctrines that are supposed to be taken completely on faith, may signal the presence of a teacher or a community that is autocratic rather than liberating. When one exercises discriminating awareness, and values one's feelings, such pathological submissiveness can be avoided. Genuine union enriches our souls and gives us more respect for and connection with other people and the world.

THE BURDEN OF THE SPIRITUALITY OF CHARACTER

Many of us have known spiritual teachers and seekers who speak of compassion and generosity yet act selfishly and immorally. They advocate a love for all beings, yet often remain in conflict with their own families or students. Ideals of spiritual perfection or virtue—eternal patience and unselfishness, kindness and forgiveness—even in the face of cruelty, betrayal, or abuse—can inspire spiritual seekers to be better people. They can also burden us with unrealistic goals, which we can't live up to—making us feel bad about ourselves. These ideals disregard our fallibility as imperfect humans and leach joy from our lives. I have worked with numerous students from an assortment of religious and contemplative traditions whose imperfect efforts to adhere to the ideals of total selflessness, perfect mindfulness, and complete purity of conduct left them feeling ashamed about their inability to achieve unreachable spiritual standards.

THE SPIRITUALITY OF MEANING AND PURPOSE CAN SEPARATE US FROM OTHER PEOPLE AND DAILY LIFE

Have you ever felt judged because you did not devote yourself to a certain cause or practice that a member of your own spiritual community regarded with great zeal? You didn't pray enough, meditate as often, or have time to volunteer? Trying to live based on a deeper meaning and purpose can cause us to be critical and condemn people who have different lives or practices. Commenting on the American Sufi community she once belonged to, Elizabeth Lesser wrote in *The New American Spirituality*: "In everything we did we took each other to task for laziness at work or worship." Lesser adds that the leader of the community, Pir Vilayat, "coined the phrase 'slugs and heroes' . . . Those who gave themselves selflessly to family and community were heroes. Slugs were chastised for thinking only about themselves, resting too much, or not participating in community activities . . . Self-judgment and the effort to rid myself of 'ego' . . . turned into an unforgiving attitude toward myself and others."

The spirituality of meaning and purpose can also make us devalue ordinary life—the human tasks and responsibilities that we face—cleaning the bathroom, making meals, answering mail, even parenting. It's easy to lose track of the beauty and meaning of daily life when we hunt for special and extraordinary spiritual experiences. Spirituality is not separate from daily life—our emotions, mundane responsibilities, and intimate relationships—and it can be experienced within a job or marriage as well as at a meditation or yoga retreat. One couple I know, for example, downscaled their lives when their daughter was a teenager so they could spend much less time at work and have more quality time at home. They practiced cherishing the moments they had together and treating whatever they encountered in the world with greater reverence, rather than focusing on enhancing their careers or professional reputations.

THE SACRED SELF CAN LEAD TO SELF-NEGLECT

While it is true that becoming more spiritual *can* be an antidote to selfish behavior, there are people for whom selflessness is harmful. The problem for many women and some men is not that they are too self-centered and need to be more spiritual and altruistic, but that they deprive themselves by making other people more important than themselves. The sacred self is not an unloved or uncared-for self. If we already struggle with self-care, the emphasis in spiritual practice on being more selfless—making other peoples' needs and issues more important than our own—often deepens self-neglect. A truly spiritual person tries to balance the needs of others and his or her own self-care requirements. My own spiritual journey, for example, has been influenced by Joel Kramer's emphasis on the importance of integrating altruism and self-care. Since they are two sides of the same coin, I now strive to both nurture myself and have empathy and compassion for other people.

A SPIRITUAL PATH CAN LEAD TO SELF-VIOLATION

There is no single spiritual path that works for everyone. A hidden assumption subscribed to by most people and rarely examined is that the seeker must fit into and conform to the path, rather than the path being adapted to the person. What worked for someone else can be a useful guide, but a dangerous master. The knowledge and wisdom of tradition—which is what many spiritual paths are built upon—can be enlightening. But each of us must choose a way of practice that is suited to who we are and what we need, one that both nourishes and challenges us; one that helps us overcome habitual conditioning and grow beyond where we are.

Otherwise, we can betray ourselves. A Buddhist meditation teacher injured his knee hiking before the evening spiritual talk he was about to give. He considered sitting in a chair during his talk but ultimately decided to sit full-lotus, which is the traditional way in Buddhism. After his talk, his knee hurt so much that he couldn't walk and he had to be carried to his room. He ignored the wisdom of his own body in trying to stay loyal to the contemplative practice he was devoted to. When the path becomes more important than the person, and we ignore either physical or emotional feedback, we violate ourselves.

How We Can Bring Spirituality Down to Earth

Through years of clinical and spiritual work I have discovered nine different ways that we can bring spirituality into our lives. For me it has been important to reconnect with why I was initially drawn to spirituality and how I can continually renew my connection to it.

1. CONNECT WITH THE CALL

A spiritual quest may often be triggered by a powerful experience that served as a wake-up call, alerting us to possibilities of the human spirit we may never have encountered. These experiences can be either positive or negative—a tremendous insight or a shattering tragedy. Some of the most spiritual people I know are victims of trauma. For one therapist I treated who had a severe history of abuse and neglect, spirituality offered a much more compelling way of being than the tarnished world of her abusers.

Connecting with the original motivating force of our spiritual journey provides a powerful impetus for our path. It can inspire commitment and link us to the deepest source of what we are seeking. It can also give us courage to confront challenges and tragedies that threaten to overwhelm us.

2. PAY ATTENTION

A psychiatrist once asked a teacher of Zen what he thought about altered states of consciousness. "I'm just trying to help my students hear the birds sing," he replied. When we pay attention we experience a richer life. Not only do we miss less, but we also sanctify the ordinary— treating it with reverence. It is how we begin to awaken our spiritual consciousness on a daily basis. More of what we encounter then takes on a more sacred character. Awareness practices such as meditation, yoga, and tai chi can refine our capacity to do this.

3. LIVE YOUR ETHICS

We can practice ethical behavior in everyday life by speaking and behaving more carefully and truthfully. Practice listening *to* other people rather than listening *for* what you already believe. Be attentive to your timing and tone and the needs and feelings of the person you are communicating with. Stick to your moral code in your interactions with others—even if you are pressured to compromise it—and refuse to be drawn into gossip, bullying, ethnic jokes, or bigoted remarks. Living our ethics helps us treat the people we come in contact with—from the bus driver to the coworker to the waitress who serves us lunch—with care and respect.

Living an ethical life—being committed to increasing the care and minimizing the harm we do to others and ourselves—not only fosters closer connections with other people and lessens the forces that threaten to divide and alienate us—such as fear and mistrust—but opens the door to more spirituality in our lives.

4. MAKE SPACE IN YOUR LIFE FOR WHAT IS IMPORTANT

Make room in your life for what really matters. It is very easy to pursue unessential projects or goals, as if they are crucial to your well-being. Turn off the TV, talk with your spouse or a friend you haven't connected with for a while, forgo your BlackBerry and play one more game with your kids, call an elderly relative or neighbor and check in to see how he or she is doing. Building time into your life for those people, activities, and causes that nourish your soul is an important way of strengthening your commitment to what is of true and enduring value.

5. CREATE A BIGGER CONTAINER

The poet Rainer Maria Rilke writes that the "point is to live everything . . . Live the questions now." Nothing is outside the spiritual journey—everything can be included within it—our triumphs and struggles, our minds and bodies, our hearts and souls. While spiritual literature can alert us to numerous distractions and seductions in daily life—such as selfishness and the attachment to false promises of fulfillment from wealth, power, and fame—it can also cause us to imagine that salvation lies outside the world and the present moment. When this happens, seekers become too detached from themselves, their lives, and their relationships.

Living a contemplative life beckons from an opposite direction. Authentic spirituality involves creating a "bigger container" within ourselves so that we can open up to more and more of life and delve into the mystery and richness of other people and the universe. Recognizing our strengths and talents, as well as fears and inhibitions, can help build a bigger vessel within us and bring more spirituality into our lives. We can go about doing this by trying to open to, instead of judging or renouncing, whatever we experience, from challenging emotions to behavior we are guilty about.

6. CELEBRATE

"In the prison of his days," writes the poet W. H. Auden, "teach the free man how to praise." Showing gratitude for life's wondrous gifts—including its beauty and magic—opens the window to the breeze of spirituality. "Every day is a good day," the Zen teacher Ummon once said. Even though many days are difficult—filled with loss and regret, pain and doubt—when we face them with a spacious mind and an open heart they become opportunities.

Make a list each evening of whom or what you are grateful for. It could be a small act of kindness, a moment of beauty, or an opportunity to help someone. Celebrating the wonders of the natural world, new dreams, moments of surprise and intimacy, and acts of empathy and generosity helps us count our blessings. It also lessens the destructive habit of focusing solely on what's wrong. Building in rituals that appreciate life's bounty—such as blessing a meal, honoring milestones including births and rites of passage like weddings, graduations, and anniversaries—allows us to experience the joy, connection, and meaning that life bestows on us in a more profound way.

7. CULTIVATE HOPE

If change is your goal, optimism is a better strategy than pessimism. In times of profound upheaval, it is tempting to sink into pessimism. We can nourish hope by meeting periodically with friends and family to reflect upon sources of possibility—constructive thoughts and ideas, inspirational practices and activities, new dreams we have for ourselves, our family, or our community. Dwelling on hope allows us to use our energy to make positive changes. Likewise, shielding ourselves from demoralizing stimuli, such as people who are chronically negative, or media that sensationalizes bad or tragic news, also contributes to cultivating hope.

8. NURTURE RESILIENCE

Resilience allows us to turn challenges into opportunities instead of defeats. It spurs us to carve out lives of greater meaning and connection even during difficult times. Inner strength can be developed or depleted by the way we live and the choices we make. Connecting with people and resources (books and movies, nature and music) that affirm life is a crucial way of cultivating resilience. Pay attention to what increases or depletes your resolve. Reflect upon what we can learn from examples of courage and strength, integrity and wisdom. Cultivating associations with like-spirited people—your parish, your temple, your workplace, your neighborhood, your volunteer organizations—reinforces inner resilience.

9. SERVICE

Authentic spirituality doesn't involve turning your back on the world, it involves engaging it empathetically and wholeheartedly. Helping others who are less fortunate and returning the gifts and opportunities we have been blessed with by friends, family, teachers, mentors, and coaches is one way we can do this. A traditional yogic belief is that if we don't share our gifts we rob the world. Imagine a world in which we all hid the goodness in our hearts. Life provides endless opportunities to practice caring and compassion, and to express our generosity of spirit by lending our concern and empathy, knowledge and skills to those in need. Service is as close at hand as quietly listening to a family member in confusion or pain, reading a friend's manuscript, or volunteering as a Big Brother or Big Sister.

Spirituality has no zip code and it flourishes in countless forms. It need not be a source of pressure or anxiety, but something we can all experience, whether as a parent or teacher, a patient with a challenging illness, or an artist creating beauty, when we live with greater attention and care, compassion, and connection.

Bringing spirituality down to earth and into our lives is one of the greatest gifts we can give ourselves and the world; filling our days with greater joy and purpose and enabling us to bring hope and inspiration to the lives of those we touch. Spirituality expands our identity, deepens our humanity, and increases our capacity for wise action—all of which are crucial to self-care—and the art of flourishing.

While spirituality is a crucial—and wondrous—gift that the universe makes available to us, it is often used to bypass challenging feelings. In order to flourish we need to understand and skillfully respond to the full range of our emotions.

5

> It is easy to get angry—anyone can do that . . . but to feel or act towards the right person to the right extent at the right time for the right reason in the right way— that is not easy, and it is not everyone that can do it.
>
> —ARISTOTLE

> **No way out but through.**
>
> —ROBERT FROST

EMOTIONAL FLOURISHING

Cultivating Self-Awareness, Empathy, and Wise Action

Nina was a vivacious, energetic thirty-four-year-old owner of a small but successful fashion accessory company. Her husband, Jerry, a thirty-six-year-old lawyer with a small private practice, specialized in wills and estates. Jerry was not adrenaline charged and he was comfortable making his own hours. While Nina had a forty-five-minute commute, Jerry worked in the same town in which they lived. He was home before Nina, and was happy to be the primary-care parent of their seven-year-old son.

"On one level, I'm doing really well," Nina told me. "I love my work and I'm excited about it. There's always something new, and I like the challenge of helping women feel good about themselves. But when I think of Jerry, I feel guilty, like I shouldn't enjoy my success because it will somehow hurt him. I sabotage myself at work by not allowing myself to be as successful as I could be. I also know that I'm cheating myself by not fully appreciating how much I have to be thankful about."

Nina was punishing herself—and doing private "penance"—for the "misdemeanor" she imagined she had committed: earning more public recognition than her less professionally ambitious partner. This is a common example of an emotional obstacle to self-care and flourishing.

Nora, an extremely competent fifty-four-year-old plastic surgeon specializing in the repair of severely scarred skin, also struggled with emotional obstacles to self-care. "When will the other shoe drop?" was a constant fear. To her patients and hospital staff, she was the epitome of cool and confidence—never ruffled by crisis, and at her best when the stakes were high.

"It might shock even my closest friends, but, I feel like a fraud and I am constantly worried that I'll be found out," she said to me. "Every time a difficult procedure goes well, I feel like I am only putting off the inevitable."

I wondered if Nora was fearing the worst so that she wouldn't be caught off guard and shocked *if* something painful happened. But in trying to protect herself she constantly focused on negative forecasts that robbed her of the ability to appreciate the rich fulfillment her work gave her.

Judy was a nurse at a large municipal hospital. She struggled with balancing the needs of her job with good self-care. While she knew that her long-deceased parents had been overly critical and intrusive and that her stubborn and rebellious stance in certain situations was often her reaction to having felt controlled by them, she still did battle with her parents in her head over issues of autonomy.

"You want me to eat well and take care of myself? How dare you try to tell me what to do? I'll show you!" The "you" that Judy was referring to was *herself*. When she gave herself advice she felt as if someone from the outside—like a critical and overinvolved parent—was trying to control her and rob her of her autonomy. Then she rebelled against her own wishes thinking that she was protecting her freedom, unwittingly sabotaging herself.

These vignettes depict the challenges of guilt, fear, and anger—three emotions that drastically interfere with self-care.

Emotions are the universal language of human beings, the glue that connects and unites us, signaling judgments of value and guiding ethical action. When we handle emotions skillfully—heed their presence, decode their meaning, and respond wisely—we create bridges of empathy and understanding, and we live more connected and contented lives.

Emotions are also frequently the barriers that divide us. Misunderstanding and conflict due to feelings of anger and hatred, humiliation and rage, for example, underlie bigotry, sadism, and war in the world, as well as mistrust, acrimony, and violence at home. Thus, skillfully responding to feelings—understanding other people and ourselves and relating well to both—is indispensable to self-care and flourishing. There are four aspects to emotional health:

1. Accepting and learning from the full range of our feelings—from happiness to outrage.
2. Handling challenging feelings—such as anger, guilt, and fear.
3. Appreciating positive emotions such as joy, happiness, and contentment, which many people tend to push away.
4. Deepening our circle of empathy and care toward other people and ourselves.

By drawing on an integration of meditative and psychotherapeutic wisdom about feelings—a crucial aspect of meditative therapy—we can better learn how to handle emotions. Feelings are two-sided: they live in the body and have a *somatic component* (for example, constricted breathing, churning stomach, and flushed face) that alerts us to their presence. They also have a *meaning,* which we often need to decipher. In meditative therapy we use yogic breathing and meditation to quiet and focus the mind and deepen our attunement to the presence of feelings, then translate what they mean.

Emotions play a profound role in dictating how we feel and behave. If we are happy we assume we are doing well; if we aren't we are certain we are doing badly. But what we consider the best of times—periods of security and comfort—could actually be the worst, as we avoid what we need to face (such as scheduling a medical appointment). Conversely, we can feel badly yet finally confront something that leads to growth (such as addressing a problem).

Feelings—which many people interpret as facts—also play a huge role in determining our actions. "Trust your gut" and "If it feels right do it" become, for many of us, touchstones for how to behave. Feelings become compasses, mistakenly seen as indisputable and unquestioned authorities for navigating our lives. When Nina felt guilty about being more accomplished than her partner, she was rushing to judgment and didn't realize that he actually appreciated her competence and wanted to stay out of the limelight. Her efforts to undermine herself came out of a misplaced desire to expiate a baseless guilt. Following our feelings can keep us passionate and engaged, or it can leave us at the mercy of emotions that we don't understand.

The problem with treating feelings as facts is that we often view them quite negatively. As the linguist George Lakoff aptly notes in *Women, Fire, and Dangerous Things,* the language we use to describe our emotional lives casts feelings as if they are opponents or illnesses: he's *wrestling with guilt, lovesick,* and *blind with rage.*

Emotions are both reliable and unreliable guides to action. While feelings can contain exquisite sensitivity to and appraisal of people's reactions to us and their underlying motives, our emotions, as psycho-analysis teaches, also contain pictures of ourselves, other people, and the world based on childhood—and sometimes childish—experiences and expectations in our family of origin. Infantile experiences often underlie adult emotions, and can cloud our views of the present. When faced with challenging feelings about a spouse, for example, we often fail to see them clearly from an adult perspective, as opposed to a pre-rational or nonrational one. In other words, our view of a loved one may be shaped by interactions with and images of our own parents so we are certain that our spouses will treat us as our parents did, and be saviors or nemeses.

Treating feelings as facts makes us prone to being swayed by what-ever superficial biases, likes, and dislikes are front and center; this sets the stage for harmful behavior—avoiding what we need to face (like a conflict with a friend or loved one) because it doesn't "feel good." More than one politician and spiritual teacher has crashed because of enslave-ment to passions or undigested emotions.

Feelings can be unruly and upsetting—the forces that distort our judgment in everything from whom we love to where we live to what we buy. Feelings can also resist our best efforts to understand and mas-ter them.

Feelings—good and bad—come unbeckoned. "When we are angry or frightened it is not by choice," Aristotle reminds us. Remember how mad Judy got when thinking about taking care of herself?

Feelings can be easy to ignite. There is often little space or time between the spark—what causes them—and the flame—our reaction. And then they hijack us and overwhelm reason, causing us to lash out irrationally at others and ourselves.

We often respond to emotions in an intellectualized and detached manner, thinking about them instead of feeling them. We often misread feelings, treating them as what Paul Ekman, one of the world's leading authorities on emotions, calls a *false positive*—assuming that a coiled rope is a snake. And then we overreact or avoid them, repress them or dump them on other people. So we have a kind of hair-trigger reaction to the presence of feelings and often would rather not have them.

Of course, none of these self-protective strategies actually work. They interfere with self-care and flourishing. When we react to feelings without awareness or compassion, we become mired in negativity, unhappiness, and harmful behavior. Left unattended, emotions alienate us from ourselves, harm our bodies, and undermine relationships.

Given the challenge that they pose, it is not surprising that there is a tendency in our culture to try to control, bypass, or eliminate feelings. That may be why, although there's a growing emphasis on what emotional intelligence is and how to cultivate it in schools and at work, there is also a flight from the full depth of emotions—especially in pop psychological, therapeutic, and spiritual attempts to master feelings through thought and detachment.

Each of these approaches has characteristic strengths and blind spots.

Cognitive approaches assume that thoughts control feelings and if we change our thoughts we can master our emotions. This overemphasizes the power of reason to manage feelings and leads us astray, because feelings are not always controllable and can often teach us something. Judy, Nina, and Nora remained angry, guilty, and fearful even after trying to control their distressing feelings. Those emotions were crucial feedback that they eventually paid attention to and ultimately benefited from.

When we assume that rational thinking can control feelings, we tend to deny or repress negative emotions and that will undermine our well-being. Nora's attempts to stem her panic by trying to convince herself that she was "making a mountain out of trivia and should just be a trouper and stop being scared" only made her become more conflicted about her fear.

Even when feelings are approached nonjudgmentally and compassionately—as in meditation—too often there is a hidden aversion to them. I have seen many meditators fall into a trap of using meditation to dodge troubling feelings.

We are often slaves to feelings—we worry about a nonexistent, imaginary future—which creates avoidable suffering. Meditation helps us be open to, stay grounded in, and feel the texture of emotions. It also provides some distance from, perspective on, and compassion toward feelings, but it can inhibit our capacity to delve deeply into what they *mean* and what they might teach us. Meditation gave Nora some distance from her fear by helping her experience it from a place of focus and clarity. As she paid attention to the bodily expression of terror—the tightening of her throat—without superimposing a story about the harm that would befall her in the future, she created a space to experience formerly terrifying emotions with less panic. But since its meaning was not illuminated during meditation, fear kept returning to constrain her life.

Reacting to emotions in these cognitive and spiritual ways can create hidden conflict and problems. Once we have abandoned the project of eliminating feelings that we don't like or that cause us difficulty, we can learn from them. The meditative-therapeutic approach to feelings— emphasizing *emotional composting*—focuses on:

- Befriending emotions, not controlling them
- Treating emotions as teachers—as feedback about how we are conditioned—and trying to understand their meaning, not just fixing or eliminating them
- Using meditative awareness to foster direct, unfiltered, and intimate contact with feelings, and therapeutic insights to decipher their meanings.

Emotional Composting

When we compost a garden we take organic refuse, such as rotting fruits and vegetables, and break it down into more basic components to nourish the soil.

In *emotional composting* we use unpleasant feelings that appear to be waste or garbage—such as anger, guilt, and fear—to enrich our lives. We study painful emotions—sadness and despair—which deepen self-understanding and expand our empathy.

Emotions that aren't composted can alienate us from ourselves and other people, sapping our vitality and interfering with intimacy. If we don't compost anger—and the hurt that often underlies it—it can lead to uncontrolled rage or withdrawal from people we are mad at. When Nina pushed away her anger at her son it resulted in her either retreating from or exploding at him. Nora isolated herself from other people—who she was convinced would "discover her fraudulence"—and then felt lonely and deprived until she composted her fear. Judy's uncomposted enmeshment with her parents—using their goals to govern her life—led to unacknowledged resentment and worry about losing herself. It also caused her to have a hypersensitivity about being controlled, and a self-destructive rebellion against her own wishes as if they were her parents.

Emotional composting is a three-stage process. It begins with *opening* to and becoming curious about our feelings; then *translating* or decoding what they mean; and finally *transforming* them by putting what we've learned into action.

OPENING

"How do you open to feelings?" a client whose family had tried to deny all emotions once asked.

I suggested that she look at the feelings directly, with a minimum of expectations, as if she was an artist examining a tree she was going to paint. Gaze at the tree. Walk around it. Survey it from various sides.

"So I try to figure out what to do with them?"

"Try to be open to them without either acting on them or burying them," I told her. "Don't deny them or feel compelled to do something with them. Just be curious about them."

Being receptive to what we are experiencing is not always easy to do because when emotions arise—like jealousy or shame—we often don't have time to contemplate them or we judge them, feel badly about ourselves, and try to rationalize or suppress them. Most of us habitually push away what we don't like and get seduced by what attracts us. (Buddha called this *aversion* and *attachment* and Freud termed it the *pleasure-pain principle*.) We don't take the time to observe our negative feelings and become blind to them.

One clue to when we are suppressing our feelings is the tone of voice we use to describe them. If "There's my anger" is said impatiently it may be proof of judgment, whereas if it is intoned descriptively then it can be an opportunity for discovery. We can try to open to feelings with curiosity rather than with condemnation.

Too often we don't really listen well *to* other people or *to* ourselves. We listen *for* what we already think or believe, which helps us hold on to a consistent and consolidated sense of ourselves, rather than to what is being said. We then deceive ourselves, thinking we have found what we actually already know. Genuine listening helps us to become more receptive to what we are truly feeling.

Feelings can be exquisite teachers. When we can be hosts to our feelings rather than judges or prosecutors our vantage point radically expands. Studying feelings in this way—which both meditation and psychotherapy at their best cultivate—fosters an attitude in which we don't immediately judge people or situations automatically or superficially, but give ourselves the time and space to figure out what is going on and what we, or someone else, really feels. For example, your husband is very quiet after dinner, seemingly staring into space. Instead of becoming angry or hurt because you assume that he is withholding from you, you might ask if he is okay and if he wants to talk. He senses your acceptance and tells you that he is upset that his friend was fired from work but wants to spare you his anger and fear that he could be next.

Here is a meditation I teach to practice the opening phase of emotional composting. I call it *emotional hosting*. Get in a physically comfortable position—your body still and your back reasonably straight. Close your eyes and relax your eyelids and your jaw. Close your mouth and breathe naturally through the nose. Now open to whatever you are experiencing, without interfering, welcoming whatever happens.

Sometimes we can't be open to what we feel because we are tired or moody, confused or demoralized. We don't have to panic or give up. We can draw on any of the tools described in chapter 1, such as listening to music, meditating, yogic breathing, or exercising.

TRANSLATING

I'm feeling unsettled and "off" and not sure why. I just spoke to a friend and we had a close encounter of a gratifying kind. I have a feeling (or is it a mood?) that I can't put into words. It ebbs and flows and eludes comprehension. I sit still, trying to be attentive to its texture. "I am slightly down," I eventually surmise. A little while later I realize that I'm actually feeling guilty. As I open to the feeling—and its bodily expression as a sinking stomach—I see that I'm feeling guilty about jealousy toward my friend's more leisured lifestyle. The self-blame intensifies. Jealousy toward a friend is at first embarrassing. It clashes with my image of who I am and want to be.

"What is jealousy and what does it mean?" I wonder. I try to open to my question and what I'm experiencing. Suddenly I have an epiphany: we are never jealous of what we don't want. Jealousy is feedback about what we want more of, namely leisure and timeless time.

Translating or decoding—figuring out the meaning of what we are experiencing—is the second quality that is necessary for emotional composting. Emotions and behavior are more complex than we realize. People who are defensive, for example, may be protecting against shame and vulnerability. Emotional betrayal or hurt may masquerade as anger. Decoding involves treating our feelings as teachers, not as tormentors, and interpreting their feedback so that we can understand and learn from them.

"A dream unanalyzed is like a letter unopened," according to the Talmud. Like dreams, feelings are letters from ourselves to ourselves about what we value, desire, and fear. Not every reaction we experience is meaningful—we can discard the junk mail—but we do need to open important letters. Powerful reactions and areas of stuckness and avoidance often signal meaningful mail.

As Judy translated her feelings of anger and her rebellion, the first thing she became aware of was that she hunched her shoulders. It reminded her of a defiant teenager saying, "I don't want to!" Like her comment, "How dare you try to tell me what to do!" she realized that she had treated her own idea of caring for herself as if it was a disturbing imposition from someone trying to control her. She then felt sad, and realized that she was rebelling against her own wishes in an attempt to preserve her freedom as if her wishes were an external impingement. But in the process, she neglected her needs and deprived herself of what helped her to flourish.

When we are open to feedback we pay attention to our bodies, minds, and feelings—and the messages they communicate. For example, after an encounter with another person, we can ask:

- Do I feel energized or depleted?
- Emotionally validated or undercut?
- Creatively inspired or discouraged?

In the same way, after we eat we might ask:

- How is my energy level?
- Do I feel mentally alert or foggy?
- Am I emotionally content or upset?

To do this, we must become what Joel Kramer calls *feedback-sensitive*—not *feedback-proof*. Feedback-sensitive means we are open to information from our bodies and feelings, allowing us to adapt and evolve, which are necessary to survival. Feedback-proof people reject any outside input. They may appear to be certain they have complete understanding and mastery of themselves and the world—but underneath they may be extremely vulnerable. They ignore feedback, which ensures that they will keep repeating what doesn't work.

Tina was a consummate caregiver who neglected herself. She had to learn to decode her experiences in order to make her life work for her. When Tina was a child she was constantly criticized and never felt understood or accepted by her self-involved parents. She assumed that she was inadequate, and always tried to please her mother and father because she felt their love was conditional. She was obedient and tried hard to get good grades. Tina was taught that the only way to be liked was to become a master caretaker who rarely asked for anything for herself. She tried to buy love by giving to other people, even if it meant that she was deprived. She realized that wanting anything was dangerous and would lead to painful disappointments. She was rewarded for being a model caregiver by being lauded for her generosity and selflessness by the people who surrounded her.

As therapy helped her stop compulsively taking care of those who took without giving, she felt guilty and lost.

Tina had to be feedback-sensitive in order to anchor herself. She had to explore what the guilt meant. Guilt is an indicator that our behavior clashes with our ideals. Most people assume that their standards are reasonable and their conduct needs to be improved, but it's more helpful to determine whether we are expecting too much or too little from ourselves—whether our standards need to be lowered or our behavior needs to be changed. Tina realized that she was expecting too much, that she wasn't a bad person if she treated herself well. As her guilt abated, she not only became more comfortable valuing herself, she took better care of herself.

Nina also greatly benefitted from trying to understand what her feelings meant. As she explored her guilt about being more financially successful than her husband, she realized that she was expecting too much of herself and that she could care about him without being responsible for his happiness and self-esteem. As she grew more comfortable with her success and stopped sabotaging herself, she noticed that she was less inclined to snap at him.

Sometimes the reverse is true and guilt is feedback indicating where our behavior needs to be improved. I have treated spouses who cheated on their partners whose guilt showed them that they needed to confront their marital unhappiness directly, instead of minimizing it and seeking alternative outlets for sensuality and emotional connection through extramarital affairs.

When Nora and I tried to translate her fear of being seen as a fraud, she felt "blank" and couldn't find anything in the present that she was scared about.

We remained silent for a while.

"I realized after meditating," she said, "that we never fear the present. We fear the future. But we never know, do we, if the future will be just more of the present, or something fundamentally different." She paused and then asked, "What do we fear in the future?"

I explained that we may fear something that we *don't want* to happen—like illness or financial crisis—and other times we fear what we *want* to happen—like love or success—won't.

"I am rushing ahead of myself and 'scripting the future'—convincing myself how my life will be before it actually happens."

I told her that her term *scripting the future* reminded me of the Buddhist parable about a painted tiger. A man went into a cave, painted a tiger on the wall, stepped back, surveyed his creation, and then ran out screaming as if the painted tiger were real. "Fear is an evolutionary necessity signaling danger and mobilizing a fight-or-flight response," I added. "But it can also be debilitating when it causes us to imagine a danger that is not there."

The more Nora and I tried to translate the meaning of her "fear of fraudulence," the less likely it seemed that it was the real problem. We came to believe that she was worried that she would disappoint her parents if she didn't live up to their standards. As Nora became clearer about this, her own goals and dreams became more paramount and her fear and worry subsided. And as she lived her own life, she not only relished her competence, but also felt much happier.

An important part of translating our emotions is learning to detect and transform our *emotional allergies,* which interfere with our sensitivity to feedback. The human body is continually exposed to foreign substances in air, water, and food. For the most part, the immune system takes care of the bacteria and viruses, and much of the rest passes through with little or no effect on it. Some people, however, react to certain substances as if they are dangerous. In physical allergies our immune systems erroneously send out signals that the organism is in danger, triggering an allergic reaction; pollen is not poisonous, but elicits an allergic response. The immune system malfunctions, overreacts, and misidentifies potential danger. So it is the immune system's *overreaction* to pollen that is the real problem.

In an emotional allergy we treat certain feelings—such as guilt and fear, sadness and shame—as threats. We overreact—for example, by denying or trying to banish them—because they are uncomfortable. Our responses, not the feelings themselves, create the problem.

My interchange with Barbara, a loving mother of two school-age children, illustrates emotional allergies.

"Sometimes it is so profoundly frustrating at home—kids screaming, TV blasting, dogs barking that I just have to..." Barbara hesitated. She trembled and looked sad and guilty.

I sat quietly, giving her the space to continue, but she remained silent. "You just have to what?" I finally asked.

"I just have to leave. I have a fantasy of getting in my car and driving away. Letting them all fend for themselves." She looked ill at ease, as if she had admitted to a crime.

"I can't believe I said that," she continued. "I must be a mean and abusive person."

"A fantasy is not an action," I said. "You are allergic to your feelings."

Barbara listened intently as I explained that we all have emotions and fantasies that we don't like, that embarrass us. But they are not shameful—they signal how we truly feel. What if we treated our feelings as teachers and tried to learn from them?

Barbara never acted on her fantasy to drive away. And she didn't abuse or neglect her children. But she did try to understand her feelings. This led to frank discussions with her husband about the burden she felt running their home. As she grew more comfortable about delegating responsibilities and her husband got more involved in sharing the parenting load, their relationship deepened and energy was freed up for Barbara to think about what she referred to as the "non-mom parts of my identity" and what she wanted for her life. She remembered how she had been supported by a high school counselor when her parents were getting divorced and she wanted to help teenage girls in a similar way. As her daughters got older she took some classes in counseling, found that she liked them, got a degree in social work, and began a career as a school social worker. Her children were well-adjusted teenagers and she was much happier.

Anita, a competent and compassionate thirty-nine-year-old woman, illustrates how spiritual practice sometimes inadvertently contributes to emotional allergies. In our first session, Anita informed me that she was coming to therapy hoping to get a handle on her listlessness and apathy after a variety of medical tests ruled out thyroid, mono, and other physical ailments. Capable and popular, with friends that she valued, Anita felt it was increasingly difficult to engage life wholeheartedly. She was in a relationship that not only seemed to be going nowhere, but—she reluctantly admitted—was hurting her. "He is verbally abusive," she sheepishly said. She longed to settle down before it was too late to have a baby.

I learned that she was haunted by her painful childhood. She had suffered massive losses—her older sister's death from leukemia when Anita was nine, and her father's death soon thereafter. Anita remembered being afflicted by uncontrollable outbursts of anger.

In graduate school, Anita discovered meditation. She practiced a Tibetan technique called "touch-and-go." She sat still, open to whatever arose—often sorrow and loneliness—connected with it momentarily, and then let it go. She pursued meditation with passion and became highly skilled at focusing and concentrating her mind. She reported that it helped her cope with the roller coaster of intense feelings she had been prone to since her early teens. "I learned," she told me very confidently, "that through meditation, I could lay my feelings about my history to rest."

Effective as it might be, Anita's meditation cut her off from feedback about her emotions, creating an emotional allergy. Connecting with her emotions was vital to figuring out what haunted her. The feelings of loss and abuse that she thought were "put to rest" returned in the form of her symptoms and suffering. Unmarried and childless, still looking for the "right" relationship, and hoping for a family, Anita had spent eighteen years anesthetizing herself with meditation, instead of dealing with the experiences of her childhood that caused her such sadness. Her apathy was a result of feelings that begged to be felt and understood. She couldn't meditate them away. She had to go through the pain to heal herself and engage her present life.

She called our therapy "touch-and-stay." As we touched upon and stayed with her feelings of sadness and loss in the past, and the neglect she was enduring with her boyfriend in the present, she was able to grieve and mourn. She initially felt worse, but began embracing her life more fully, and passion and vitality replaced listlessness and apathy. She left her boyfriend and eventually began dating a man who really cherished her.

TRANSFORMING

"Understanding is not enough," said a patient who, in spite of knowing her psychological dynamics, felt powerless to change. In our instant-gratification-oriented age of self-help gurus, charismatic workshop leaders, and psychiatrists who prescribe quick fixes, it is important to keep in mind that insight is often a crucial ingredient in lasting change.

But insight is not a panacea. By itself it is not always sufficient for change. *Transformation,* or putting into action what we have learned, is the final stage in the process of emotional composting. We must apply what we have discovered, otherwise, it remains merely intellectual knowledge and we won't change. This application takes many forms, from handling challenging feelings to changing harmful behavior.

"I wish there was a statute of limitations on my habitual bad patterns," a patient once said to me. Unfortunately there's not. Most of us continue to do what's bad for us. It reminds me of Nasruddin, a character in Sufi stories, who keeps eating hot peppers. At first, Nasruddin flinches. Then his eyes tear.

"Why do you keep eating them?" his companion asks.

"I'm waiting for a cool one," he says.

Like Nasruddin, we keep doing the same thing, hoping for a different result.

Without a commitment to action, the seductive pull of old psychological conditioning, personal habits, and social conventions can overwhelm us. Flourishing often requires action. Transformation takes different forms depending on the person and the situation. Sometimes we need to turn adversity into learning and growth so that it enriches our lives—what I call *emotionally recycling our experience.* At other times we need to flow more with life—accepting what we are pushing away. And sometimes we must challenge habits by going against the grain of what is familiar—testing our limits. This might involve letting go of old and hurtful habits and patterns or venturing beyond the boundaries of areas of familiarity and comfort.

Emotional Recycling

No one goes through life without confronting difficulties. Everyone faces obstacles. Many of us hope to get beyond them. Certain religions and spiritual traditions promise the possibility of eliminating misery and attaining complete peace, but neither human folly—including self-deceit and selfishness—nor mortality can be completely avoided or transcended.

Lin Evola was troubled, even outraged—an emotion society trains us to squelch—by brutality and war. Seeing Los Angeles torn up by gangs and street violence in 1992, she committed herself to drawing attention to the importance of peace. She collected weapons from gang members and cluster bombs, land mines, and missile casings from the U.S. Army. She melted these materials and created inspirational sculptures called "Peace Angels," icons for peace, custom designed for particular locations and reflecting the area's culture, people, and sources of violence.

By making sculptures for peace, and creatively working with her outrage, Lin Evola recycled her emotional experience as well as weapons.

Toward the end of his life Joseph Campbell, the writer and scholar of mythology, reportedly said that he should have encouraged his readers to "Follow your blisters" instead of "Follow your bliss." He was pointing to the potential value of challenges and suffering.

We can practice emotional recycling by treating both our adversity and our symptoms—from sadness to outrage—as our teachers. Instead of denying or trying to get rid of such feelings, we can ask what they teach us about how we are conditioned and what we need to change. Recycling our experiences allows us to learn from what we normally avoid.

Going with the Grain

Violate the reality of things
And you will never find
the true Way.

—IKKYŪ

Many of us fight a daily war in which life—as well as our feelings—is the enemy. We strive to force and direct our world, mightily trying to get what we want even when it isn't possible. There is a very constructive aspect to this: it can sometimes inspire us to challenge artificial limits, such as our beliefs that we can't accomplish a goal because we have internalized other people's low expectations of us. It can help us break through these unnecessary barriers, but it can also result in our not accepting reality as it is and blaming the world (or ourselves). Greed is our wanting our lives to be other than the way they are, suggested the Indian spiritual teacher Jiddu Krishnamurti. If our wishes are thwarted we often become emotionally frustrated or furious. Our not accepting reality as it is puts us at odds with our lives.

What we lose sight of in our war with our world or ourselves is that our lives have a natural grain. Consider our bodies. If we go to bed when we are tired we fall asleep more easily and awake rested. If we stay off an injured ankle we heal more readily. There's less effort required to go with the flow rather than against it. Part of flourishing is developing an understanding of when to move with—rather than resist—the nature of the universe.

Edgar Allan Poe's "A Descent into the Maelstrom" illustrates how to flow with life. In the story, a sailor saved himself from near-certain death by studying the action of the deadly whirlpool his boat was pulled into, and cooperating with it instead of fighting it. We may apply what the sailor did to our lives. Zen Buddhism urges us to "Laugh when joyful, cry when sad." In a way it teaches adults what comes naturally to children before they've been conditioned to ignore their own instinctive and unself-conscious and wholehearted response.

When we go with the grain of life we accept reality when we can't change it, and we live more organically—respecting our natural rhythms and our feelings. This tempers the human tendency to fight nature. Consequently we exert less unnecessary pressure on ourselves. We don't use our minds to override feedback from our bodies. When we are physically worn down we let ourselves recover instead of forcing ourselves to do what we don't want to do.

As Judy began to listen to her feelings she distinguished her parents' wishes for her from her own. She started taking the things she valued seriously. Not only did most of her empty rebellion stop, but she also followed her intuition and lived more freely and passionately.

We can reflect upon a time when we were fighting life, when we

didn't accept it as it was. We can notice when we feel that we are denying unchanging barriers (like a sprained ankle) and forcing situations.
There is a difference between working hard to overcome obstacles and
going against the tide when we should be going with the flow.

Going against the Grain

In the film *Groundhog Day*, the protagonist (played by Bill Murray)
keeps repeating the same day until he gets it right. In reality, most
of us keep doing what doesn't work. This is because the lives that we
lead are self-reinforcing. We choose partners and vocations that often
perpetuate—as well as attempt to heal or transform—what troubles us.
For example, if we tend to engage in pathological accommodation to the
needs of other people, we inevitably leave ourselves out of relationships
even when someone we're involved with cares about us. Likewise, fears
that commitment will result in entrapment might keep us distant from
potentially nurturing people.

Sometimes when a car is stuck in a ditch, putting it in reverse gets it
out of the rut. Another aspect of flourishing is *going against the grain*—
doing the opposite of our tendencies by challenging negative habits,
beliefs, and expectations. Going against the grain is a counterweight to
harmful tendencies or actions. Without conscious effort—disciplines
and relationships that challenge, rather than reinforce our injurious
patterns and inclinations—we often fall victim to our psychological
conditioning and reenact it. Going against the grain is a useful approach
when insight hasn't led to change and we feel defenseless against harmful habits.

We need to go against the grain of success *and* failure. Sometimes,
as Lao Tzu noted, "Success is as dangerous as failure," because it causes
us to cling to past triumphs—even when they no longer serve us—
and this inhibits risk and experimentation. Yesterday's success can be
an obstacle to today's creativity. We remain stuck in a job, an attitude,
or a relationship that no longer flourishes, because of habit or because
we receive certain benefits from it.

Going against the grain of difficulties lets us challenge destructive behaviors and gain clarity about what keeps us stuck. Sometimes

self-reinforcing patterns can be broken by insight. When Tina, who compulsively gave to other people and neglected herself, realized that her deprivation signaled she was starving herself of vital emotional nutrients, her realization loosened the grip of her harmful pattern. She practiced respecting instead of slighting or forsaking herself, and her self-care improved and she became more engaged. As I mentioned earlier, there are times when negative patterns aren't altered by insight. We still stay up late even though we know that we are trying to cheat time and stretch out the day. We go to work when we're sick, which causes us to get sicker and we miss more work than if we had just taken care of ourselves in the first place.

Action can be helpful when insight fails because it liberates us from bad patterns and can increase insight into the underlying forces that keep us stuck. Tina got insight into her self-neglect after she began taking better care of herself. She never felt the fear and guilt beneath her automatic caretaking until she went against the grain of the habits and tendencies that made her feel guilty about being "selfish" and anxious that other people wouldn't like her.

Going against the grain requires awareness of patterns, waking up to other possibilities, and a willingness to challenge beliefs and habits. We need to reflect upon where we feel stuck and imbalanced, detect what we are avoiding, and imagine what we need to be more balanced and whole. Only then can we choose appropriate counterpractices.

We can ask ourselves:

- What bad habits need to be unlinked?
- What am I avoiding?
- What is distracting me?
- Is there clutter in my life?
- What needs to be subtracted from my life?
- What behavior that used to work has stopped working?
- Where do I feel stuck?
- Where am I imbalanced?

As Cecil, the sleep-deprived artist, considered these questions, he saw he wasted time during the day surfing the Net when he was anxious about the quality of his work. When he stopped anesthetizing himself with eBay and solitaire he had more time to paint and study art. By late evening he felt more fulfilled, making it easier to go to bed when he was tired.

After getting clear about what needs to be subtracted, added, or unlinked, we can take a habit or pattern and find a way of creatively playing with it. We might practice going just one day without checking email in the morning before doing yoga. Or go against the grain of (sometimes productive) isolation by consciously reminding ourselves to call our friends more regularly. Instead of weighing ourselves daily and feeling shame when we think that we are too heavy, we can practice going against the grain by eating more carefully but not consulting our scales.

We can deepen the practice of going against the grain by renewing our contract to challenge or unlink ingrained habits or patterns on a daily basis. We can observe the results of our experiments and modify them accordingly.

Tina challenged her conviction that she caused the problems that those around her struggled with. She also questioned her self-image. She asked herself why she only deserved emotional crumbs and examined why she tolerated deprivation. She put her discoveries into action by building self-care into her life and abstaining from self-neglectful giving.

For people who overwork and take lousy care of themselves, going against the grain might entail a lifestyle makeover. Lenore had been to several doctors who had ruled out a physiological cause for her chronic fatigue and a slew of gastrointestinal symptoms and disorders. As we explored the way her lifestyle—including brutally long work hours and insufficient downtime—was undermining her health, she was able to expand her view of life to include what she wanted for herself apart from work. She reevaluated her financial success and changed her lifestyle. She ate in a more mindful way and got regular sleep and exercise. She stopped working compulsively and devoted time to her partner and hobbies.

Eileen, a successful senior vice president at a computer company, led a highly "wired" existence packed with unending interactions via cellphones and email. She complained that they were drowning her. I recommended that she go against the grain by having pockets of time with her family—and even with herself—in which she didn't use any of her favorite technology.

The aggressive, type A lawyer who plays squash as if her life depended on it might challenge the comfort of the known by studying tai chi or playing squash without attention to the score. The shy and passive person who avoids conflict might grow more from studying the martial arts rather than yoga. Initially these kinds of challenges to familiar habits will feel awkward or uncomfortable. At first a person like Cecil who stops painting and goes to bed at a reasonable hour might feel deprived. Eventually he will develop another side of himself that would have been ignored if he stayed within the confines of the known.

Several years ago I noticed an elderly man in the gym teaching boxing to a teenager. He moved with uncommon grace and dexterity. His footwork was extraordinary. I learned that eighty-nine-year-old Phil Nestel was a former trainer. I thought it might be fun to study with him because I knew he had a special talent, and I wanted to learn how he moved, but I never followed up on my intention. I asked about him at the gym and found out that he had recently died. I realized, with some sorrow, that I should have gone against the grain of my normal tendency to take time for granted by following up on my intuition.

Another way of going against the grain is by facing feelings or situations that we can't yet handle. When we can't cope with powerful emotions, we may need to develop more of a capacity to sit with them, even ride them out. *Behavioral Buddhism* is a powerful way to do this.

Behavioral Buddhism

Ordinarily when we can't handle powerful feelings such as pain or fear we avoid them because they overwhelm us or make us feel bad. This creates a self-reinforcing cycle of anxiety and avoidance, guilt and shame. For example, Cecil had trouble admitting that he had "slipped" and gone to bed in the middle of the night because he was ashamed that he felt out of control. Behavioral Buddhism is a constructive way of challenging this destructive pattern because it teaches us how to consciously develop the capacity to sit with, just *be* with, what we once avoided.

The seeds of behavioral Buddhism come from two sources. Many years ago—early on in my meditation practice—I stepped out of the shower, avoided a sneaker, and stubbed my toe very badly. The throbbing radiated throughout my whole body. I had a highly counterintuitive (and meditative) response: I went into, instead of away from, the pain. To my surprise it dissolved immediately. Then an even stranger thing happened. While I felt an intense impetus to get mad at the person who left the sneaker near the shower, the absurdity of doing so immediately became apparent because I no longer felt any pain. This was my first glimpse into what I call *phantom emotional pain*. Phantom limb pain is the feeling of pain in an absent limb or portion of a limb; phantom emotional pain is the experience of negative reactions even after the event triggering them—and the feelings themselves—are no longer present. We get angry, as I did after the stubbed toe, even when there might be nothing to be upset about.

The second source of behavioral Buddhism was of a more clinical, though no less personal origin. Some years ago I treated a client who was emotionally scarred by early life trauma, had a lot of rage, little self-awareness and less self-control, and was verbally abusive in a way I have never encountered before or since. Seemingly out of nowhere she would launch into blistering attacks and scream at me continuously. I tried everything I knew to manage the situation, but nothing worked. I explored whether she felt hurt, let down, or endangered by me and whether I was enraging her. I wondered if she was trying to let me feel what she had endured at the hands of an abuser. Perhaps she was eschewing human connections—while desperately hungering for them—to avoid retraumatizing herself. I even speculated whether she was living what the philosopher Søren Kierkegaard called the "despair that is unaware of itself as being despair." Empathy, kindness, understanding, setting limits, and letting her know her impact on me failed to stem her verbal assaults. They—and both her and my suffering—persisted.

After I had weathered several of these excruciating assaults, I learned that she had seen and sued several therapists including a colleague's friend, an esteemed practitioner. My colleague earnestly informed me that I was doing good work because she hadn't yet sued me, but that reassurance, as you can imagine, didn't make it easier to sit through our sessions.

I asked one of my Buddhist teachers, Shinzen Young, how he would engage this meditatively. He recommended a practice to develop progressive awareness and equanimity amid the noise and distractions of daily life. "Meditate with your eyes closed, for ten to twenty minutes," he suggested, "listening to any and all sound, savoring it and soaking it in. Treat the sound not as an interference, but an opportunity to develop focus and concentration. When the attention wanders—as it inevitably does—return, with as little judgment as is possible, to paying attention to sound. Then do the same thing sitting with your eyes open. Then standing with your eyes open. Then walking inside. Then walking outside. Then walking outside near the noise. Stand near a noisy place and practice." I sought out louder and more cacophonous sounds because they offered more challenging opportunities to cultivate equanimity. With practice I could maintain equanimity in the face of a great deal of noise in daily life.

Shinzen's method made it infinitely easier for me to stay more centered amid my patient's verbal abuse. I was able to remain open to her and think clearly when she went on a tirade. I became empathic toward her pain and sadism without feeling that I was drowning in it.

My glimpse of phantom emotional pain and the process of cultivating progressively greater awareness in everyday life became the foundations of behavioral Buddhism. Human experience, according to one version of the classical Buddhist model of the mind, as I suggested in chapter 1, occurs in one of six areas—the five senses plus thinking. If we add "feeling" then we have seven potential domains to pay attention to.

Try this experiment. Take a piece of paper and make seven columns down the page. Think about areas of experience that are easiest and hardest for you to handle. Now list them at the top of each column—going from easiest to most difficult. For example, if sound is easier to handle than sight, write it on the left. If feelings are harder to handle than sight, write it on the right. Do this with the five senses as well as thinking and feeling.

Now do the same thing within each column—write the easiest type of experience within each category on the top row and the hardest on the bottom. For example, if the first column is sound, your favorite music might be the easiest sound to handle, which would be listed in the top row of the column followed by something slightly more difficult, say police sirens outside your home, or cellphones nearby when you are trying to concentrate. Jackhammers outside your home when you are trying to work might be underneath. At the bottom of the column, write the most difficult sound, say screaming. In the "feeling" column joy might be at the top of the column and shame and humiliation might be at the bottom.

Here is a list of the seven zones of experience, followed by a sample chart:

Thinking · Feeling · Seeing · Touching · Hearing · Smelling · Tasting

Which of the above seven zones of experience (the five senses plus thinking and feeling) are you most comfortable with? Write it in the top left-hand box. Pick the next area of the seven that you are most comfortable with and write it in the next topmost box. Continue until you have filled in all seven boxes across the top of the chart. The last box on the right will contain the realm you are least comfortable in.

Easiest ((((((((((((((((((**Zones of experience**)))))))))))))))))))) Hardest

SOUND	SMELL	SIGHT	TASTE	TOUCH	THOUGHT	FEELING
Favorite music	Lilacs	Sunset	Good food	Gentle massage	Creativity	Love
Melodious voices	Good food	Face of loved one	Sweets	Clean, smooth sheets	Sexual fantasies	Joy
Birds	Soap	Fine art	Tasteless food	Warm shower	Planning	Contentment
Cellphones	Cigarette smoke	Messy house	Salty foods	Cold	Problem solving	Anxiety
Jackhammers	Burning smells	Urban blight	Burnt food	Heat	Bad memories	Guilt
Screaming	Rotting meat	Pictures of war	Bitter medicine	Bodily pain	Fearful thoughts	Shame

Now do the same thing within each column. Starting under each of the seven zones of experience write in the top box the easiest experience to tackle within that area. Underneath the top box, list a slightly more difficult experience. Underneath that, list an even more challenging one. Beneath that, list a harder experience. On the bottom row, list the hardest experience within that zone of experience. What we now have is a chart of the seven different zones of experience and a descending list of challenging aspects of each. Take the first item in the first column, for example, sight. The easiest may be a beautiful landscape, a more challenging one could be something that you don't find attractive, and the most difficult one might be a sight that disturbs you, say pictures of bloodshed or children living in poverty.

Do a few minutes of yogic breathing followed by meditating on your favorite music. Sit in a comfortable chair and try to really hear the music when you are listening to it. If your mind wanders, return without any judgment to concentrating on the music.

What we usually don't realize is that we can grow our capacity for equanimity—for sitting with and through challenging experiences. If we can open to the easiest aspect of one of the seven areas of experience—for example, favorite music—then we can be receptive to something slightly more difficult. If we can do that, then we can open to something harder because it is the same capacity—one that can be trained.

The way to practice behavioral Buddhism is to work down the first column on the left—your easiest domain of experience—until you feel you can handle more difficult experiences. Move on to the next column when you feel comfortable. And so on.

After Nina translated what her guilt meant, and realized that she characteristically had difficulty accepting—and routinely dismissed—positive feelings, she practiced behavioral Buddhism by slowly building a greater capacity to sit with positive feelings without pushing them away. Nina had a highly developed sense of smell. She started by smelling lilacs, flowers that she loved. When she could take them in, she moved on to aromas from Indian food, which she also loved. Then she moved on to smells that were distasteful, like cat litter. Once she felt at home with smells, she moved on to sights, then sounds—focusing on music she cherished such as eighties' groups and chanting monks. Then she focused on the joy she felt hearing the laughter of her favorite niece. She then moved on to her own happiness about her sister's wonderful marriage, and finally she learned to become comfortable sit-ting with her own success.

Eleanor, a survivor of childhood trauma, used behavioral Buddhism to work directly with fear. Eleanor suffered devastating loss when she was twelve—while riding his bicycle her older brother was hit by a car and died. He was Eleanor's best friend, an enormously supportive pres-ence in their single-parent home. Her mother, whose husband had died when Eleanor was a baby, was so overwhelmed and bereft when she lost her son that she had little psychic energy to help her dazed daughter. Eleanor felt completely alone.

Through the love and devotion of family and friends, Eleanor and her mother survived, but scars remained—particularly a tendency for Eleanor to anticipate loss and trauma so she wouldn't be shocked if it happened.

Mark Twain pointed to the unnecessary suffering self-induced phan-tom emotional pain fosters when he quipped, "I am an old man and have known a great many troubles, but most of them never happened." The pictures we create of the future are usually based on how we feel and what we think in the present. Projecting the present into the future may help us to maintain a feeling of continuity and predictability con-cerning other people, the world, and ourselves, but it can obscure con-structive possibilities.

The future we construct is often too pessimistic. As an older friend wisely pointed out to me before I moved to a new home, "You can only focus on what you'll lose when you move, because what you'll gain—for example the new friends you'll make—hasn't happened yet."

History—the unfolding story of the world and our lives—has a wonderful unpredictability. Most of us never thought we'd see an Afri-can American president of the United States or South African apart-heid overturned or the peaceful end to the Cold War, and so we have to build into our thinking about the future the inevitability that it will have positive and constructive features that we can't foresee.

Eleanor and I spent a good deal of time exploring the experiences of her childhood and the accompanying feelings she still needed to under-stand, which helped her detect phantom emotional pain and refine her awareness of when she was superimposing her traumatic past onto the open and unknown present and future. By understanding that the future always contained unimagined treasures and opportunities, she short-circuited her tendency to assume negative events would occur. Together we realized that she needed concrete tools to handle her tendency to rush ahead of herself and brace for losses that hadn't happened.

Our capacity to stay grounded in the present—which we are all capable of—is an invaluable aid in helping us avoid scripting the future or anticipating problems.

Yogic breathing and Buddhist meditation are two wonderful ways of practicing this. They can be used whenever we are getting ahead of ourselves.

Here's a brief meditation to practice staying grounded in the present:

- Turn off your cellphone, sit in a physically comfortable position, close your eyes and your mouth, and gently breathe through your nose, pulling the air into the back of your throat. Begin with a long exhale, gently press your abdomen toward your spine, and then take twelve quiet and relaxed breaths.
- Continue breathing through the nose if that is comfortable. If not, breathe normally. Bring your attention to your body, noticing any places of restfulness.
- Savor them and soak them in. If your mind wanders—anticipating the future or replaying the past—gently, and without judgment, return to paying attention to restful states in your body. Do this for several minutes.

Empathy and Emotional Flourishing

Once we have developed the ability to compost emotions and take more seriously and respond more skillfully to feelings centered on I—*I wish, I need, I feel*—we can deepen our capacities for empathy and compassion, hallmarks of emotional health and flourishing. It is easier to understand and accept in other people what we are at peace with within ourselves. It's hard to respond skillfully to the qualities in others that we can't stand in ourselves. For example, the more I can be at peace with my own fear and vulnerability, joy and contentment, the more I can be empathic with yours. At this stage our concern and attention expand from *I* to *we*—empathy for and care toward loved ones, friends, and even acquaintances.

Empathy extends our capacity to enter into the experience of another person, who may be very different from us. Compassion grows in this soil, as do concern and responsibility—literally the ability to respond. Compassion also reveals our shared humanity—we all love and bleed, hope and fear—and it increases our solidarity.

"Obligation to others" is the mantra of systems of universal ethics. For many of us, this may feel like an abstract principle. Solidarity with others, on the other hand, can be a heart-filled impetus that feels more compelling and takes us beyond "local" empathy to a region that spiritual traditions East and West point to—namely to care for people outside our religion, ethnic group, and nation, which includes all people, and even animals and the natural world. Enriched self-care and continual practice composting challenging emotions can provide a brief glimpse into an expanded and ultimately enduring compassion and a more encompassing concept of care.

Feelings are an amazing birthright and a wonderful resource for taking better care of ourselves and deepening intimacy. When we become more adept at composting feelings and fully experiencing the range of human emotions that we are graced by—from joy and jealousy to outrage and fear—we not only deepen insight into ourselves and other people, we expand our capacity for empathy and compassion, all of which play an indispensable role in flourishing.

Now that we are becoming more attuned to our emotions and more caring toward other people and ourselves, we are ready to pursue our passions, the fuel that drives our efforts to flourish.

Feel yourself quietly drawn by the deeper pull of what you truly love.

—Jalāl ad-Dīn Rūmī

Following Our Passion

Passion, by which I mean what excites and inspires us, is crucial to flourishing. To lead a creative and fulfilling life we need to discover what truly delights us. Our passions propel us into new experiences and relationships, making our lives rich and full.

Not all passions are equal. While the line between healthy and unhealthy passions is not always immediately clear, there are certain indications. Addictions and obsessions are destructive passions. Constructive passions are those that we freely pursue, rather than compulsively engage in. They resonate with our values—they support what is important to us—and energize rather than enslave us. Whether or not we pursue our passions for our own enjoyment or a higher purpose, healthy passions are worthwhile, don't hurt other people or ourselves, and help us to flourish, because they are engaged in for the right reasons. This can take the form of giving back to other people or a cause, as well as nourishing our own emotional, intellectual, or spiritual growth and development.

We can be passionate about a lover or a moral ideal, a hobby that we pursue with heart and soul, or a mission that gives us something to live for beyond ourselves. Nothing transports us quite like passion, and it is potentially accessible to us all.

John Miller is a seventy-four-year-old jewelry artist whose passion saved his life. The gallery he created is an expression of what inspired him and kept him alive. Located off a main thoroughfare in Princeton, New Jersey, Tomorrow's Heirlooms is an elegant setting for the riches of color, design, and artistry found within the gallery. Its one-of-a-kind pieces of jewelry are made with semiprecious gemstones, lovingly cut, polished, and set to bring out their inner beauty.

The seed of the idea for it was planted sixty years ago, when, at the age of fourteen, John was on a camping trip in California where he found an oddly shaped piece of what seemed to be petrified wood. He was mildly curious and took it to the University of Southern California, where he was informed that it was part of the hip joint of a Tyrannosaurus rex. But John's interest was not really piqued until the geologists offered to cut the calcified bone—now a rock—so he could see the inside. During the process of slicing and then polishing the specimen so the ring of marrow could be revealed, John found himself enthralled with the transformation from dull and uninteresting to beautiful and inspiring.

"Amazing to take a rock that was ugly on the outside and polish it and reveal something beautiful. It's totally different—just the act of polishing changes the optic and the color and everything else," he told me, a grown man whose voice still reflected the wonderment of that fourteen-year-old boy.

That's how John's lifelong passion for rocks and minerals started, and working with them became an enduring hobby.

John had always believed that "reality dictates you can't do pretty things" and make a living, so despite his fascination with stone, he joined the Marines, got an education, and ended up working in a senior management position for a large corporation.

"I hated every day I went to work. I wasn't creating anything. Oh, sure, I created systems, but it wasn't the same thing." After twenty-three years of corporate life, John realized that he needed to make his beloved hobby his vocation. He gave his employer notice that he would be retiring in one year's time. John's company, refusing to believe he would not be jumping ship to a competitor, gave him one year in severance pay and immediately released him from his position.

At first John felt unbelievably free. Family and friends were highly supportive; it was obvious to everyone that he had a huge passion for his stonework. He was worried that he would not be able to make a go of it, but the enticement of spending his time and energy doing what he loved soon stilled his doubts.

The road was not without bumps and detours, but twenty years later, John Miller is a young and robust seventy-four. He does not work fewer hours than he did before, but he is doing something he loves passionately, and this love nourishes him in a way his corporate job and its financial security could not. "Now, my work is my passion. I love what I do."

Many of us don't know what we are passionate about. We lack inspiration and are disengaged from our lives. Several things can sabotage our efforts to do what John Miller did. The first one happens to us all.

The Adult Fall, or Passion Lost

"**G**row up. Stop being so immature and childish," I overheard a mother saying to her son in the park as I played basketball nearby. The elementary school–aged kid was all over the place, rolling in the grass, chewing on god-knows-what, laughing hysterically, chasing after butterflies, and playing tag with imaginary companions.

At first the frustrated mother's remarks seem reasonable. We can all empathize with her exasperation. Many of us have said or thought similar things. Her son was exhausting to be with and might at times do things that endangered his safety—what exactly did he have in his mouth?

Consider for a moment what happens when a person actually "grows up" and becomes an adult. Childhood is often a state of wonder in which almost everything is new. Children revel in what harried adults rush past. Most adults abandon or dampen childlike curiosity and the passion it often gives birth to, so that the business or work of adulthood can get under way.

Grown-ups tend to value practicality, competence, and responsibility. They want to earn a living, succeed at work, find a mate, and raise a family. From this perspective, if we veer off the prescribed course to follow our dreams, we are being silly and unrealistic, wasting time and money. As adults, unlike the boy in the park, we treat imagination and exuberance as signs of immaturity, of an inability to take life seriously, instead of as a part of the vitality of a lively and passionate human being. The question is: What are we missing?

Growing up has a secret cost that few people consider—we often lose the freethinking, imaginative, I-can-do-anything attitude of childhood. The passion we forsake as we become responsible and mature may contribute to an unconscious melancholy that permeates the lives of many adults.

In order to recapture some of that passion from childhood, we must understand that an adult can be childlike (unself-conscious, unaffected, and spontaneous) without being childish (silly and immature).

Practice observing the elements of your daily life—what you see, feel, and do—as if you are looking at them for the first time. Linger on what you might normally rush past or take for granted. Allow yourself to not only feel what excites or impassions you but explore and cultivate it.

The second thief of passion is also one that many of us know intimately.

The Caretaker

Tina, the consummate caregiver who neglected herself, had a dream that illustrated her self-neglect in a particularly stark and poignant manner: "I cooked a delicious dinner of spaghetti and meatballs. While my guests sat in the dining room enjoying the food, I licked the sauce off the ladle while standing at the kitchen stove."

In her dream, Tina fed her guests and neglected herself. She was so absent from her own life that she was reduced to accepting the scraps of emotional food that she ate on the sly. As a result, Tina experienced the very deprivation that she was attempting to avoid. Her caretaking not only left her feeling emotionally deprived and unloved but interfered with her ability to nourish herself. Because she was so busy tending to other people, she did not question, let alone pursue, what she wanted for her own life. When she began therapy with me in her late twenties she was in a nursing program, but didn't feel excited by or committed to it. It is no wonder that she felt adrift, without direction.

At first Tina tried to take care of me. She was too apologetic when she was late for a session and excessively concerned about whether she had hurt my feelings or wasted my time. We repeatedly explored her guilt and her almost crippling sense of duty. This made her feel both liberated and lost, "like an actor without a script." As she began to spend less time trying to be attuned to me, she recognized more of the deprivation in her own life, especially the way that giving to others helped her neglect herself.

Over a period of a few months, Tina began exploring various interests including tai chi and feminist history. She was surprised and gratified that no one died when she nurtured herself. This made it easier for her to deepen her commitment to her new passions. She became happier and more energized in our sessions. She also left nursing school, a wise decision, because for Tina, being a professional caretaker was the last thing she needed to do.

The most important action a caretaker can take is "retire" from compulsively serving other people. This will help them to focus more on taking better care of themselves. There are obviously times when going the extra distance for someone else is not only healthy, but necessary. One-sided giving, however, in which the caretaker is being exploited by the receiver and also neglecting herself is not really beneficial for either person.

What I have observed clinically is that if we are constantly doing favors for other people who are unappreciative and we feel deprived and resentful, then we might need to ask ourselves, "Is this constructive for me—or the other person—or does it deplete my energy?" If we repeatedly overrun our own healthy boundaries we may need to reestablish new ones by being conscious of what we are giving to others, and exploring how much caretaking actually costs us, both emotionally and energetically.

People who are caretakers must circumvent the automatic response of giving to others and neglecting themselves. If you fall into this trap, you can ask at the beginning of each day: "What do I need and want?" The answers may not emerge immediately, but we have to consider how we feel in order to begin the process.

When we bring ourselves into the equation, we can more easily and steadily focus on our own passions and interests, which will nurture and enrich our lives. And then we will be more generous with those around us. I have repeatedly witnessed the ways those people who truly take care of themselves are more genuinely connected to, and giving toward, other people.

Although some people fail to discover their passions because they are busy caretaking, others do not find what they are passionate about because they want to remain self-sufficient and free from what they perceive as external control.

The Free Agent

As a child, Joseph felt that nothing was ever good enough for his father, a hypercritical man and a highly accomplished writer. By the time he was in the seventh grade, Joseph remembers feeling that he just couldn't win. His father conveyed through words and scowls that Joseph never measured up, that he was not achieving enough and was not okay as he was. Joseph was either criticized for failing to meet his father's demanding standards or ignored when he did well because it was simply expected.

During middle school Joseph dropped out emotionally saying, "I'll be anything but what he wants me to be." He continued to go to class, and carried out his daily responsibilities at home, but he began smoking pot daily. He became a chronic underachiever whose grades slipped precipitously as he rebelled against what he saw as the unrealistic expectations and the absence of emotional support from his father.

Joseph came to see me for therapy when he was in his late thirties. He felt disgusted with his life and devoid of any plans for what he wanted to do when he "grew up." After several months of talking we realized that saying no to life was his way of carving out his autonomy, protecting himself against the relentless onslaught of his father's shattering criticisms, and sabotaging his father's plans and dreams for him. Joseph had become a free agent, someone who never committed to or joined anything so that he wouldn't be controlled or rejected. Commitment felt like a jail sentence.

By remaining uncommitted to anything and anyone, Joseph protected himself from his father's relentless rejection and warded off the horrendous feeling that he was fundamentally inadequate. But defining himself by what he was not led to what Joseph called a "life of musical chairs" in which he was not focused on what he wanted for himself and unsure about what he hoped to do for the rest of his life.

At first, Joseph played out his conflict over commitment with me. While he seemed very dedicated to therapy, he only halfheartedly worked on discovering his passion. Nothing changed, and he remained stuck and passionless, until we understood the way he was invested in remaining a free agent. Engaging anything was scary for him because it opened up the dreaded danger of being seen as a failure, risking humiliation, and losing his freedom.

Joseph slowly began to realize the price of being so detached; while it protected him against what he feared, it also deprived him of the joy and fulfillment of being involved in meaningful pursuits. He began trying new activities, such as volunteering on a hotline for troubled teens and playing the guitar. As he pursued what he called his new enthusiasms, he noticed that he didn't lose his freedom. Best of all, he felt as if he was beginning to really live his own life, rather than be a free agent who never felt any passion because he never committed to anything. He eventually became the director of the hotline and derived great fulfillment helping young adults find direction and meaning.

I've learned that free agents are not truly free. They are so busy holding back from committing to anything for fear of losing themselves or being controlled that they cut themselves off from possible sources of passion. Real freedom is the capacity to be connected to something—engaged by it—while being oneself.

There are several obstacles to doing this. What we truly want to do—what inspires us—as opposed to what we think we should do, is often not built into our lives. It is replaced by what we think we should do, which both freezes up a vast amount of energy and causes us to sometimes not recognize what we truly *want* to do. Human beings spend a vast amount of time demanding that they should do certain things which they actually don't want to do—and then rebel against what they are supposed to do whether it is good for them or not. Free agents can practice committing to those activities that interest or excite them and see that they can retain their autonomy and self-respect.

We can't always reconcile what we should do with what we want to do. Some "shoulds" can be immediately dispensed with because they are not truly necessary or of interest to us. Others appear less onerous once we realize that they are personally chosen wishes, rather than coercive externally imposed constraints. Some of those shoulds that remain become slightly less distasteful when we remember that they are steps toward goals that bring us fulfillment or reduce pressure that has been haunting us.

The Sleepwalker

M any people live their everyday lives as if they are under a spell. From the outside they may seem successful and content, but they sleepwalk through life, going through the motions without vitality or authenticity or passion. They are merely pursuing goals and fulfilling responsibilities, paying little or no attention to what they feel or want. Because they fall asleep to their genuine feelings and needs, they don't know what they are passionate about.

Since Ellie had graduated from college, her life had followed a positive trajectory. She married a great guy, maintained her athletic body, and enjoyed her job at a radio station. At their tenth college reunion, her former roommate confided that she was envious of Ellie's life. At first Ellie was flattered, but several days later, she wondered why the comment made her feel uncomfortable. She and her husband, Steve, had been talking about when to start a family, but for some reason, Ellie was hesitant to make a decision. She felt suffocated. She worried she might not be fit to be a mother.

As therapy continued, she realized that she wanted a child, just not yet. Her hesitancy was not due to fear of mothering or ambivalence about her close relationship with Steve, but because seriously contemplating motherhood elicited the feeling that she had not yet really lived.

Ellie was not really there—present, conscious. She was going through the motions, not really paying attention to what she truly wanted. When the possibility of motherhood and all that it meant—adding one more person to her family, putting herself second for at least several years, losing herself to the needs of a baby—intruded on her consciousness, something in Ellie woke up. She realized that to have a child before she felt more fulfilled would leave her more alienated from herself and her dreams, and make it even more difficult to discover what she was passionate about.

Ellie began practicing paying attention to everything from the mundane to the deepest aspects of her life. She made a game of it. Throughout the day she asked herself how she felt about what she was eating; whom she was talking to; what she was doing at any given moment, at work, at play, and at home, from the weekly night out with three friends to how she felt working out. Her goal was to know what she was doing when she was doing it.

At first, Ellie felt more unhappy, but she was not sure why. Awakening from her self-imposed sleep was overwhelming. She became sad at how much life she had missed and was both scared and lost. She was not sure what to do and had no compass to point her in the right direction. She questioned her work and her relationships. She allowed herself to wonder if she should change jobs and move to another part of the country.

As Ellie practiced paying attention to her movement through the world, she began to notice subtle shades of feeling: enjoying something; disliking something else; being confused, fearful, happy, and even passionate. This made it easier to edge toward what was satisfying and fulfilling. As time went on she grew more grounded in her experience.

Ellie realized that she did not like certain aspects of her job, such as boring meetings, but loved others, such as contributing to innovative radio programming. This enabled her to decide to stay with the company, but change her job.

She also recognized that she had secretly felt that she wanted to engage in more competitive sports. After several tries, Ellie settled on volleyball and joined a team at her gym. She lived in an area rich with natural beauty and she persuaded Steve to try hiking, which they discovered they enjoyed doing together. Three years later, she told Steve that she was ready to start a family.

Sleepwalkers avoid what excites them. They are adept at doing without feeling. The best antidote for this is to continually pay attention to actions and thoughts, and engage in life. We can check in with ourselves frequently and take our emotional temperature throughout the day. We can ask ourselves how we feel about what we do or the people we come in contact with. This will help take us off autopilot and give us feedback about what we are experiencing.

Be patient, because there will be times when we do not feel any-thing, but eventually we will begin to notice more and more of how we feel. These realizations will give us the clues we need to decipher what we really want and need, and will aid us in discovering our interests and recognizing and intensifying our passions.

The Perfectionist

"I'm not perfect, so why try? I lose before I begin," Michael, a tal-ented painter in his late twenties, told me. He rarely painted any longer, even though it was his first love. "I see ideal pictures of what I want to draw in my head," he said, "but whatever I draw falls short. The completed product is always inferior, not only to what I want it to be, but what I think it could be. It's incredibly frustrating and painful, so I avoid painting. Then I don't feel so bad—but then I step back and look at my life and feel that it is empty, without any passion."

Michael had cut himself off from the activity he was most passionate about because he couldn't do it perfectly. He continued behaving in this way for several months, during which we talked about why he needed to be perfect and what dilemma he imagined his perfection would solve, namely his wish to be more loveable.

When he realized both the impossibility of perfection and the way he was striving for it to prove that he was worthwhile, he felt lost and empty. He didn't know what to do. We spoke about the difference between ideals being an inspiration and being a suffocating force.

"Having goals is not a bad thing," I said. "They can provide direction, something to strive for. But they have to be realistic—potentially reach-able." Michael, who had an interest in meditation, said this reminded him of the emphasis in Eastern thought on enjoying the process rather than on being consumed with the product. Over time, that enjoyment and "just being good enough" replaced his quest for perfection.

"I am realizing that the process is the road to pursuing your pas-sions," he said to me. "As long as I sought perfection—no mistakes—I couldn't see that people are meant to stumble and fall. But maybe in the process of picking yourself up, you see things differently and you learn something new. I certainly have."

We can challenge the perfectionist urge by focusing on the texture of our efforts—whether learning a new skill or practicing a familiar one—rather than on the results, which we can't usually control.

Recovering perfectionists need to focus on being good enough rather than being perfect. Trying our best and wholeheartedly engaging the process is what really matters. Then, as the yogic tradition teaches us, we can pursue what we value without being so consumed with the outcome, which is out of our hands.

Setting realistic goals and pursuing them in stages—as we discussed in chapter 3—rather than all at once helps perfectionists slow down, feel less pressure, and enjoy the process. Not only will the result be enhanced, but we will feel more incentive to risk trying something new, even if there is no guarantee that we can master it. When we venture beyond the safe and constricting confines of the known, we'll live with greater joy and vitality.

Finding Your Passion

John Miller's career shift reminds us that passion usually springs from what we love. We need to pay attention to what energizes us and excites us; what makes us feel fulfilled and alive. When we take this seriously it can provide clues to potential enthusiasms.

When he was in his twenties, John Douglas Thompson was earning a comfortable living as a marketing representative for a software company. "I didn't feel passionate about it so much as, 'This is what I'm supposed to be doing,'" he said. One evening Thompson invited a date to Yale Repertory's performance of August Wilson's *Joe Turner's Come and Gone*. The date stood him up and he concentrated on the play—only the second live one he'd ever seen. When the performance ended he realized that more than anything he wanted to be an actor.

Though he confronted long stretches of unemployment and ate a lot of Ramen Pride and pasta, he stayed the course. "I was scared because it was like throwing away this career I had, going into the unknown," John said. "But the drive for me to figure this out and discover it was more powerful than the reality of 'Well, John, you've got to get another job.'"

Now forty-seven, John has had several screen credits, numerous regional theater roles, become a Shakespeare specialist, and won several Obie and Lucille Lortel awards for his performance of Othello.

There are several ways that we can detect what our passions are in the midst of the frenetic pace of our lives. We can notice what grabs our attention; those activities that speak to us, that pique our interest. At first, there may only be hints and inklings. Follow these clues. Trial and error are necessary. We need to take that hike or foreign language class we have been fantasizing about. Try various activities until one really resonates.

Here are some signs that we have found our passion:

- Our spirit lightens.
- We look forward to engaging in the activity.
- Once we are doing it, time appears to slow down and we lose track of it.
- We think, "This is what I am supposed to do," or "This is what I am meant to do."
- It feels "right" to lose ourselves in the activity.
- We don't mind the grunt-work part of it.
- We can't wait to get back to it.
- The place we do it can feel like a sanctuary where the best part of us is engaged.
- There may be a part of us that is expressed only when we do this particular activity.

If nothing seems to be inspiring, reflect on whether there was something in the past that you loved to do or be immersed in that made you feel some of these signs of passion. Some people can regain the passion that is missing from their lives by pinpointing the moment they lost contact with it. We may find clues in earlier interests and paths not taken. Consider exploring that activity now—even if just on a basic level. For example, did you love collecting coins when you were a child? Or did you prefer listening to music?

JoAnn, a successful advertising executive, once told me, "I'm really good at what I do and I earn a lot of money, but something is missing. In spite of my success I never really feel pleased or turned on by what I do. I feel trapped and frustrated, like I'm not leading the life I want to lead. My life has no real purpose. When my friend Sam died last year, I couldn't stop thinking that he never got to do what he constantly talked about doing—spending more time in his workshop to start his cabinet-making business. He seemed so happy when he talked about starting his new business, but he never did it. I began asking myself what I really wanted to do that I have been putting off."

I needed to find where JoAnn lost her passion so I could help her regain a link to it.

JoAnn was driven to succeed by her achievement-oriented parents, who made it obvious that their love and acceptance was conditional upon her accomplishments. Throughout her youth they drummed home the importance of ambition and focus. They discouraged her enthusiasm for creative writing, which they said was impractical. "Most novelists don't make any money," they told her.

An obedient child, JoAnn complied with their wishes and gave up her dream in hopes of winning their approval. She decided to find a viable career, be "successful," and earn a great living. When she received a perfect score on the verbal portion of the SAT, the educational service administering the test listed advertising as a possible profession. Her parents didn't discourage her from that career.

JoAnn succeeded at defining narrow goals and making appropriate decisions. After attending a prestigious college, she got on the "achievement track," won a lucrative job, and eventually bought a large, expensive apartment.

A part of her felt that something fundamental had been forsaken, but as soon as pangs of regret struck she redoubled her efforts to succeed at the life her parents had encouraged. After a while she became so immersed in her professional strivings that she no longer thought about her earlier passion. Each business success moved her up the approval ladder and further away from what she loved and what nourished her.

JoAnn and I focused on clarifying her passion. At first she was hopeless about escaping the rut she was in, but once she began thinking about the topic, she felt faint hope and engaged it more enthusiastically.

She even decided to write down everything she had been passionate about in her life. She noticed some recurrent themes. "I have always written—in private journals, essays, a few short stories. I don't know what to do with them, but I seem to keep going back to them. I also love to read serious literature."

"Are you doing any of the things you have been passionate about?" I asked.

"Very little, I mostly read in my field—trade magazines and so on. I don't seem to have time to read what I love."

"What is standing in your way?" I wondered.

"I am busy with work, but I sense there's more, but I don't know what it is."

"What makes you come alive?"

Her voice was conspicuously more animated when she replied, "Reading literature and writing fiction."

"What do you do in your spare time, at night, on the weekends, during vacations, and when you lose track of time because you are playing effortlessly?"

"I take work with me wherever I go, but I try to read a little quality literature and I jot little things down here and there—ideas for stories."

"Are there recurring images in your dreams that are trying to tell you something?" I asked.

"I don't remember my dreams. What else have you found helpful in discovering your passions?" she asked.

"What are you jealous of in other people?" I asked. "What is the jealousy telling you that you really want or need?"

"Other people seem to have more fun—their work isn't everything. And they seem to be doing what they love. That's what I'd like to be doing."

Joann's answers clustered around her passion for reading and writing. She loved to do both. "They are my lifeblood," she said as we discussed her responses, "a source of solace and direction."

In therapy she began to review her choices and her direction. She asked herself, "Am I working at this job because I think I should and want to please my parents, or because I want to?" She realized, with a great deal of sadness, that "I have caved in to what my parents wanted, and never really considered what I needed."

As a result of therapy and taking her passions more seriously, in her spare time JoAnn began reading literature again. She started attending poetry readings. She eventually took a short-story class and wrote a piece about a woman who felt buried alive until she pursued her dreams. One day in a session she said to me, "I have decided to apply to several master's programs in creative writing. I know it won't be easy, but I have to do it—it's just what my soul was meant to do."

She didn't get into any school on the first round. Though discouraged, she forged ahead, participating in a writing workshop and working hard at her craft. A year later she finally got into one program.

JoAnn's efforts to take seriously what inspired her were not without sacrifice. She took a job at a smaller, less prestigious ad agency, downscaled her lifestyle, and had to live on a tighter budget and draw from savings. There were times when she could not do certain activities she had taken for granted when she had earned a much more lucrative income, but she began to feel more alive and inspired. Her happiness doing what she loved illustrated the wisdom in Nietzsche's remark, "He who has a why to live for can bear almost any how."

JoAnn found her passion by discovering when she had lost contact with it. Another important clue to what we might be passionate about is to notice what we do effortlessly—what we gravitate toward on vacation, at night, and on the weekends. John Miller, for example, worked with gemstones whenever he had time outside of his job; JoAnn went to poetry readings. Those activities we pursue without any effort—a feeling of *have* to or *should*—are often clues that can reveal our passions.

We know what we love; we are ready to give it lots of energy and focus. What we need now is purpose—an idea of how we want to live and what we hope to accomplish—that helps us channel our passion in the way best suited to our personal ideal of flourishing.

7

Purpose is what gives life meaning.

—C. H. Parkhurst

Discovering Our Purpose

When we have a plan for how to live our "one wild and precious life," what I call *purpose,* we not only channel our passion, we flourish. Purpose is based on what we cherish and value, and it shapes the choices we make about how we live. It is what directs passion. Passion needs to be directed by an aim—an idea or at least an inkling of a direction to take—in order to grow into something tangible and inspiring. A person without such a vision is a creative force without an outlet; unfocused, unharnessed passion soon fades or goes underground. "If you bring forth what is within you, what you bring forth will save you," Christ said in the *Gospel of John.* "If you do not bring forth what is within you, what you do not bring forth will destroy you." People who neglect their passion do not truly live.

Many of us don't have any idea of where we are going—or where we want to end up in our lives. We are preoccupied with what we think we should do based on someone else's images and ideals or what we think we have to do to survive; we've lost our purpose. You can survive without purpose—many people do—but your life will probably feel more directionless and less full of passion and meaning.

My understanding about the importance of purpose came from an unexpected place—a hearing with the local draft board. I was eighteen years old when the Selective Service informed me that my lottery number was thirty-six. It was the fall of 1972 and it was likely that I would be drafted to serve in the Vietnam War. There was only one problem: I was a passionate pacifist who took bugs outside to free them rather than squash them inside, and I vehemently objected to the war in Vietnam, which had been an ongoing tragedy for much of my youth. I was interviewed by my local draft board regarding my application for conscientious objector status. I later learned that they had not granted any COs in ten years. I remember little of what happened, except for one snippet of conversation:

"Tell us, Mr. Rubin, why should we grant you a draft deferment?"

"Life is like a gigantic canvas," I replied. "Everyone contributes a unique brushstroke. When you kill someone you eliminate their brushstroke, which steals from life. I can't be a part of that."

I eventually received a letter granting me a CO.

I still believe several decades later that everyone has a unique brushstroke to contribute to the canvas of life. What I have observed in myself and other people is that when we make our contributions, we not only experience inspiration and delight, engagement and vitality, but we help to create a better world.

Defining Your Purpose

In order to flourish it is crucial for us to identify our goals, ideals, and conception of how we want to live, which serves as a beacon lighting our path, an internal guidance system that carries us through the rough times when self-doubt or circumstances out of our control make it difficult for us to persevere.

Some people form a vision for their lives when they are young, knowing even in high school that they want to be a writer or a veterinarian, a lawyer or an artist. Other people take longer, finally recognizing it after following different paths. Whenever the realization arrives, we must pursue it with focus and determination. When we know what we value, when our vision is clear, we need to follow it, protect it, and build upon it. As we do this, it will grow stronger and play a more central role in our lives.

The story of an accountant named Rick illustrates what we can do when we fail to connect with our vision. Rick felt utterly lost after divorcing his wife of ten years. Although he had been in an increasingly unhappy marriage, he still suffered a huge void in his life after the divorce. Suddenly he was at loose ends with no specific goals or direc-tion. He was confused and depressed. While he was married, he had focused on carrying out the role of good husband and provider, which he had learned from his father. And much like his passive and depen-dent father, he had never explored what he really wanted. Accounting afforded him a good income but it didn't excite him. He didn't feel as if he was really making an impact, which is not vital to everyone, but was to him. When Rick finally realized that he had always secretly aspired to touching people's lives, he recognized that his life needed to go in a radically different direction.

"You've been talking to me about finding and living my vision," Rick said one day. "Can you tell me more about what vision is and how I can find mine?"

I told him that I believe vision is a genuine expression of our goals and ideals and how we want to live. It isn't a ripe fruit just sitting on the vine waiting to be picked. It needs to be created based on what we truly value, but before we can figure that out we need to find out what is truly important to us.

For the next few weeks we focused on clarifying Rick's values and ideals, as well as uncovering what was most important to him about how he wanted to live.

"What really matters to you?" I asked. "And does your current life reflect this?"

"Feeling like what I do makes an impact. My life does not embody the values I hold dear. I don't feel like my life adds genuine value to the world or touches anyone's life in a positive way. That's what's missing," Rick replied.

"The route to that," I said, "is to get clearer about your unique tal-ents and gifts and how you could bring them more into your life."

Rick went on to tell me that he was a systematic thinker—he liked putting things into context. He truly cared about making the world bet-ter and felt that he could be of service in the right situation. He just needed to pursue a field in which he could do that. When he thought about the people who had inspired him and whom he truly admired and the qualities in them he most respected, he recalled a remarkable history teacher he'd had in high school. He supported Rick at a really rough time and made him feel that he mattered. The teacher taught Rick that making a difference in people's lives was a noble thing to do.

"And when I think about what figures in history I'd like to meet," Rick said, "Abraham Lincoln comes to mind. I'd like to talk to him about how he took a massive risk to follow what he believed. I need to forge my path and not worry about public opinion."

"That's inspiring, but you look sad," I said.

"I keep feeling like there's more to life than I am tapping into, but I can't put my finger on what exactly it is. I think it would be making a difference."

"Was there ever a time when your life felt right? What was that like? How could you make that happen now?"

"I have never really felt that. Looking back now it's easy to see that my life was off course because I didn't do what I really loved."

I asked him if he had ever sensed that there was a song or a dance within him that had never been expressed, and if there was, how he could bring that into his life now.

"I sense that there is more to life than living by rote—just doing what you are supposed to do. I think I have always been following someone else's beat. I want to follow my own and be excited by life," Rick replied.

"One doorway into that is to visualize those special and rare moments that changed your life for the better," I said. "What happened? What did you learn? How did it change you? How can you draw sustenance from that now?"

Rick told me that there were two moments that came to mind. "One is when I realized I didn't have to be an accountant the rest of my life, and two, when I asked my friend—your former patient—how he had changed and he gave me your phone number."

I then asked him to imagine, without any barriers, the kind of life he'd like to have.

"Fulfilled in my work, making a difference and inspiring young people, and having a loving relationship with someone who shares these values. That would be perfect for me."

Then I asked him to imagine that he was at the end of his life, looking back. What would he regret? How could he change his life now so that he would not have those regrets when he was older?

"I regret that I blamed myself for my parents' divorce, that I stayed too long in my marriage and especially in a job that has not fulfilled me. I could live in a way that would lessen this regret by using the tools that I am learning from you about following my passion and identifying my vision. In other words, finding out what I love and doing it, because I'm tired of living halfway and I want to live a full and happy life."

Rick mulled over our conversation for several weeks. "That dialogue has helped me clarify my core values and purpose," he told me one day. "I want to make a difference and I think I want to teach history. But how can I know that's my purpose?"

"Not so fast," I said. "Let's examine how you actually spend your time on a daily and weekly basis, as opposed to how you would *like* to spend it. This will help us figure out where you put your energy and whether you are living what you value."

Rick made a pie chart of how he wanted to spend his time and how he actually spent it.

We realized two things: First of all, there was a discrepancy between what he valued and how he was spending his time. Second, while he loved reading history and watching movies with historical themes, both activities occupied only a relatively small amount of his day. His schedule was dominated by both accommodating the needs of other people and wasting a lot of time surfing the Net. Noting this gap between how he actually lived and how he wanted to live was at first discouraging. He understood that he was cheating himself and that he would never have what he wanted if he didn't change. Rick became inspired to find more time for what he truly valued.

Now we were ready to address his important question: "How can I know that's my purpose?"

"There are two signs," I said. "One is positive and the other is negative. The positive sign is that you feel passion and aliveness when your life is based on your vision. You are more connected to what you are doing and you know in your heart that you are going in the right direction. The negative sign is that your life feels off course, inauthentic, and depleting when you are disconnected from your authentic vision. You dread going to work and you try to kill time—filling it with activities that you are not invested in—rather than joyfully engaging in it. And you later feel deprived, rather than rejuvenated and enriched."

"How do I know if my vision is sufficient?" Rick asked. "Earlier in my life—perhaps because of my facility with numbers—I expected perfection. No mistakes. That feels too rigid and strict. I guess it's not surprising that I often feel deprived. I need another way of thinking about it."

I suggested he ask himself if it is good enough—gratifying and fulfilling—even if it is not perfect.

Rick ultimately decided to change the direction of his life and become a high school teacher so he could inspire young adults. When Rick told a group of his friends about his plan to change careers they were openly skeptical. They acted as if he was deluded, which made him severely doubt his decision. He almost lost faith in his dream. In therapy we treated his new career choice like a fragile seedling that he had to water and nurture and protect. We spent many months exploring how he could solidify his new direction by making it a priority, devoting time and energy to learning about it and mastering the skills and knowledge necessary for him to succeed, including getting a master's degree in history and developing both a broad base of historical knowledge and particular areas of specialization and expertise.

Now, some years later, Rick is a happy and successful teacher and husband, married to a fellow teacher who shares and complements his vision. He is grateful that he took the risk and altered his life. Igniting students' interest in history has given him a great deal more meaning and purpose than he had known in his previous work. "If I had to do my life over again I'd trade a financially lucrative position at a boring job for the chance to make a difference in people's lives," he said during our final session. "And of course my arm doesn't have to be twisted to take time off in the summer," he added with a grin.

Rick discovered his path by clarifying in therapy what he valued. This enabled him to identify a vision for his life that fulfilled him. Some of the other ways we can discover our vision include studying dreams, meditation, getting feedback from trusted friends or colleagues, and paying attention to what disturbs us about our lives and what we desire that other people have.

Dreams and Your Purpose

M any writers, artists, and scientists inform us that their most creative discoveries come to them in dreams (and waking visual
images), rather than in words or concepts. One of the most famous rev-
elations occurred in a dream of the nineteenth-century chemist August
Kekulé von Stradonitz:

> But look! What was that? One of the snakes had seized hold of its own
> tail, and the form whirled mockingly before my eyes. As if by a flash of
> lightning I awoke. . . . Let us learn to dream, gentlemen.

Kekulé had long been struggling to understand certain molecules
when he had this dream. The image he saw translated into an enormous breakthrough in the understanding of molecular structure and
the astonishing discovery of the benzene ring.

We don't have to be a scientist or an artist for our dreams and daytime images to reveal clues to our visions. We are all night-shift artists,
creating dreamscapes each evening that capture our problems and fears,
our desires and potentials, with exquisite precision and evocativeness.

Pay attention to your dreams—they never lie and they offer an
unsurpassed opportunity to honestly assess the state of your being.
And they simultaneously shed light on where we are stuck and suggest
how we might free ourselves.

Delving into our dreams and figuring out what they might teach us
offers clues to our vision by symbolically presenting hidden interests
and potentials and pointing us in the direction of what we value but
may have been neglecting or ignoring.

There are three ways we can explore dreams:

- in therapy, as Rick did
- in lay experiential dream groups described in Monte Ullman's
  Appreciating Dreams
- on our own

Considered the father of the group dream work movement by the
International Association for the Study of Dreams, Monte Ullman

devoted his life to bringing dream work into the world beyond therapy. Grounded in traditional psychoanalytic perspectives on dreams, he became increasingly disenchanted with them. In 1974, while teaching in Sweden, he developed his own innovative approach based on the belief that "dreaming consciousness" is a "natural healing mechanism confronting us with information about the personal and social realities that shape our lives." He fervently believed that group dream work was an experience that ordinary people could participate in outside of individual psychotherapy to aid one another in understanding their dreams.

I trained with Monte, became certified in his visionary method, and currently lead one such group, which is a profound pathway to self-awareness and transformation. Participants regularly experience remarkable breakthroughs.

Each dream is unique. In my clinical experience, there are no standard symbols and meanings; an image or event in your dream will likely have a completely different meaning to someone else. For example, water in your dream might represent a life-giving force, while in another person's dream it could signify a deadly danger. We can learn the significance of our dreams only by compiling our unique associations or reactions to each element in them.

Here is a technique you can use to analyze dreams on your own:

- As soon as you awake write down the dream as best as you can remember it. Include every detail even if it feels insignificant or is hazy. Fragments of a dream can be potentially illuminating. Leave space on the paper so you can make notes after you have written everything down.
- Read each detail of the dream, then write down your associations to each. Since there are no one-size-fits-all interpretations of our dreams, the real meanings are going to be specific to you and your life.
- Try to reconstruct your emotional state and what you were doing right before you fell asleep and during the day before you had the dream. This is called the *day residue*—literally fragments of what you did and how you felt before you went to sleep. Often, the day residue

contains triggers that may have spurred certain parts of your dream, or can put your dream in a context that will help you understand it better.

Reconstructing the context and fleshing out the possible meanings of the symbols in your dreams helps you to illuminate what you are trying to communicate to yourself about what you might not be paying attention to in your waking life.

While we were attempting to figure out his vision, Rick had the following dream:

I am trying to get home. I am having a lot of trouble. Finally, I see a train with numbers printed on the outside. It looks like my train. I get on it. Inside all the seats are empty and I'm alone. I don't recognize the towns we pass through. I see the station for my town, but the train keeps going and doesn't stop. I wake up disoriented and disturbed.

Rick decided to test the method and tackle the dream on his own. The dream made him think of three things: the numbers printed on the outside of the train triggered an image of accounting; the train was going in the wrong direction; and he couldn't get home. Each of these associations clicked, but the dream still felt murky to him until he considered the major context in his life at that time—namely his efforts to figure out his direction and purpose. Then the dream made sense to him. He realized that he was going in the wrong direction with his job, which felt "empty on the inside." To get "home" he needed to "go in the right direction" and do what he loved.

Waking Images Are a Window into Purpose

Like dreams, sometimes amid daily life waking images seem to arise spontaneously. Most people usually pay them no attention and let them go. But if we heed them and try to decode what they are communicating, we can gain insight into old or current interests that we haven't taken seriously. We might have a body memory of being more active, getting into a flow while dancing or running or playing a sport we miss. We might have a recurring picture of doing something we think we are good at or enjoy. These images, fantasies, and daydreams can be reflections of past success or visions of things we haven't done but want to pursue.

Yvette, a college student I once worked with, was lost and lacked direction. She saw no value in taking part in her daily activities. She cut classes, her grades were failing, and she was depressed. As I got to know her, the only time she seemed animated was when she talked about skiing, which she dreamed and daydreamed about frequently. What became very clear was that skiing was the only thing that excited Yvette.

Yvette had been raised with the expectation that she would get a good education, work hard, and be affluent. By the time she graduated from high school she realized that she would not be able to earn a living skiing professionally. As a result, she had dismissed skiing from her life. She felt she had to "put my dreams away" and focus on the business of growing up and becoming a responsible adult. So she literally cut herself off from her greatest source of passion.

But the passion did not leave her. Images of skiing—the rush of speeding down the mountain, the psychic warmth of being outside in beautiful surroundings, the camaraderie with her friends—cast Yvette's present life in a negative light. It had none of the passion and exhilaration of skiing. In our sessions we began to focus on helping her reconnect with the sport. Could she still be involved even if she could not ski professionally?

At first she fought this idea. "Isn't adulthood a time when you grow up? Become responsible and give up your dreams?"

"I hope not," I said. "Why can't adults earn a living doing what they love? Everyone needs to dream and play—it's healthy."

Eventually Yvette took her passions more seriously. Since she already knew what she loved, we focused more on the trial-and-error process of sharpening her vision rather than discovering it. In other words, Yvette and I didn't have to figure out what she valued; her daydreams had taught us that. We concentrated instead on what aspect of skiing she would pursue. I suggested that she read ski magazines and interview people in various ski-related occupations—from instructors to shop owners to equipment distributors.

After doing this research and learning a great deal more about the advantages and disadvantages of various kinds of work involving skiing, Yvette eventually expressed an interest in owning a ski shop. We explored how classes in business, computers, marketing, and economics might help make this burgeoning dream a reality. And Yvette excitedly pointed out how she had to test new equipment and therefore needed to ski on a regular basis.

She began to change. She engaged her life more fully and focused more intensely on her classes. School became part of a means toward an end as she was spending her life engaged in her passion. Her new-found success increased her self-esteem, which was reflected in a more friendly and outgoing personality.

Yvette contacted me recently to tell me that she was the proud owner of a ski shop in a beautiful resort town. She had married a man who also loved skiing, was skiing a lot herself and giving lessons, and had taught her young daughter to ski. She felt very focused and happy in her life. She was flourishing.

Meditation and Your Vision

Not everyone has dreams or images that lead them toward their purpose or passion, but there are other tools that can help us. Meditation is also a potent method to increase our self-awareness and help us discover what we really value and how we want to live. Meditation does this in at least two ways:

- It slows down the often frenetic clutter of thoughts, feelings, and fantasies that obscure what is really going on inside of us.
- By greatly reducing this mental interference or static, we are then able to check in with ourselves calmly and objectively, to more accurately assess our deeper thoughts and feelings.

There are two main types of meditation: *concentrative* and *insight*. In concentrative meditation we focus on a single object, such as the breath or a mantra, with wholehearted attention. When we notice that our minds have wandered, we return to the breath. Concentrative meditation cultivates a high degree of mental focus. In traditional Buddhist practice, we often begin with concentrative meditation. When the attentiveness is developed and stabilized, we practice insight meditation.

In insight meditation, we pay attention—without attachment or aversion—to whatever thoughts, feelings, fantasies, or somatic sensations we are experiencing. When I teach meditation I emphasize that the purpose of such a practice, contrary to popular misconception, is not to make anything happen—such as silencing or emptying the chattering mind—but to help us relate to these thoughts and feelings (no matter how painful) with clarity and acceptance. Given our normal state of distractedness and self-judgment, this is not an easy task. It requires discipline and practice to train the mind to be truly present and self-accepting. But we do not have to perfect it in order to reap the benefits. Along the road to becoming adept at meditating, we will gain insight about ourselves.

Meditation does not have to be practiced solely in a retreatlike setting. While such intensive practice does have the advantage of rigorous immersion in the technique without many of the distractions of daily life, meditation can be practiced at home.

In order to meditate, sit physically still in an upright position. Pay attention to the immediate flow of moment-to-moment experience, attending to the breathing process, silently noting the experience of inhalation and exhalation at the nostrils or abdomen. The effort is not to control the breathing but to be aware of it. Meditation proceeds in stages. At the beginning it is difficult to stay focused for even several seconds.

As meditators know all too well, we soon become distracted. An apparently endless flood of thoughts, feelings, and fantasies arise. Memories, daydreams, anxieties, and insights beckon. We replay old experiences or plan new ventures. One of these usually hijacks us and before we know it we have traveled down a path that takes us away from what we are focused on.

As soon as we notice that our attention has wandered, resume observing the breath. After a few seconds the same process may occur. Like a child who reaches for one toy, becomes bored, and reaches for another, and then another, the mind keeps jumping from one thought, feeling, or fantasy to the next. Like a loving parent, take the child's hand

and guide it back to the breath. Noticing that we have been inattentive is part of the process of becoming more aware and focused.

As concentration increases and becomes more refined we can use this capacity to focus the mind so that we can more thoroughly observe the nature of our consciousness. Like a movie that is slowed down, we can see how one frame of our consciousness leads into another—how particular feelings trigger specific reactions. We might become aware, for example, that when we feel guilty about getting angry with our kids, we later overindulge them.

As our awareness becomes clearer and more focused, we experience a sense of psychological spaciousness: we do not become as entangled in reactive patterns of feeling and thinking. We have opened up inner space. For instance, when someone praises us, we might allow ourselves to bask in its warm glow instead of automatically devaluing it.

We become more psychologically resilient: when we are unsettled or distracted we regain clarity more quickly. We can begin to notice within the first few seconds that we are unthinkingly attacking ourselves, thus avoiding getting caught in a downward spiral of self-contempt and self-destructive behavior.

In meditation what was formerly hidden becomes conscious, revealing what is really important to us. By enabling us to examine our deepest thoughts and feelings calmly and clearly, we can gain deep insight into what we value and how we want to live.

The Value of Compassionate Feedback

The human capacity for self-deception is endless. A healthy dose of skepticism about who we think we are is a valuable ally in becoming more conscious and self-aware. "Don't always believe everything you tell yourself about yourself," Joel Kramer once suggested to me. "Watch how you behave." If we value truth more than being right or "winning," we will be much better able to detect who we actually are underneath our self-images and justifications. The anger we display under duress in a relationship, for instance, teaches us more about our personality than our conception of ourselves as a kind and gentle human being.

We can solicit feedback about our strengths and weaknesses from people we trust who really know us. We need to be selective about the people whom we choose. They must be neither overly critical nor overly protective. Excessively negativistic people may give feedback that is not only unhelpful but also destructive. Overly protective feed-back is not truly informative, because it focuses on making us feel good rather than on telling us the truth. We can ask the people we choose to give us an honest assessment about their impressions of our talents and limitations—and their evidence for it. Whenever possible, concrete information and the reasons for it are helpful. You might like the idea of being a professional musician, but a friend will remind you that you hate to practice or don't like to perform in front of other people. Or you might want to work in an office, but a colleague will point out that you are happiest when you are on your own. We need to compare the feedback we get from several people and see if there is a common thread.

Spirituality and Your Vision

M any of us have had a special experience—I think of it as a spiritual or mystical moment—that transcended our ordinary existence. In chapter 4 I called this *natural wakefulness*. What triggers the moment may be mundane, such as hiking on a beautiful day, or miraculous, such as the birth of a child. It can happen watching a sunrise or playing sports, listening to music or making love.

After such an experience, we might see ourselves and our day-to-day existences in a different light. We might suddenly feel as if we are look-ing down on our lives from a great height and have a panoramic per-spective. We realize what is important and what is not. We vow to drop petty concerns and focus on that which we hold dear. These moments can get us back on track in our lives and be a powerful impetus for change.

Unfortunately these experiences often fade from memory. It can be difficult to hold on to them. But we can reconnect and draw from them by writing them down and remembering how they made us feel and what they showed us about our lives. A friend of mine recently spoke of such an experience with regret.

"When I was visiting my sister in Seattle last summer, there was a day when she couldn't be with me. I decided to explore on my own. I walked and walked for hours and I felt this incredible sense of freedom and peace. I suddenly realized that I was not living the way I should be, wasting too much time on the small stuff, worrying about garbage, and not focusing on enjoying my life on a daily basis. I decided that as soon as I got home, I was going to start living in a very different way.

"But when I got home, I was tired from the trip, and had a backlog of mail and bills and problems I had to deal with. I let all the old habits take over, and before I knew it, I had started thinking about that day in Seattle as if it was a distant memory instead of a real gift to me. So I have started again, and every morning, I make myself sit and remember where I was when I had that feeling. It's not easy, but I am making changes little by little. I have come to think of that experience as a wake-up call that came from some spiritual place inside me and I am treating it more sacredly than I had been. It's funny, but I find myself smiling more during the day, even taking long, deep breaths, because I feel like I was given a special gift and my life can be better and more 'me' than before."

If we have had an experience where we were able to gain perspective on our lives, we should trust its authenticity and think about what we learned. What was the most important insight we arrived at and how have we used it in our lives? We can ask ourselves how we could begin making changes based on what we learned.

The Power of Discontent

We may be able to ultimately connect with our purpose by paying attention to our discontent, which can signal that we are leading a life that violates who we are and what we value. That sense that we have lost our way, or are off our paths, is for certain people the place to begin creating a life that feels more authentic and alive. We need to take our discontent and use it to teach and guide us. We may learn that old goals and ideals are bankrupt and no longer inspire us. Despair and sorrow are not signs of our weakness. They are the starting points to reconnect with our vision. They suggest that we must either let go of familiar things that no longer nurture us or change our lives to reflect new interests and directions. Or both.

Monica, a dedicated mental health professional, woke up one day in her early forties and realized that during the past three years she had drifted away from what she had once valued, namely sports and political action. She had gained thirty pounds, and to her horror, had become a couch potato like her deceased father.

We couldn't yet work on pinpointing her vision because she so quickly dismissed her feelings of discontent and deprivation.

"I can't believe how much I'm whining and complaining," she said contemptuously.

I was silent.

"I should be over this," she continued. "I'm such a wimp."

"By mocking yourself and dismissing your feelings—treating them as evidence of your badness—are you hiding your emotional reality and making it more difficult to heal what is distressing you?" I asked.

She began crying. "I guess my hunger really is emotional," she said.

As she began taking her feelings of unhappiness and deprivation more seriously she began looking at her life. At first she felt lost, not herself, off her path.

Monica's disgust with herself eventually led her to what she once valued but had been neglecting. She volunteered at a local hospital, and met other people who shared her ideals. She renewed an old friendship and attended more plays and movies. As she began to be more physically active she was more centered and alive. She gradually lost the excess weight and felt more like her old self. All of these changes increased her vitality and sense of fulfillment. By attending to her disgust with herself, she was able to clarify what she wanted. Her discontent dramatically taught her that she needed to change her life, that it was not in line with what she valued.

For other people, jealousy—that feeling of wanting what other people have—is crucial to finding our own vision. We often confuse jealousy with envy. They are not synonymous. One way of differentiating them according to psychoanalyst Melanie Klein is that in envy we wish to take away and spoil what the other person possesses, while jealousy involves wanting what someone else has.

Normally we lose sight of what jealousy can teach us because we feel guilty about it. It may seem shameful, but by paying attention to who or what we are jealous of, we can become clearer about what we want for our own lives. Monica first became aware of her discontent when she noticed jealousy toward her best friend, Anne, who seemed, at least from the outside, to live a more physically active and interesting life. "I feel jealous of people who are bouncy and energetic, like my friend Anne. Anne is always doing something that sounds like fun—something I wouldn't have thought of doing. She also works out regularly and looks really good and hasn't gained weight like I have. And she has tons of energy and volunteers at her church. She has a whole circle of friends from doing that, and I feel left out." Monica's jealousy led her to clarify what she wanted more of in her life.

We began this chapter by exploring the importance of pursuing our purpose, our conception of how we want to live. Next we discussed the way various tools—including dreams, meditation, feedback from trusted friends and colleagues, discontent, and jealousy—could assist us in illuminating what we value. Now we are ready to begin clarifying where our purpose lies.

As we did in the previous chapter, let's do a practice that can open up inner space, which will help us refine our vision:

Write down how you feel emotionally and physically.
When you are finished close your eyes.
Relax your eyelids and jaw.
Let your shoulders drop.
Let the chair or cushion or couch hold you.
Close your mouth.
Breathe through your nose and pull the air to the back of your
    throat.
Relax your shoulders and chest.
Let your breath be gentle and fine.
Do that for a few minutes.
Very good . . .
Keeping your eyes closed, bring your attention to your body.
Notice any restful places.
If your mind wanders, as soon as you notice that you have drifted

away, gently return without any judgment to the experience of
savoring and soaking in restful states in your body.

Do this for a few minutes.

Keeping your eyes closed, now attend to sound. Welcome it, don't
resist it.

Experience sound directly, making it the sole focus of your
attention.

Gently and slowly open your eyes and return your attention to the
room.

Write down how you feel emotionally and physically.

Any changes?

As you may have experienced, yogic breathing and meditation can
offer clues about purpose and direction, as well as refine your awareness
and self-acceptance. Pay attention to any images or intuitions you have
accessed while meditating.

Discovering Your Purpose

Take some time to pinpoint your purpose. Sit quietly without any
distractions. Turn off your cellphone and your computer. Both help
expand inner space. Ask yourself the following questions one at a time.
Savor each question. Reflect on them. Pay attention to the answers,
images, and associations that arise. If you have any difficulties answering them remember that there are no right or wrong responses. Since
new insights don't always reveal themselves right away, give yourself
the time and space to think about them more deeply. If you feel flooded
with too much information or get stuck or tired, take a break and return
when you feel more energetic.

Write down your answers without censoring them. After a while—
perhaps a few hours or even a few days—examine your answers and see
what they might be trying to tell you.

- What really matters to me? Does my current life reflect this?
- What are my unique talents and gifts—the brushstrokes I could

contribute to the canvas of life? How could I bring them more into my life?

- Who are the people who inspired me and whom I truly admire? What are the qualities in them I most respect? What did I learn from them?
- What figures in history would I like to meet? What would I want to talk with them about and what would I ask them? How can I bring whatever I admire in them into my life?
- Do I feel that the life I am leading is all there is? If I feel that there's something more, what do I sense is missing?
- Was there ever a time when my life felt right? What was that like? How could I make that happen now?
- Have I ever sensed that there is a song or a dance within me that has never been expressed? How could I bring that into my life now?
- What happened in those special and rare moments that changed my life? What did I learn? How did it affect me? How can I draw sustenance from that now?
- In an ideal world what kind of life would I like to have?
- How could I alter my life now so that I will not have regrets when I am older?

Once you have answered these questions, notice common threads or patterns that could reveal your purpose. Perhaps there is a link you have been ignoring between what really matters to you and someone you really admire. Or maybe what you admire in other people is a clue to unexplored potentials lying dormant within you. Pay particular attention to where you are missing what you value and how you might bring it into your life.

If you are not using your gifts, reflect on how you might. If your dreams, jealousies, or regrets hint at what you need to bring into your life, try to imagine living in such a way that you feel more of a sense of authentic meaning and purpose. Ask yourself what you need to change to make that possible. Break this down into small, manageable steps and tackle them one at a time.

If the patterns of your answers to the questions are vague or unclear, treat them as clues that you will attempt to learn from as you read the rest of the book. Be patient and remember that change often occurs gradually and incrementally—as it did for Yvette and Rich—and that it takes time and patience.

Keep your answers in mind as you read the following chapters and continually ask yourself how to make your life more of a genuine reflection of your passions.

> The best lack all conviction, while the worst
> Are full of passionate intensity.
>
> —W. B. YEATS

EMBODYING OUR VALUES

Closing the Ethical Gap

A few years ago my friend and colleague Reverend Tom Downes invited me to speak to the Committee on Spirituality, Values, and Global Concerns at the United Nations. In preparation for this meeting Tom asked me to read The Universal Declaration of Human Rights, the founding document of the U.N.

The Universal Declaration of Human Rights is an immensely inspiring document advocating the highest ideals of justice, freedom, and respect for the sacredness of human beings. If the world were organized according to its precepts it would be a much more peaceful, loving, and beautiful place.

Regardless of how many countries have endorsed The Universal Declaration of Human Rights and how dear we hold its ideals, the vast majority of people live without even the most basic protections endorsed by it. The United States is far from alone in its violation of the values in this document. Some countries are better; many countries are much, much worse.

Why can't we put these inspiring ideals into practice? I am not an expert in the political obstacles to creating a more just and humane world, so I felt silly talking about that at the United Nations. But I did see strong parallels between the ways that nations failed to live up to the values they espouse, and the ways that individual people do the same thing—both with devastating results. I think it can not only shed light on how things work in the international and political spheres, but teach us about an indispensable aspect of flourishing, namely embodying our values.

"To know who you are is to be oriented in moral space," notes the philosopher Charles Taylor in *Sources of the Self: The Making of the Modern Identity*. We are what we value. We all have our personal views on what is right and what is wrong, whether they are derived from religion or personal feelings, philosophy, or a combination of factors. We make moral judgments all the time, and if they are not always perfectly consistent, then they are also far from random. Values are compasses that help us find meaning and direction in our lives. If I consider people as *ends unto themselves*, I will live very differently than if I see the world as a huge amusement park, the sole purpose of which is to entertain me and satisfy my appetites. In the first case I will be moved to respect people and the world around me. In the second I will view everything and everybody as nothing more than resources I can tap for my own personal gratification. Almost everyone will claim to hold the first view—that people are sacred and important as individuals—and yet there are literally millions of women and children enslaved in brothels around the world and thousands of people killed every day because of religious beliefs and racial bigotry, or because they are pawns caught between warring factions.

While most people embrace exemplary moral ideals, they imperfectly embody them. Flourishing necessitates that we strive for a deeper commitment to an ethical way of living.

Our values and ethics are not just laudable sentiments that conflict with our personal hungers; they also have a practical side to them. They are the glue that holds together relationships and families, communities and societies. Ethical behavior—what I think of as *accountability to self and to others* and *integrity in action*—engenders trust and makes our relationships deeper, smoother, and more fulfilling.

A few years ago I treated a wealthy and successful man in his forties. He had a great deal of pride about his father and the lessons he'd learned from him. He told me about when they had gone to a car dealership to work out a price for a new car and the value of his father's current vehicle as a trade-in. They went on a warm, sunny day and haggled with the dealer until they found a price acceptable to both. When they returned to the dealership to complete the transaction and pick up the new car, they drove there in the trade-in vehicle. It was a rainy day. The car dealer immediately noticed that the car's window was rolled down and asked why it wasn't up.

"It's broken," the father replied proudly. "We already signed the papers, though, so it's your problem now."

My client viewed this as a positive lesson from his father. He didn't seem to understand why someone might think it would be better to tell the car dealer about the broken window during the negotiations. His ethics were essentially "If you can get away with it then it's acceptable, and if you get exploited then you are a chump and deserved it."

We live in an increasingly amoral world with little consensus—and much acrimony—about what to do. Our values are skewed, our priorities are in disarray. It's as if a virus of immorality and lack of accountability has swept through the culture causing the ceaseless pursuit of *more* to pervert our judgment and degrade our souls.

The backlash has been enormous. In the first decade of the twenty-first century, not only were tens of millions of loyal workers cheated out of hard-earned retirement funds and college savings for their children, but insatiably greedy predators created a moral-free-for-all that has profited no one except the obscenely rich—and at a huge cost to us—and also to them, which they rarely, if ever, consider.

I want to first examine the personal cost of the lack of ethical accountability. Let's return to my client, whose father embodied how to cheat car salesmen. The morality his father taught him did help to make my client wealthy, but left him with emotional scars. He was always suspicious that someone was trying to cheat him and obsessed with preventing that from happening. He didn't want to be a chump, because for him that meant not just getting cheated; it also provided evidence that he deserved to be swindled. He was reluctant to be vulnerable around people, and only really opened up to those he thought he could control. He was caught in the grip of a perversion of the golden rule: exploit others before they take advantage of you. His twisted ethics had simultaneously brought him financial success and robbed him of the joy that success might bring. The way he saw the world meant that he couldn't trust or open up to other people. He had trapped himself inside a prison of his own making. It seems a heavy price for the ability to win at certain business dealings, but it's a price I've seen many unethical people pay.

A society in general can be ill or sick, argues Erich Fromm in *The Sane Society,* insofar as it promotes destructive values and fails to foster needs that are crucial to human growth and development. The epidemic of immorality alienates us from what might truly nourish our souls, seducing us into thinking that the more we acquire and consume the better we will feel. This is a pathological form of self-care. It not only starves us of vital emotional and spiritual nutrients—a topic we'll soon explore—it erodes the foundation of trust and safety that is essential to the flourishing of a democratic culture in an increasingly complex and diverse world. It pits us against each other and breeds a devastating suspicion of the very people we actually are dependent on to flourish. Not following our values and not being accountable to ourselves or other people also causes us to think and act in more jaded and self-protective ways.

Shunning values also narrows the horizon of hope for young people. A few years ago I taught a graduate seminar at Union Theological Seminary entitled "Staying Sane in an Insane World: Insights from Psychotherapy, Yoga, and Buddhism." In one class I was talking about the rampant immorality in American culture. The students (all of whom, except for one, ranged in age from midtwenties to early thirties) were subtly resistant to my argument. All of them, except a woman in her fifties, believed the moral climate had always been as grim and things had not gotten worse. I realized that they were relatively insensitive to how immoral things had become because it was all they have ever known. This may be the greatest crime the immoral masters of the universe have committed—shredding hope and lowering expectations in the young. But the idealism, aspirations, and energy of our youth are the lifeblood of democracy. Without them our society is robbed of an indispensable and priceless resource.

It is not an exaggeration to say that we are at a *moral crossroads.* The ethics of I-will-get-mine-no-matter-what-the-cost to you—or me— is unworkable and unsustainable. It's a degraded way of living that is warping our relationships with each other and ourselves.

Yet it is important to note that this ethic is not an alien concept to any of us. In the *Gulag Archipelago* Alexander Solzhenitsyn wrote,

"If only there were evil people somewhere insidiously committing evil deeds and it were necessary only to separate them from the rest of us and destroy them; but the line dividing good and evil cuts through the heart of every human being." We all have blind spots and ethical lapses, so while it is enormously tempting to moralize about the flaws of other people, we would do well to first understand—and then struggle to transform—our own.

There is obviously a gap between what most people say they value and their actions. And this gap exists in all of us. Most people are not criminals, but I'd wager that everyone reading this has cut an ethical corner he or she regretted, or done something that went in a different direction than his or her moral compass pointed. I am not an exception.

There may be a chasm between our soaring ideals and the sordid realities we confront on a daily basis, but I believe it is possible to make our highest ethical and spiritual aspirations come alive in today's world, and if we cannot do that, then we can at least strive to get closer to them.

A young adult I treated told me the following story, which gives me hope that my idealism is realistic.

He returned a policeman's wallet that he found late at night. "Here's forty dollars," the detective said when they met.

"If I wanted the money I would have taken the wallet," my patient replied.

He was astonished that he should be rewarded for simply doing the right thing.

Why We Are Not Living Our Ideals and What We Can Do about It

Humans routinely deceive themselves. The person who claims to be religious and moral, for example, may not only pray on the weekend, and lie, cheat, and steal during the week, but he may be able to convince himself that the two things are not related, or that the one balances out the other. This makes many people either minimize their own ethical lapses or discount them altogether with the rationalization that everybody does it or it's not a big deal even if, objectively, it is. The process of *cognitive dissonance*—changing the facts to fit the theory—works in tandem with self-deception to keep people from objectively judging themselves.

There is a widespread miscalculation of the value, and in this instance I don't mean moral value, but rather the worth of certain choices we make in how we live. "You can never get enough of what you don't need to make you happy," wrote Eric Hoffer in *The True Believer*. An important reason people betray their values is because of a failure to understand what they really need.

Lack of self-knowledge leaves us prone to misrecognize and miscalculate our needs—believing that the more we acquire and consume the happier we will be. That is *cotton candy for the soul*—it looks and tastes good but it is a poor substitute for something that is vital (such as nourishing human connections or having a sense of meaning and purpose) and it leaves us starved for what helps us truly flourish.

In addition, the mad and endless quest for more, which fueled the recent Wall Street debacle and so many disasters throughout history, leads those in its insidious grip to dehumanize or render invisible their fellow human beings. It is harder to exploit people if we recognize their worth and needs.

Lack of self-knowledge also causes us to misperceive how we fit into the universe. We assume that we are separate and independent from other people and the world. Einstein wrote:

A human being is a part of a whole, called by us "universe," a part limited in time and space. He experiences himself, his thoughts and feelings as something separated from the rest . . . a kind of optical delusion of his consciousness. This delusion is a kind of prison for us, restricting us to our personal desires and to affection for a few persons nearest to us. Our task must be to free ourselves from this prison by widening our circle of compassion to embrace all living creatures and the whole of nature in its beauty.

We do not recognize our connection with each other—as you fare, so do I—and thus we are oblivious to the consequences of operating as if we are separate from the rest of the world. One form this takes is a pathologically narrow conception of citizenship—too many of us only focus on what we are owed, rather than on what we might give.

Let's reflect upon the set of qualities and attributes that might aid us in being more moral in an immoral age. We can do this individually and our example can inspire other people to engage this worthwhile and realistic pursuit.

Self-knowledge—what I think of as wise attention to who we are and how we behave—teaches us what we *truly* need, how we fit into the world, and our characteristic blind spots and temptations.

Self-awareness can help us treat ourselves better, which means respecting and nourishing, rather than indulging and exploiting ourselves. My clinical experience has amply demonstrated that compulsive working, shopping, and substance abuse are often poor medicine for feeling emotionally invisible, voiceless, and alienated from meaningful human connections. These substitute gratifications inevitably disappoint us and do not fill our emotional holes.

In order to nurture ourselves it is crucial that we know what truly helps us flourish, as opposed to what Herbert Marcuse called the "false needs" that advertising and consumer culture try to convince us are necessary. I suspect few people on their deathbeds lament that they didn't have more money, gadgets, or possessions. I am fairly certain they wish they had more time, meaning and purpose, and fulfilling relationships.

Another crucial aspect of ethically useful self-knowledge is the recognition of our fundamental interdependence—we are not really separate from other people, in fact we are interconnected. Understanding what the Buddhist teacher Thich Nhat Hanh calls our "interbeing," our essential interrelationship with each other, makes it more difficult to exploit other people because taking advantage of them demeans us, which is like exploiting ourselves. If we help create a toxic society, then we—and our families—can't help but be poisoned by it too.

Understanding ourselves also entails recognizing our characteristic temptations—whether sex or money, drugs or gossip—which are different for everyone. The Dalai Lama was teaching in L.A. some time ago. Each day, on his way home from the hotel where he was staying, he was driven down a street filled with shops selling high-tech gadgets. At first he was simply curious about all the different things he saw in the store windows as he rode by. By the end of the week he found himself wanting things even though he didn't know what they were!

Desire grips us all. It is human, and it is universal. It is essential for our survival, fueling, at its best, intimacy and constructive change. When we understand the particular desires we are prone to be seduced by, we can, like Odysseus, tie ourselves to the mast so that we can avoid the siren song of unhealthy appetites and mechanical behavior.

Distinguishing between healthy and pathological forms of desire is crucial. Healthy desires—for example, the wish to understand, grow, practice an awareness discipline, achieve goals, and connect—help us flourish, fuel both self-care and constructive features of human evolution, and leave no traces of guilt. There are several signs of unhealthy desires—gratifying them harms us, they have an addictive quality (we can't do without them), and afterward we feel conflict, guilt, and regret.

Skillfully responding to human selfishness, as well as mastering desire and temptation, is a crucial part of living our values because our egocentricity often sabotages our highest ethical ideals.

Narcissism haunts our world in various destructive guises. In its wake we witness, on a daily basis, rapacious greed and unconscionable hard-heartedness toward the downtrodden and oppressed. From the highest political offices to college and professional sports, our world resembles a moral free-for-all in which the interests of the autonomous individual take precedence over virtue or civic well-being.

Conquering selfishness is one important purpose of religious ethics. Many religions assume that when human beings are left to their own devices, they will be destructively egocentric—even evil. A deep puritanical streak permeates Western civilization—there is what Fromm in "Selfishness, Self-Love, and Self-Interest" terms a "taboo on selfishness" in modern culture. Many people believe that to be self-centered is to be sinful and to be self-less is to be virtuous.

It is often true that self-centered behavior taken to an extreme can be destructive in a variety of ways. This is probably a huge reason that The Universal Declaration of Human Rights so rarely guides actual behavior. Selfishness can cause us to place our needs at the center of our actions, allowing nothing to stand between us and our goals. The needs and feelings of other people may even become irrelevant. Taken to its extreme this leads to dictatorships and fundamentalists, wars and imperialism.

However, it is worth noting that appropriate self-centeredness is actually healthy for a person's development, and sometimes there is a hidden cost to a religious approach that attempts to eradicate or re-nounce self-centeredness, which is an irreducible part of being a human being. Trying to eliminate self-centered behavior often leads to *greater* self-deprivation and self-preoccupation. Because self-concern, self-protection, and self-esteem are indispensable for survival (as is human connection and concern), they can't—and shouldn't—be purged, but rather must be handled more wisely.

Concern for the well-being of other people is a counterreaction to the habitual, taken-for-granted, and thus unconscious narcissism of individualism, where personal preferences underwrite and guide our values. This is an indispensable corrective to the egocentricity and immorality that pervades our world. Undreamed-of possibilities for mitigating strife and forging new bonds of human understanding and connectedness become possible when our own desires are central to, although not the center of, our moral universe. When room is cre-ated within us to consider the feelings and needs of other people who may see the world very differently, not only might we treat them with greater kinship but we are more receptive to their potential influence. Then we might see the flourishing of what Tibetan Buddhists call *nying je chenmo* or "great [or universal] compassion," which is a deep and abid-ing concern for the welfare of everyone, not simply "local" compassion for those closest to us.

Over the last few years I have repeatedly witnessed two different things that make me question the completeness of the selfless religious or spiritual prescription for morality. I have observed enormous ego-centricity and interpersonal myopia in some Buddhist communities—numerous scandals involving supposedly enlightened masters sexually exploiting students and stealing funds from the community, as Sandy Boucher noted in *Turning the Wheel: American Women Creating the New Bud-dhism*. Jung's great insight about the interpenetration of opposites that we explored in chapter 3 sheds some light on this troubling tension between a movement that consciously stresses egolessness and loving-kindness and yet is permeated by self-centeredness and an absence of empathy for others. Jung taught us that the opposite of whatever we consciously value will unconsciously return to haunt us. The conscious emphasis on selflessness in Buddhism generates its polar opposite, the unconscious emergence of selfishness.

While I have observed more egocentricity than one might expect in many Buddhists, I have also witnessed the enormous pain and suffering of many clients in psychotherapy and psychoanalysis who struggle with not feeling that they even have the right to their lives. Their behaviors suggest that the answer to the question "Whose life is it anyway?" is a resounding "Not mine!" The problem for these people is not that they are too self-centered, but that they are too self-negligent. Spiritual practice involving selfless attunement to other people can breed further self-neglect and especially impoverished self-care.

We seem to be caught in an irreconcilable dilemma. The narcissism of secular individualism cultivates egocentricity and immorality, while spiritual alternatives like those the Dalai Lama recommends might unwittingly foster self-neglect.

Skillfully responding to selfishness entails a method that strives to approach it constructively without attempting to renounce or eliminate our humanity, as opposed to the view of much religious thinking. One of the hallmarks of psychoanalysis is the awareness that we cannot eliminate our essential humanness, which includes the evolutionary need for self-concern, self-protection, and self-esteem. If we try, it returns with a vengeance and emerges in distorted forms like the very pathological selfishness that spiritual ethics evolved to remedy. From this perspective altruism and self-care are two sides of the same coin and we must open to others without forsaking the self. Walt Whitman pointed toward this stereophonic perspective in "Song of Myself" when he wrote, "Clear and sweet is my soul, and clear and sweet is all that / is not my soul." In *The Ethics of the Talmud: Sayings of the Fathers*, Hillel wrote, "If I am not for myself who is for me? and when I am for myself what am I? and if not now, when?" In order to flourish we need to promote the cultivation of empathy and compassion for others (including those outside our circle of family and friends) even as we cherish, celebrate, and nourish ourselves. An integrative approach has the potential to be a profound way of living our values and a revolutionary force in the new millennium.

Living our values also entails having the *integrity and accountability* to learn from our mistakes and commit to discovering and encouraging the best within us and other people. This is the *feedback-sensitive* approach to the body and emotions we discussed in chapter 5.

Our self-image—who we think we are—is a central part of our identity. Humans typically try to confirm their conception of themselves. If I believe I am kind and disciplined, I will feel badly when I notice myself being insensitive and unfocused. Since most of us don't want to feel lousy, we gravitate toward pleasure and the familiar and away from pain and the unfamiliar, as Freud reminded us: without conscious effort we are all predisposed to ignore feedback that clashes with our cherished ideals about who we are. One crucial way of living our values is by becoming very curious about gaps between our ideals and our behavior, which are often signaled by remorse and regret. I learn more about myself when I study those times when I don't live up to my self-image and ideals than I do when I either live up to them or don't and deny or rationalize it.

Paying attention to our dreams is another indispensable way of detecting such disparities between who we think we are and who we are. Dreams are an early warning system about emotional conflict and areas of guilt. Studying and composting this aspect of dreams keeps us honest.

Our efforts to read such feedback and learn from our experience are aided by being part of *communities of accountability*—relationships with individuals and groups of people who value the truth and doing the right thing, not simply making more money or garnering more power or fame. Many of us feel more elevated and inspired when we are with people who are highly principled, than when we are with individuals with shifting values. And our truth-seeking friends and mentors can steer us in an ethical direction when our own moral compass is failing.

Next we need to enlarge our *moral imagination,* which is illustrated by a story about Gandhi. A man was hired to assassinate Gandhi. He attended one of his talks, but he was so moved by the power and the spirit of Gandhi's teachings that he scrapped his plan. As Gandhi finished speaking, the assassin went up to him, prostrated himself, and told Gandhi of his aborted assassination.

Imagine yourself in the same situation. What would you feel? What would you say? What was Gandhi's response to the man?

"What are you going to tell your boss about your failed plan?"

That to me is *ethics—integrity in action.*

While we don't know the actual impact on Gandhi of adopting an ethical relation to the other person—a man, in this case, who wanted to kill him—I imagine that he felt more at peace with himself and the world than he would have if he had had a more conventional response and was filled with consuming rage and the desire for vengeance. And while such magnanimity can make a figure such as Gandhi seem saintlike, distant, and remote from our own experiences, he was a human being, flawed and complicated like anyone else, and the only things that made him different in his morality were the choices he made. The flip side of Solzhenitsyn's statement about good and evil is that if there are no devils, only people, then there are also no angels, only people. Each of us is personally capable of whatever morality we choose to pursue. It is a matter of awareness, choice, and the capacity to learn from experience.

An exposure to a wider range of stories and lives through literature and travel, anthropology and film cultivates an expanded moral imagination and helps us live our values. Exposure to the particular and unique life and world of people different from us promotes human solidarity, which is, as I wrote in chapter 5, a firmer foundation for compassion and caring than appeals to abstract ethical guidelines. In a world that contains *The Diary of Anne Frank,* the description of alienation and anomie in Ralph Ellison's *Invisible Man,* and the depiction of the descent into madness in Sylvia Plath's *The Bell Jar,* we know more about the holocaust, the African American experience, and women and mental illness than we would if they had never been written.

Developing greater empathy, striving to understand other people from within their frames of reference, is another invaluable asset in extending our moral imagination. An important aspect of this is becoming attuned to the impact of our actions on other people.

I suspect that there is more harmony within and without when we each pursue our highest values and are accountable to each other and ourselves. Accountability to each other engenders trust and makes our relationships more reliable and fulfilling.

Cicero's *The Dream of Scipio*, an imagined dream vision of the Roman general Scipio Aemilianus, points even further to human beings as *planet stewards*. When we see ourselves as cocreators of the kind of world we wish for, we may more passionately commit to living our values and thereby contribute to a better universe.

The practices that I have recommended for cultivating greater integrity in action—ranging from studying our dreams and the gaps between our ideals and our behavior, to participating in communities of accountability and embracing stewardship of the planet—take time and patience, but will yield substantial benefits personally and collectively.

When I finished my talk at the U.N., I thought that I had expressed everything that I wanted to say about embodying our values. That is, until a twenty-something Slavic man in the audience asked me what to do when one's ethics clash with his culture. After answering his question I realized that he had helped me put into words what for me are five of the crucial aspects of ethical decision making and living our values. I told him about my CO experience and then described the following principles:

1. Understand the context of our actions and the possible impact on all concerned. When I applied for conscientious objector status, should I have considered that I might hurt someone else by refusing to kill?

2. Recognize our true motive, as opposed to what we tell ourselves or would like to believe. Was my application for a CO position sincere or self-serving? Was it based on moral conviction or expediency and escapism?

3. Seek and await clarity before taking action. Does my action come out of expanded inner space and a state of wakefulness, or is it reactive and rushed and based on accommodation to, or rebellion against, the viewpoints of other people?

4. Study the actual impact of one's actions. What were the ramifications for me and the other people involved in my decision to be a CO—from the members of the draft board to my father, who attended the draft board hearing with me?

5. Be willing to adjust one's subsequent behavior based on what is learned. I still live my life based on the conviction that violence begets violence, and hate is never healed by hate, as Christ and the Buddha recognized. But if my life or the lives of those I love were threatened, I suspect I would use physical force.

Several years ago I taught a workshop for therapists on self-care at the Harlem Family Institute, a psychoanalytic center in New York City that trains therapists to offer affordable treatment for poor people. We met in the Dietrich Bonhoffer room at Union Theological Seminary. As I waited for the workshop to begin, I contemplated the life of this Protestant theologian who fought against the Nazis and literally gave his life to help others in mortal danger; it struck me that the final stage of self-care is *going beyond exclusive preoccupation with oneself*. In our me-first culture it is tempting to think that being ethical is a huge sacrifice, but it is actually *in our own best interest* because it is a foundation of flourishing.

We are living our values. Now we are ready to harmonize our passion and purpose, talents and skills, and create a symphony of self.

9

THE SYMPHONY OF THE SELF

We are pursuing our passions—the what-we-love-to-do part of our lives—with focus and determination. This has clarified our visions of how we want to live and the directions we want to take that passion. Now it is time to turn our visions into action by creating harmony within ourselves.

Imagine a symphony orchestra, a large ensemble of musicians playing string, wind, brass, and percussion instruments together. How do the musicians work as a cohesive whole without any single instrument dominating or remaining in the background? The conductor or maestro—another name for master—has a vision and knows what each instrument can do and what to ask of each musician to make the piece harmonious. Without a conductor, disharmony and even cacophony could prevail.

There are many "instruments" or aspects that make up a human being, including passion and vision, talents and skills. Each of us has his or her unique "sound" and purpose. Passion adds richness and fullness to our lives. Vision directs our enthusiasms in a constructive direction. Talents and skills help us live what we value by putting it into practice.

If we do not play some of these instruments, our lives won't be as full and rich as they could be. Our visions of how we want to live must be fueled by our passions, otherwise they lack gusto and authenticity, but our passions have to be supported by a good foundation—the cultivation of the necessary talents and skills to master what we aspire to do. Passion, talents, and skills need to be properly channeled toward constructive purpose—our vision—otherwise we would travel in the wrong direction, away from what we genuinely love.

The best music in our lives occurs when no instrument of our being is dominant or excluded—when we follow our enthusiasms, nurture our gifts, hone our abilities, and embody our purposes—and when we, as our own conductors, bring balance and harmony to our lives.

Consider professional ambition—the drive to succeed at work—which often causes us to be quite self-focused and myopic. Ambition needs to be in proper proportion to intimacy, the wish to have close relationships with family and friends. Otherwise, we overemphasize work, the emotional aspects of ourselves that are only nurtured by close relationships languish, important relationships suffer, and we deprive ourselves of an essential source of emotional sustenance. Bringing balance and harmony to our lives means, among other things, that we create realistic visions that are aligned with our values and then develop the necessary skills to implement them.

When our passion, vision, talent, and skills are harmoniously blended, we create a symphony of our selves. Then we live in greater harmony as the different parts coexist in a splendid balance and play together cooperatively. The psychoanalyst Erich Fromm's description of his friend the esteemed Zen scholar and teacher D. T. Suzuki depicted a symphony of self in action:

> Perhaps I should mention his ever-present interest in everything—he was delighted to see a Mexican rug, or piece of pottery, or silverware. It was not only a matter of seeing it, but of touching it, feeling its texture and its form. He gave life to everything by his interest, by his active relatedness; a person, a cat, a tree, a flower—they all came to life through his own aliveness . . .
>
> He was always himself, humble, never an "authority"; he never insisted that his views must be followed; he was a man who never aroused fear in anybody; there was nothing of the irrational and mystifying aura of the "great man" about him; there was never a sense of obligation to accept what he said because he said it. He was an authority purely by his being, and never because he promised approval or threatened disapproval.

Trying to pinpoint the source of Suzuki's unique quality, Fromm wrote:

> Was it his lack of narcissism and selfishness, his kindness, and his love of life? It was all of these, but often I have thought of still another aspect: the child-like quality in him. This needs some comment. The process of living hardens the heart of most people. As children we still have an open and malleable heart; we still have faith in the genuineness of mother's smile, in the reliability of promises, in the unconditional love, which is our birthright. But this "original faith" is shattered sooner or later in our childhood. Most of us lose the softness and flexibility of our hearts; to become an adult is often synonymous with becoming hardened. Some escape this fate; they keep their heart open and do not let it harden. But in order to be able to do so, they do not see reality fully as it is. They become as Don Quixote, seeing the noble and the beautiful where they are not; they are dreamers who never awaken fully to see reality including all its ugliness and meanness. There is a third solution, but an exceedingly rare one. The persons who take this road retain the softness of a child's heart, and yet they see reality in all clarity and without illusions. They are children first, then they become adults, and yet they return to being children without ever losing the realism of adulthood. This is a difficult way, and that is why it is so rare. I believe it was this, which characterized Dr. Suzuki's personality. He was hard as rock and soft as wax; he was the realistic, mature man, who was able to look at the world with the innocence and faith of the child.

And this quality touched and inspired others.

Getting in Our Own Way

Can we orchestrate a graceful, novel, and harmonious composition without any discord? Some of us might be able to, but most of us will face certain typical core conflicts as we attempt to fashion a life that honors our unique gifts and accomplishes our goals amid the challenges—and often conflicting demands and loyalties—of work, family, success, and intimacy.

Five typical obstacles often stand in our way and prevent us from making our lives into symphonies:

1. A person focused only on seeking his *true self*, what he believes is his essential identity—which is presumed to provide infallible guidance and direction—ignores or rejects other, vital aspects of himself that don't fit into this restricted conception.
2. People who suffer from a *scattered self* often go in so many directions that their goals can't be achieved.
3. People with *lopsided selves* have underdeveloped skills and so lack the tools to carry out their purpose.
4. Those split into good and bad sides—a *divided self*—fight a perpetual inner war that sabotages their efforts to pursue their visions.
5. The *doubting Thomas* is undermined by a lack of self-trust. It is nearly impossible to follow our bliss or pursue our aspirations when we don't trust our capacity to succeed.

Many of us face one or more of these challenges, which can make it difficult to realize the lives to which we aspire.

The True Self

JoAnn was the successful advertising executive who left a lucrative but unfulfilling job to pursue a career in writing. She put an unnecessary burden on herself by assuming that within her past lay a blueprint for who she "really" was and how she should live; and that if she could only discover it, everything would fall neatly into place. I learned about this when she described an interchange with a friend. During a time of conflict and confusion, the friend challenged JoAnn's comment, "All I have to do is find my true self—that will tell me how to lead my life." But a true self doesn't exist, although our culture perpetuates this misconception.

"You be you," the Nike commercials advise us—as if we are one essential thing, like a captain of industry or a homemaker but never both.

The language of everyday life—conversations, movies, books, television commercials, and even spiritual retreats and psychotherapy sessions—is filled with slogans exhorting people to find and be themselves.

Many people spend a lot of time and energy searching for their true selves. There is something profoundly seductive about the possibility of uncovering who we *really* are. We assume—without carefully thinking about it—that there is a true self hidden within each one of us, and that once that true self is discovered it will serve as a perfect compass for how we should live. This is enormously comforting in an age when people juggle multiple roles and responsibilities, are pulled in many directions, and are confused about who they are and how they should live. The search for the true self is also prevalent among people who feel that they never got to do something vital or important, or somehow took a wrong turn. They imagine that if they discover it their lives will be redeemed.

Searching for our true selves is a misguided enterprise that can actually narrow the breadth of our vision and limit us. While we may in fact be alienated from ourselves—living a life that feels false or inauthentic and clashes with or even violates what we value—the solution to our estrangement from ourselves does not lie solely in discovering a singular and essential version of ourselves.

The self that we discover when we try to figure out who we really are is only a snapshot from our past—a picture of who we were—not a guide for our futures. These versions are neither better nor truer, nor do they somehow magically provide unerring guidance for how to live in the present. They are, in fact, simply earlier, less mature versions of ourselves.

Do you ever find yourself believing that there is a true self underneath the person you are now, and if you could just access it, it would provide a blueprint for how to live? The danger for a seeker of the true self is that instead of taking responsibility in the present for creating who one wants to be, one can passively await the revelation of an imaginary inner essence.

"I am large," wrote the poet Walt Whitman in "Song of Myself," "I contain multitudes." Because we are multidimensional beings, we don't have a singular true self. Shakespeare wrote: "To thine own self be true." Yes. And I'd add: "To thine own selves be true." The same person might be a parent, a spouse with friends, hobbies, a job, and other interests—all in one. And none of these roles, taken on their own, define the totality of who we are.

When we conceive of ourselves too narrowly, our vision for what is possible is severely restricted. We set limiting goals—such as making as much money as possible or being a mother—which might aid us in reaching that particular goal, but leave other parts of ourselves underdeveloped.

When we conceive of ourselves more broadly, and strive to nurture the different parts of ourselves, we not only avoid the trap of seeking our nonexistent singular essence, we expand the possibilities for depth, meaning, and fulfillment.

Until she realized that she was more than just her job, JoAnn defined herself too narrowly—slotting herself into a constricting mold. And as she discovered the various facets of herself—including the wish for intimacy as well as professional success—she was freed up to seek a better balance between work and relationships.

The Scattered Self

Some people face the opposite challenge—their vision is too broad and diffuse. "I could see myself living a thousand different lives," a client once told me. When we have too many passions and too broad an image of how we want to live, we can be all over the place, too scattered and unfocused. Too many visions can lead to paralysis.

I struggled with this for many years. I wore three professional hats—therapist, professor, and writer—and my interests ranged from Western psychoanalysis to Eastern meditative disciplines. Over nearly three decades I had worked with several different exceptional psychotherapeutic, meditative, yogic, and martial arts teachers. These studies were enormously illuminating and nurturing. I passionately filled my nonwork and nonfamily hours with exercise, and studying and writing about psychoanalysis, meditation, and yoga.

Even though I found each activity profoundly enriching, I was too scattered and had difficulty reconciling my different passions and aspects of myself. Aspiring to being a healer and scholar, contemplative and athlete, left me feeling pulled in different, often opposite directions. And my capacity to deepen my understanding and practice of each passion was probably compromised by my not having a cohesive vision. It was as if I knew I wanted to play music, but could never choose an instrument, so I tried to play them all simultaneously. The challenge for me was how to make a coherent life out of varied passions and a wide vision.

The danger of a scattered self is that we never manage to unite our different passions and interests into a coherent whole; we feel directionless. When we focus our vision—prioritizing our different interests and passions and weaving them into a harmonious composition—we not only waste less emotional energy, we operate more effectively.

The Lopsided Self

The lopsided self develops talents and skills in a highly imbalanced manner. The lopsided development of some strengths might cause us to neglect other vital skills necessary for actualizing our vision. Anyone, from a renowned spiritual teacher to a great athlete, can do this—exercising certain psychological (or physical) muscles while neglecting other ones, which, of course, atrophy. Such people practice what feels good while neglecting what doesn't. One reason many professional athletes experience a psychological death and feel completely lost after they retire from professional sports is that the only parts of themselves that they ever developed were their athletic skills and their bodies. For a large part of their adolescence and young adulthood their identities were limited to being a specific kind of physical performer. When their ability to execute on the athletic field ended, they had little else to give them self-esteem. Their sense of themselves was suddenly eroded, they felt lost and had difficulty knowing what to do with their lives.

When we are a lopsided self we develop unevenly. For example, we might become a caretaker who neglects his own needs; or an intellectual who skillfully solves problems but ignores her physical health; or a very physically attractive person with low self-esteem whose needs for intellectual or cultural stimulation are disregarded in the pursuit of being physically admired.

JoAnn was lopsided in three ways: she developed her artistic side to the exclusion of relationships, spent little time staying connected to friends or dating, and had large gaps in her knowledge of literature, in spite of her passion for it.

Unfortunately most of us are attracted to practices that foster our one-sided development and perpetuate our lopsidedness. People who are comfortable in their heads but not grounded in their bodies typically pursue cognitive rather than physically oriented activities. I once heard such a man, who saw himself as an intellectual, proudly proclaim: "The only muscles I need are between my ears." Athletically inclined individuals who are out of touch with their emotions tend to engage in demanding physical disciplines such as martial arts, rather than psychotherapy. It feels gratifying to do something we are already skilled at, but it doesn't stretch us or contribute to our growth or bring out other sides of ourselves.

Incomplete development has a high cost. When we cultivate only parts of ourselves, as when an orchestra uses only a few of its instruments, our lives are restricted and impoverished.

JoAnn's one-sided development left her feeling emotionally isolated, secretly vulnerable, and anxious about the intellectual challenges of her master's degree program.

Do you ever feel that you have developed unevenly, with highly competent areas coexisting with huge gaps in skills that you need?

The danger when we are a lopsided self is that we have neglected to develop those abilities that are necessary for what we really want to do. Developing different sides of ourselves—particularly those talents and skills that are essential to carry out our vision—aids us in reaching our goals.

The Divided Self

The divided self is the fourth barrier to composing our lives. Rick, the accountant who became a high school history teacher, had a disturbing lifelong pattern of not doing what was good for him and not following through on what he wanted for himself—from exercise programs to professional opportunities. This hindered his marriage and career and left him feeling shame and self-doubt.

There's a reason we have so much trouble following through on our New Year's resolutions to eat healthier foods or exercise more regularly, and procrastinate about doing things that we know are good for us. From a moralistic pillar of the community who is an unfaithful spouse to a yo-yo dieter, there are many people who seem to have two disconnected and antagonistic existences. A divided self is compartmentalized into two separate and warring factions, the *good self* and the *bad self*. The good self, according to Joel Kramer and Diana Alstad in *The Guru Papers,* is the hardworking, disciplined, and unselfish part of ourselves that we believe is good and virtuous. The other aspect, the bad self, doesn't live up to these values. When we are undisciplined about eating or exercise or when we procrastinate, for instance, the self-righteous good-self aspect of ourselves labels us as bad, lazy, and self-centered.

Most people ordinarily assume that the reason that they have so much difficulty doing what is healthy is because of what they believe is the "bad" part of them. They think that they need to subdue this aspect of themselves, and this triggers them to redouble the good self's efforts to control and tame the bad self, making sure it doesn't emerge. But what happens if the good self succeeds in subjugating the bad, so we vow to, for example, never have dessert again? Not only will we feel imprisoned and deprived, we will eventually rebel against the oppressive and unrealistic demands of the tyrannical good self. And even if the good self fails to crush the rebellious part of us we still lose because we act against our best interests—we then overeat because we feel deprived and rebellious, not because we are actually hungry.

A major reason most people seem to sabotage themselves and not take care of themselves is that the coerced and oppressed parts of them feel imprisoned and dominated, and rebel against the tyranny of the good self's puritanical, unrealistic, and depriving demands for perfect compliance and rigid self-control. The tragedy is that when we procrastinate about following through on what we value so we can defeat the controlling part of ourselves—like Judy in chapter 5—we often act in a way that clashes with what we actually want and what is healthy for us. That is one of the central reasons many people don't do what is good for them.

When we are a divided self, we are in continual conflict. Not only is our physical health often compromised, we are so busying bouncing between tyrannical demands for perfection and obstinate rebellion that we are distracted from pursuing our passions or discovering our visions. We have great difficulty remaining focused on our goals and we unconsciously undermine and sabotage our own aspirations. We can become whole, undivided selves and end the eternal tug-of-war by following our passions and setting realistic goals, instead of seeking unattainable purity and perfection.

The Doubting Thomas Self

"I'm filled with doubt," Rick confided in me during a moment of rare vulnerability. "I don't believe in myself and I fear I'll fail." When we are a doubting Thomas self we mistrust ourselves, and neither treat ourselves seriously enough nor feel entitled to fully claiming our lives. The danger then is that lack of self-trust greatly limits what we might strive for and achieve. This can make us risk-averse and sabotages our efforts to lead creative and fulfilling lives. This was one reason Rick, for example, spent so many years in an unhappy marriage and job.

We can cultivate belief in ourselves by following through on what we tell ourselves we will do, and by learning to access and trust our own resources for creativity and self-healing. Drawing sustenance from what we learn and how we feel when we expand inner space, appreciate beauty, compost challenging feelings, and study our dreams and daydreams can help us to do this.

Each of the five obstacles—the true self, the scattered self, the lopsided self, the divided self, and the doubting Thomas self—diminish our abilities to create harmonious lives and to flourish. The antidote is self-awareness.

Self-Knowledge

A symphony of the self requires planning, effort, and persistence. And for this we need self-knowledge, discipline, and flexibility.

Self-awareness aids us in drawing on our strengths to skillfully respond to the roadblocks in our paths. Discipline enables us to put self-knowledge into practice. And adaptability is crucial when unexpected contingencies arise.

The first step in composing our lives is self-knowledge, specifically an awareness of our strengths and weaknesses and the challenges and constraints we confront, which will enhance our abilities to be successful in creating harmonious lives.

Is our vision too narrow or broad? Do we have the skills to achieve our goals? Do we have the self-trust to persevere in the midst of a dark night of the soul? We need to understand how we can best use our particular talents and skills to face the obstacles that stand in our way. This process takes time and demands patience. But it will leave us with a clear map of our journeys, including bumpy roads, as well as the best route to our destinations.

We need to see ourselves in a realistic light to gain such self-awareness. We begin the process with an honest self-assessment, appreciating our strengths and recognizing our weaknesses.

This is not always an easy task. Humans, unlike other animals, have a stunning capacity to remake themselves in idealistic—and distorted—images. Some people, for example, see themselves in an excessively and unrealistically positive light. Such individuals routinely neglect their faults, rationalize away their mistakes, blame other people for their inadequacies, and continue doing what doesn't work—even when it no longer serves them. Other people exhibit the opposite form of self-blindness and see themselves in an unrealistically negative light. Such people are often their own worst enemies, condemning themselves for imperfections that they accept in others. It is not surprising that they neglect their strengths, rarely take credit for their triumphs and achievements, and feel flawed and inadequate. We need both an accurate assessment of our "inner wealth" and a clear idea of what we need to bolster ourselves as resources for the journey toward flourishing.

In my work with JoAnn, we began by reflecting on her talents and skills, accomplishments and positive traits.

I asked her what the most important accomplishments of her life were and which activities gave her the strongest sense of personal goodness.

"I was always an A student, won various academic awards, and got a perfect score on my SAT," she replied.

"What are your talents and skills?"

"I am hardworking, perform well under pressure, and rise to the occasion. I love to read and write, and am a talented short-story writer."

"Can you reflect upon situations that illustrate them in action?"

"My academic success."

"I wonder if there is any inner wealth that you are not appreciating and what you'd need to do to embrace it."

"My guts and drive. Realize what I have already accomplished."

Since JoAnn also needed to know which of her liabilities had to be remedied, I asked her to reflect on her negative attitudes and traits, beliefs and behavioral patterns as well. Here is how our conversation went:

"What are your weaknesses?"

"I cover over and avoid my vulnerabilities including my academic imbalances.

"I don't feel up to the challenge of graduate school. I'm an avoider—I stay away from things I have trouble doing. I can also be impatient if I feel I'm moving too slowly or not getting to where I think I need to be fast enough."

"Describe a recent incident that revealed that particular flaw."

"The summer before graduate school I wrote short stories and avoided novels and poetry."

"What would you like to change about yourself?"

"Confront my weaknesses instead of working around them."

From her responses, JoAnn realized that despite her fears of not being up to the challenge, she had a strong work ethic—in particular, an admirable capacity to concentrate and focus. She also recognized that she could rise to the occasion when she confronted roadblocks. Deadlines in her former job had mobilized her to do her best work.

Her intellectual strengths were that she loved to read and write. She also had received a good deal of feedback from talented, published writers that she had a gift for writing short stories. Her weakness was that she had no experience writing novels. In addition, she had a large gap in her knowledge of fiction and poetry.

JoAnn faced two external challenges: her financial resources would be limited while she was in graduate school and beginning a career, and she felt responsible for a beloved but ailing aunt who lived alone and whose health-care decisions often fell to JoAnn. Her aunt received a small pension and JoAnn often covered certain necessary expenses.

The two internal issues that JoAnn had to grapple with were the narrow way she viewed herself (her search for her true self) and the lopsided way she had developed her skills.

Before discussing how JoAnn used self-knowledge, discipline, and flexibility to create harmony in her life, it will be helpful to consider how self-knowledge aided Rick in creating a symphony of his self.

Rick too needed to increase awareness of his strengths, weaknesses, and the forces that obstructed his efforts to guide his life in the direction he chose.

I asked him to tell me about his important accomplishments, and the activities that gave him the strongest sense of personal goodness.

"I don't yet feel I've really done very much," he replied.

"What are your talents and skills?"

"I have the capacity to immerse myself in what I'm doing. I can synthesize a lot of information."

"What are your positive traits?"

"Good concentration and focus."

"Can you reflect upon situations that illustrate them in action?"

"I was able to study for my accounting degree for hours each day."

"Is there any inner wealth that you are not appreciating and what would you need to do to embrace it?"

"I guess my capacity for concentration and focus."

In order to illuminate what he struggled with, I asked Rick to reflect on his negative attitudes, traits, beliefs, and behavioral patterns.

"What are your weaknesses?"

"Foreign languages are an Achilles' heel. I sabotage myself and don't follow through on certain things that are good for me."

"What are your least appealing traits?"

"I isolate myself during times of duress and have few friends."

"Can you think of a recent incident that revealed that particular flaw?"

"I kept to myself during and after my divorce."

"What would you like to change about yourself?" I asked.

"I would like to follow through on what is good for me."

In exploring the career changes he hoped to make, Rick realized that he had a strong capacity for concentration and was undaunted by the need for both a great deal of memorization and the capacity to synthesize a range of information. But he was not proficient in—and felt vulnerable about—learning foreign languages, a prerequisite for graduating from his master's program. He had barely passed French and Latin in high school and believed he was "language challenged." His narrow view of history was also a liability. Until partway through his first semester in grad school he read only one type of history—quantitative approaches that relied on numbers to the exclusion of other methods.

At first we thought that the biggest emotional challenge he faced was a fear of being too emotionally isolated while he immersed himself in the master's program. Rick had few friends and a tendency to disengage, especially since his divorce. But there were deeper issues underlying his need to withdraw, namely the way in which he was afflicted by two ailments of the self—the divided self and the doubting Thomas self—which undermined his efforts to reach his goals.

Once we know our strengths and weaknesses and the internal and external challenges that we are confronting, we can use this self-knowledge to figure out how to make the best of our assets and untapped potentials to remove the obstacles that stand in the way of integrating our passion, vision, talents, and skills.

As JoAnn began to recognize the cost of her one-sided intellectual and emotional development—the way it narrowed her vision—she started feeling disenchanted with false either-or choices such as "I can have either success at work or intimacy at home. Life is not so neat or simple," she said. She slowly began to define herself in wider terms by seeking intimacy as well as professional excellence and success. She had avoided long-term commitments because she put all of her energy into her work. Once she dropped her either-or stance, she was able to allow the possibility of a serious relationship.

She also realized that her talents and skills were lagging behind her passion and vision and that she had to appreciate her abilities and uniqueness and use her strengths to shore up her weaknesses.

It is not enough to know what we need to do. We have to make it happen. While self-knowledge is quite valuable, without action we often remain stuck. Daydreaming about being an artist or an entrepreneur, without cultivating the necessary skills, is about as gratifying as looking at a menu in a restaurant without ordering.

Discipline is an indispensable ingredient to constructive action.

Discipline

Mastery of others is strength;
mastery of yourself is true power.

—LAO TZU

Discipline helps us translate self-knowledge into action. There are different forms discipline can take. These include:

- Repetitive training and practice
- Persevering until we reach our goal
- Learning from and then letting go of past disappointments and failures so that they don't sabotage future possibilities

When combined, these aspects of discipline support our efforts to develop our talents.

In *Values of the Game,* former U.S. senator and Hall of Fame basketball player Bill Bradley, a person of legendary determination, described the "virtuous circle" of discipline as, "the harder you work, the sooner your skills improve . . . As your skills grow, you get a rush of self-confidence, which spurs you to continue working, and your skills increase all the faster." Determination and focus are indispensable allies in this process. "Determination sits at the core of discipline, and the will to excel sits at the core of determination," Bradley wrote.

Even if we lack the will to excel, there are still two things we can do. Reconnecting with our passion and vision will reinspire and energize our commitment, reminding us of the larger purpose propelling our efforts. Concentration, what the Japanese call *isshin* or single-heartedness, is one of the most important skills we can develop. It aids us in remaining consistent, a prerequisite for honing our skills and cultivating our talents in the service of our visions. Concentration can be trained and refined by any of the meditations we have done in this book and in any activity that cultivates paying attention.

Creative efforts are subverted not only by narrow visions and conflicting commitments but by self-doubt. Dedication and consistency result in competence and mastery. This, in turn, strengthens our trust and belief in ourselves and makes us resilient, and then it is exponentially easier to persevere. The gratification we experience practicing—and honing—the *scales of our lives* encourages us to work harder, which helps us learn more, feel better about ourselves, and strive for further mastery.

JoAnn used her knowledge of herself to shore up her artistic weaknesses and deepen her assets. She began tentative forays into new and unfamiliar territory—working on her intellectual gaps and shortcomings and trying to become more emotionally and intellectually well rounded. She accomplished this goal by striving for a better balance between her personal relationships and schoolwork. In addition, she immersed herself in more novels and poetry and practiced more fiction and verse writing in order to be properly prepared for the academic rigors of graduate school. She handled her financial challenges by moving to a smaller apartment, selling her luxury car and buying a more fuel-efficient one.

She used her weekly visits to her aunt as a break from her intense academic schedule and an opportunity to read while her aunt rested or slept. In this way she was able to be with her aunt and juggle work and professional responsibilities.

All of this was gratifying, as well as scary. When JoAnn no longer avoided her weaknesses, the fulfillment she felt helped her brave the period of discomfort and transition. As she became more comfortable with both her need for intimacy and her academic imbalances, she began to feel more stable and resilient—eager to confront the challenges on her new path.

Rick's increased knowledge of his strengths and weaknesses also helped him address them. He slowly realized that "there are many different aspects to being a human being. We contain the capacity to be loving and angry, rational and passionate, self-centered and altruistic."

He recognized that these different facets of ourselves are not so much outgrown and renounced as we grow up as they are integrated into who we are, and are central ingredients to who we become.

Rick practiced accepting the different parts of himself by acknowledging that "the parts of me that I used to consider bad are often reactions to my being too tough on myself. They neither can nor should be eliminated. In fact, they serve a purpose of letting me know I am treating myself too repressively." Rick thus lessened the tyranny of the good self and experienced fewer swings between strict discipline and reactive, self-destructive rebellion. His life was less of an emotional and physical roller coaster. He occasionally had a piece of carrot cake without needing to eat the whole thing. And when he "slipped" and overate, he tried to learn from it: Was he really starved? Was he feeling emotionally deprived? Or had he waited too long to eat?

Over the next few months Rick lost twenty pounds and got on a balanced and regular exercise regime. "I have never felt better," he told me.

Rick handled his fear of foreign languages by hiring a private tutor, a master's student in the French Department who had a reputation as an excellent teacher. After studying for a year Rick developed a reading knowledge of French. He followed his adviser's suggestions that he take a broad survey course first semester. This gave him a much-needed wider and more complete view of history.

In his personal life, Rick made a conscious effort to renew old friendships and become more receptive to getting to know some of the people in his program. He was also able to admit that he might soon be ready to start dating. "Maybe this time I'll be able to choose a better partner," he said.

I n my own life, discipline was crucial in fashioning a symphony of myself. Since my vision was too broad and unfocused, an important aspect of composing my life was prioritizing my purpose based on my values. I asked myself: Are there any unifying themes or unexpected points of linkage or convergence in my passions and vision? How do my various interests serve, or obscure, my attempts to flourish?

One day after meditating I realized that there were two unifying themes among my disparate interests and the different aspects of myself:

1. I was passionately interested in plumbing life's depths and figuring out its mysteries.
2. I wanted to help other people lessen their pain and access their deepest potential for self-knowledge and aliveness, authenticity and wisdom.

All my interests were unified by the twin mandate of understanding and living the art of flourishing, and helping other people. Meditation, yoga, psychoanalysis, exercise, and reading were the five aspects of my personal efforts to accomplish the first goal, while teaching, writing, and practicing therapy aided me in achieving the second one.

As the conductor of my own symphony, I had to use self-knowledge and discipline to make the various instruments of my being play in tune. Awareness of my strengths and weaknesses helped me recognize the need for prioritizing. "If you pursue all your dreams you might get lost," sings Neil Young. Once I had identified the two underlying threads connecting my disparate passions I realized that I needed to be more focused and selective about them.

Discipline helped me follow my enthusiasms and avoid distractions and diversions. Then I could eliminate tangential interests and activities, make better use of my time, and be more protective of key passions. When peripheral interests tempted me, I maintained my direction by periodically reflecting on the nature of the life I was trying to compose. The most important way I practiced this was through a traditional Indian meditation I have made my own called *Dharma meditation*. In the yogic tradition the word *dharma* means, among other things (including cosmic order, virtue, and righteousness), one's responsibilities. We all have many facets to our dharma—from the dharma of being a parent to the dharma associated with our job, to the dharma of the close relationships in our lives. Every morning I do yoga and meditation. At the end of each session I reflect on my dharma for the day and ask myself, "What must I do today and how will I do it?" I reflect on three things: the various responsibilities that I have; the spirit that is necessary to fully honor them; and what I need to nourish my mind, body, and psyche. I write this down on an index card, which I consult throughout the day. This keeps me focused on my passions and purpose, as well as on my relationships with other people and myself.

Discipline enabled me to hone my abilities and nurture my gifts so that I could deepen my understanding of meditation, yoga, and psychotherapy. It also helped me refine my capacity to communicate about them with other people through therapy, teaching, and writing.

Flexibility

We must be willing to let go of the life we have planned,
so as to have the life that is waiting for us.

—E. M. FORSTER

We need one last tool in order to compose our lives: flexibility: the ability to adapt to changing circumstances, and where necessary reinvent, or at least reconceive ourselves.

In a world of tremendous flux, when industries change and jobs evaporate, clearly defined goals and rigid plans can become blinders instead of guides. The traditional idea of a set path is unrealistic for many people—think of them as cultural refugees—displaced by changes in work, the economy, and society. Flexibility is necessary because illness and setbacks, natural catastrophes and external challenges—such as divorce and financial struggles—sabotage our plans.

While JoAnn was in graduate school her aunt died. She had been a steadying presence during JoAnn's adolescence and a beloved surrogate mother. When JoAnn took time off from school for several months after her aunt's death, she felt guilty about interrupting her studies. In our sessions JoAnn and I spoke a great deal about the inevitability of change, the rarity of living one's life in a straight line, and the need for adaptability and resilience. As she gradually became more comfortable with the importance of embracing transitions, her guilt receded and she saw her aunt's death in a different light. It not only chastened her—bringing home the inevitability of death—but deepened her commitment to her vision as she embraced the reality of her own mortality. Her writing became more emotional and powerful, evoking deeper feelings in her readers.

At the beginning of his master's degree program, Rick was mourning the end of his marriage. His short-term memory was poor as a result of his emotional state, so he had to organize his schedule so he could study for shorter and more frequent periods to accommodate his inability to stay focused. By adapting to his unique needs, Rick successfully pursued his dreams.

The Music of Our Lives

What happens when you create a symphony of your self? What were the fruits of JoAnn and Rick's self-knowledge, discipline, and adaptability?

Rick's and JoAnn's passion and vision, talents and skills were now harmoniously blended. Each instrument of their beings worked together cooperatively and synergistically—supporting the music as a whole. Since their purpose was fueled by what inspired them, Rick and JoAnn engaged life more wholeheartedly and excitedly. The cultivation of their talents and skills helped them to master their challenges. Their passion, talents, and skills were directed toward what they truly valued and who they wanted to be—and they each experienced levels of success and happiness they never expected.

When the many parts of yourself are playing together in harmony like a symphony orchestra, your life embodies your own unique music. All it needs now is rhythm.

Rhythm

Rhythm is essential to human life. We all march to the beat of our individual drummers. When Rick was grieving for his failed marriage, he needed family and friends to accept the slow pace of his recovery from his divorce so he would not be forced to hide his feelings in order to make everyone else feel more comfortable in his presence. Tina, the caretaker we met earlier, who spent the first three decades of her life serving other people and neglecting herself, was not unexpectedly a late bloomer. She suffered immensely when her highly achievement-oriented father challenged her pace of emotional development.

Some of my clients periodically tell me that they've been living other people's rhythms. Their consistent hyperattunement to the needs of other people has often become so automatic and extensive that they no longer know what they owe themselves. They feel confused about who they are and what they want and need.

It is classic sports strategy to exert intense and unrelenting defensive pressure on the opposing team. Their tempo speeds up, and they abandon their game plan, play into their opponent's rhythm, and make more mistakes. In much the same way, many of us feel pressured by the pace and tempo of life and we tend to accommodate to it. We make a tragic Faustian bargain—in exchange for security and stability we conform to the rhythm of others and become emotional pinballs, careening to and fro. Our natural trajectory is knocked off balance by the artificial speed of the outside world. We lose ourselves; we drift or come unglued. Worst of all we are made to feel "less than" because we can't keep up, even though the pace is often inhuman and counterproductive.

When we don't follow our own rhythms we lose our way: lovemaking becomes obligatory and mechanical; playing becomes working out; the vocations that might inspire us become mere jobs. As we rush from obligation to obligation, life becomes dissatisfying. There is no time for what nourishes us.

Finding our own rhythm and living at our own pace is a crucial element in the art of flourishing. It enables us to work in harmony with ourselves, which in turn allows us to carry out our mission.

The rhythms of people on vacations, between jobs, or recovering from illnesses will be different from the tempos of those starting a new business or in the grip of a creative phase at work or an ecstatic romance. We can use our sense of our own rhythms as compasses to see if our lives are off course. To this end, we can ask ourselves what our unique rhythms are and what pace nourishes our self-care and relationships. We can explore whether we are giving ourselves the time to appreciate and enjoy life. It is crucial to consider what pace nourishes our souls or wears us down.

The rhythm of JoAnn's new life as a graduate student was very different from that of her old job. The high-powered, energetic, fourteen-hour-a-day schedule of an advertising executive meeting deadlines, supervising staff, and answering to her boss didn't seamlessly segue into her new lifestyle. While she worked just as hard in graduate school, she became aware that the rhythm of her days needed to change—she had to slow down and allow herself time to immerse herself in and reflect on her work; to spend hours writing and reading in an introverted state. Finding a pace that was more effective helped JoAnn feel centered so she could fully express her thoughts and ideas.

When we are living the rhythm that is ours alone, we can experience life as magical and inspired. We feel graced by a flow and serenity that nourishes our souls. We are efficient and creative, moving through our days with less wasted motion.

The Symphony of the Self

We began this chapter by discussing the instruments that we need to play in harmony to create a symphony of ourselves—passion and vision, talents and skills. Next we examined the five obstacles to creating that harmony—the true self, the scattered self, the lopsided self, the divided self, and the doubting Thomas self. Then we analyzed how to pinpoint our strengths and weaknesses and use self-knowledge, discipline, and flexibility to fashion our passion and vision, talents and skills into a harmonious composition, a symphony of our selves. We concluded by discussing how we find and live our own unique rhythm.

Now you are ready to begin to try this on your own. Reflect over a period of a few days on your strengths and weaknesses. Give yourself time to connect with your talents, abilities, and vulnerabilities. Are there any other instruments of your being that are neglected, out of tune, or that need to play together in harmony? Try to treat your imperfections with compassion not contempt. They are potential teachers, not proof of inadequacy. If clarity about your strengths and weaknesses eludes you, be patient and persistent. Write down your answers. Use them to help create a harmonious composition between your passion and vision, talents and skills.

Discovering Your Strengths:
- ☛ Write down the most important accomplishments of your life and the activities that give you the strongest sense of personal goodness.
- ☛ List your talents and skills.

- List your positive traits.
- Write down and reflect upon situations that illustrate these talents, traits, and skills in action.
- Ask yourself: What inner wealth am I not appreciating and what do I need to do to embrace it?

Pinpointing Your Vulnerabilities:
- Reflect on your negative attitudes and traits, beliefs and behavioral patterns.
- List your least appealing traits.
- Beside each, describe a recent incident that revealed that particular flaw.
- What would you like to change about yourself?

Determining Your Rhythm:
- What is my own unique rhythm?
- What pace nourishes my self-care and intimacy?
- Am I giving myself time to appreciate and enjoy my life?
- What pace wears me down?
- Am I constantly moving either too quickly or too slowly?
- Am I forcing myself to answer questions about my life or solve problems too quickly without allowing the question to germinate so that the answer can express my genuine needs?

Remember that there are many instruments that make up a human being—passion, purpose, talents, and skills. We play the best music when no instrument is dominant and none are excluded, and when we as our own conductors bring balance and harmony. So in order to create a symphony of our selves, we must have a vision that reflects our passions and values, and develop the necessary skills to implement them. Self-knowledge, discipline, and flexibility aid us in creating a symphony of our selves.

The fruits of this symphony are an authentic life, the focus of the next chapter.

10

> To be nobody but yourself in a world which is doing
> its best, night and day, to make you everybody else,
> is the hardest battle which any human being can fight;
> and never stop fighting.
>
> —e. e. cummings

A LIFE OF ONE'S OWN

Authenticity in a World of Spam

Authenticity—truly being ourselves—is crucial to, and an expression of, flourishing. When our life is our own—when we pursue what we are passionate about and embody our values—we feel more real and alive, centered and inspired, brimming with purpose and vitality.

When we are inauthentic—living a life designed or dictated by someone else—we dismiss or ignore what really matters to us. As a result, we become alienated from ourselves and live without vitality and passion, and that is emotionally deadly and physically unhealthy.

When we are authentic we listen to our feelings and make healthy, self-respectful decisions based on our genuine needs and what our passions, vision, and core values compel us to do.

A friend of mine chose a nontraditional school for her daughter that resonated with her and her husband's values, rather than a more academically elite one that my friend's parents preferred and would have impressed her neighbors and colleagues.

Another friend of mine gave up a lucrative job at a law firm to earn much less money to do work that had more meaning and fulfillment for her—defending vulnerable, indigent clients.

Living authentically doesn't necessarily have to involve compromise, as Barbara illustrated. Barbara was a very successful practitioner of alternative medicine. After her son went off to college she realized that she didn't want to take care of other people anymore (except her son and husband), and focused on taking care of herself; that involved pursuing something that she loved and that also nurtured her. She now has a burgeoning career as a writer.

Another person I know illustrated the cost of inauthenticity. She denied her feelings of unhappiness and stayed in a marriage and job that she never found fulfilling because both afforded a luxurious lifestyle that she was afraid of losing. I was troubled—although not surprised— that her health suffered.

When we listen to and heed our feelings ("Eat when hungry, sleep when tired," the ninth-century Zen master Rinzai reminds us), protect our boundaries, and embody our values we are authentic. It's not always easy—being true to ourselves and giving the world our own fullest life is, as cummings recognized, "the hardest battle which any human being can fight; and never stop fighting." That's why it shouldn't be surprising that a therapist who has written a great deal about authenticity once admitted that music—which he loved but never pursued—rather than analysis, was his true calling.

Societal Obstacles to Authenticity

Authenticity is under attack in our world. It's very difficult to be your truest self and manifest your uniqueness when you are living at an inhuman pace, assaulted with stimulation, and expecting immediate gratification, as we explored in chapter 1.

Our collective, burgeoning distractibility and hyperactivity—and the other attacks on authenticity—like the pervasive cultural emphasis on conformity and sound bites, and the lack of time for, or interest in, introspection—sabotage mental and physical health. They impair our clarity and judgment, negatively affect our moods, and undermine our capacity to care for ourselves and thrive. Our efforts to escape these impingements cause us to neglect ourselves and become more insular and disconnected from crucial concerns such as how we might flourish, and most important, to miss out on our only chance to lead the lives we are capable of leading.

The enormous and unyielding pressure on women to conform to unrealistic, contrived, and distorted images of beauty—to resemble airbrushed, anorectic, preteen bodies, have perfect hair, clothing, and makeup and above all, not show signs of aging—also sabotages authenticity. (As does the male version revolving around how much money men make, what they own, and their sexual potency, which must be maintained at the level of a teenager in order for a man to be perceived as "still in the game," not washed up, and again, certainly not aging.) Women and men are diverted from pursuing what they truly love and value by the insane quest to be what they are not, and in reality what no one could ever be.

Guilt is also a huge and usually misunderstood obstacle to authenticity. "I see it with so many friends," Gail, a forty-something woman told me. "They don't do what they really want because they are guilty about disappointing other people and failing to live up to their own idealized images of who they think they should be; and then they are angry and depressed." They are self-denying—which inevitably leads to feeling entrapped, deprived, and angry—rather than self-nurturing, which triggers guilt.

Another source of guilt is our perceived failure to live up to our own standards—many of which we often don't consciously choose. This is what the psychoanalyst Karen Horney called the "tyranny of the shoulds." The "shouldaholic" self is haunted by, and bases his or her life on, artificial self-imposed rules instead of what he or she authentically feels or wants. "I should be nice, good, self-sacrificing, and disciplined." These shoulds make us appear to be kind and respectable people, but they also become a hidden blueprint seemingly guiding us, but often enslaving us too. We are not free to respond honestly and authentically to our lives and other people. The shouldaholic self may often feel virtuous—even better than other people—but also feels like a failure when he or she cannot meet these self-imposed ideals. And even if one could embody them, they are inauthentic.

Blind conformity and accommodation interfere with authenticity as well. In 1835, the great political thinker Alexis de Tocqueville commented on the unprecedented conformity of Americans. Almost two hundred years later, the truth of his observation still holds. The timidity and moral failure of leaders in the financial sector and government—who knew that individuals and institutions were on a destructive economic and moral course yet did not challenge their corrupt compatriots— illustrates the continuing truth of de Tocqueville's observation. The essential ingredient in fostering authenticity is what I call *self-creation*.

Self-Creation

Self-creation has both a healthy and a neurotic version. The neurotic version—*self-splinting*—occurs when we attempt to fix or protect childhood emotional injuries by damage control. Emotional self-splinting is what Karen Horney called a temporary neurotic *solution* to, rather than a healthy *resolution* of, our problems, such as when we respond to childhood rejection by isolating ourselves as adults so that we will not be dependent on other people and emotionally vulnerable again. When the psychoanalyst Masud Khan wrote that therapists must heal their patients of their "practice of self-cure," he was referring to transforming these partial, makeshift solutions to our dilemmas of living.

Many people in our culture often consciously or unconsciously subscribe to a view of human beings as arrested, damaged babies, who are passive and vulnerable victims of cruel treatment. When we view people struggling with authenticity through that lens—which, of course, may sometimes have clinical validity—we often miss their own contribution to their misery; the way they unconsciously re-create their imprisonment and suffering. Their parents could be deceased or live a million miles away, but the abused or neglected person continues their parents' harmful treatment of them without the parents even being present. In a psychoanalytic twist on Dostoevsky's political insight, the oppressed become the despots—toward themselves. And unless a person's role in that is acknowledged and transformed, she is prone to intellectually understand the sources of her struggles yet continue to repeat them.

Take the case of Talia, a young woman I worked with who told me that she was afraid of really being herself because she'd hurt other people who would be jealous of her competence and vitality because they were unhappy with their lives. She unilaterally decided that she couldn't ask for what she wanted or needed with me, which she only admitted after our relationship deepened.

"Don't ask, don't receive, is where this leaves you," I said. I wanted her to understand that she was denying herself her freedom and ultimately her opportunity to be authentic.

"What I'm doing to myself is sad," she replied. "I contributed to my own imprisonment when I subscribed to my father's denigrated image of me, viewing myself through his skewed eyes. I am learning what was done to me and understanding my role in perpetuating my struggles. It's about finding myself."

"It's about *creating* yourself," I said, explaining that she needed to pursue her passions, rather than expect that a younger version of herself—what I spoke of earlier as the buried true self—would serve as a blueprint for how to live. What inspired her would serve as the doorway to her purpose and authenticity.

As Talia's tendency to bury herself alive became clear, she began to break her pernicious pattern of self-imprisonment. "I am looking to myself more," she said several months into her treatment, "learning new ways of being; exploring what is important to me, instead of assuming the answers are out there."

She had succeeded in embracing what she valued and pursuing what really mattered to her. We could think of this as the movement from *authoritarianism* to *authenticity*—by trusting ourselves and making ourselves, rather than other people (such as our parents, teachers, doctors, religious and spiritual leaders or therapists), the final authority on our lives.

Once someone works through the kind of self-oppression Talia struggled with, a healthier form of self-fashioning becomes more possible. This can include creatively reworking and transforming the past as it has shaped us through healthier choices, better self-care, more reciprocal and fulfilling relationships, and commitments based on one's genuine values, goals, and interests. From this perspective both the past and *the appropriation of the past in the present* shape who we are.

I once told a man who had enormous heart and soul and who was struggling with authenticity that we can engage in self-creation by sifting through the crumbs we don't know we've dropped—the music that stirs our soul, the artifacts decorating our home and office that enliven us, the stories and poems we cherish.

"And the tattoos we have," he chimed in. And he was right—his tattoos gave him a clue about the direction he needed to trust as he risked breaking free from the stranglehold of his father's excruciatingly negative view and treatment of him and began exploring the exhilarating and scary world of authenticity. "I love that there is something vital of me in each tattoo," he added. "My tattoos and other parts of me yet to be discovered offer traces of what direction to pursue."

Living is more like extemporaneously constructing a building out of materials from the past and present in the present—including the enduring images of self and others and the associated feelings that shape our personal, subjective worlds—than like discovering a frozen, nascent self-state from the past. Such discovery, however, may add a crucial element to a person's ongoing self-creative efforts. Self-creation in the present plays a more significant role in self-experience than is accounted for in popular or traditional psychotherapeutic notions of discovering the buried "true self" that I discussed in chapter 9.

Living Authentically

> *Truth is a pathless land, and you cannot*
> *approach it by any path whatsoever,*
> *by any religion, by any sect . . .*
>
> —JIDDU KRISHNAMURTI

To be fully yourself in everyday life is an individual pursuit. What's real and genuine for me may be inauthentic for you—there's no existing map and no route can be prescribed. Every person's path is unique, but we can point out some common signposts and pitfalls. Insights from meditation and psychoanalysis have enriched my awareness of each. Both disciplines cultivate self-knowledge, self-trust, and wise action, which are indispensable to authenticity.

Imagine that you are watching a movie that is fast-forwarded. You would fleetingly notice rapid visuals and miss most of the details. The texture of the movie would elude you. That's basically how we live most of the time—sped up and oblivious to the particulars—and that's a breeding ground for being on automatic pilot and living inauthentically.

Imagine that you watched a movie in slow motion. You would obviously perceive many more of the subtleties, and such heightened awareness is a crucial ingredient in authenticity.

"Someone once asked [the Zen master] Sasaki Roshi whether he ever went to the movies," meditation teacher Joseph Goldstein wrote in *A Heart Full of Peace*. "'No,'" Sasaki replied, "'I give interviews.'" Sasaki observed the movie of the human mind in the formal meetings he had with his students.

Meditative awareness is a special—and eminently trainable—state of mind that is always potentially available, but often not accessed. It is like a mirror that reflects back only what is presented. Learning to systematically pay attention without commentary or interference to what we experience moment by moment—which meditation trains with exquisite precision—is an indispensable tool in fostering authenticity, for it slows us down and opens us up. Meditative awareness allows us not only to examine our feelings and reactions microscopically, but to watch the film that is our mind in slower motion and more clearly. "Just as the focused lens of a microscope enables us to see hidden levels of reality," notes Goldstein, "so too a concentrated mind opens us to deeper levels of experience and more subtle movements of thought and emotion."

The implications of meditative-contemplative perception, as opposed to our ordinary scattered mode, are enormous, as David Lynch's film *The Straight Story* brilliantly illustrates.

Alvin Straight, a frail seventy-three-year-old man without a driver's license or the financial wherewithal to fly or take public transportation, drove three hundred miles from Laurens, Iowa, to Mt. Zion, Wisconsin, at five miles per hour on a homemade lawn mower to visit his estranged, ailing brother. The film is narrated through Alvin's eyes—and pace of traveling. He slowed down and took in the countryside in a way that would not have been possible if he had traveled by car or by train. The viewer of *The Straight Story* begins seeing the world in a meditative way.

A poignant scene demonstrates the consequences of the rashness with which we ordinarily approach the world. One night in the midst of his solo sojourn, Alvin spoke in a bar with a fellow World War II vet about the harshness of war and the price it exacted from their souls. A sniper in the war, Alvin confesses a fatal mistake he made that has haunted him ever since—accidentally killing a fellow soldier because he was hasty.

Authenticity rests on a foundation of self-knowledge, which helps us understand what motivates us and the patterns of how we care for (or neglect) ourselves and relate to other people. This is the arena in which authenticity unfolds or is subverted. Awareness "gives us the option of *choosing wisely*," as Joseph Goldstein aptly notes.

When we give ourselves the space and time to engage more intimately with whatever we encounter—from our guilt about being authentic to our fear that we will alienate other people if we are truly ourselves—we use our awareness to transform or remove obstacles to authenticity. In my own ongoing efforts to live authentically, I have found it helpful to continually ask the following questions: Am I driven to take care of other people and how does that impact both of us? Am I valuing and trusting myself and bringing out my voice, or am I submerging myself and accommodating to the wishes of other people? Are there any areas in which I have a submissive relationship to authorities and tradition—including the authority of the past and spiritual and religious, or medical and psychological, wisdom? The more these aspects of our lives remain hidden from awareness, the greater our enslavement to them.

Guilt, as I suggested earlier, is a huge inhibitor of authenticity. It operates like an invisible psychological fence that shocks us every time we think or act outside the perimeters of our images of who we believe we should be; this keeps us fenced in emotionally. Choosing wisely helps us be more comfortable with healthy self-centeredness and not take the bait of neurotic guilt. Then we can avoid the "tyranny of the shoulds." When guilt arises in everyday life, we can compost it and see whether it is feedback that we need to change our behavior or lower our standards. For example, a client of mine nearly sabotaged his successful career as an entrepreneur because his success threatened his fragile sister's self-esteem. He was able to let himself succeed once he realized that guilt was not feedback that his standards were destructive to either him or his envious sister, but rather due to an unrealistic mandate to be responsible for his sister's self-esteem. Living through neurotic guilt and resisting the seductive pull of shoulds—whether they originate from the culture or our families of origin—opens up the possibility of responding authentically.

Once we become more adept at this—which takes practice and patience—we can begin to distinguish what we feel and need from what other people wish for or demand from us. Such self-delineation builds self-confidence and increases our trust in ourselves. Since it may, at least for a while, be fragile, it needs to be protected. Setting appropriate boundaries—especially learning to take ourselves into account in interactions with other people and sometimes saying no to the demands and guilt-inducing behavior of even those we love—does that. Then we are less apt to get swept up into the agendas and desires of other people when they threaten to hijack our quest for authenticity. And we don't have to prematurely push people away as an artificial way of protecting ourselves. When we have healthy boundaries and are not continually enslaved by images of how we think we are supposed to be, we naturally access and honor our authentic feelings and needs. It then becomes easier to know and embody our values.

Many years ago I treated a young adult, Dani, who was at a crossroads in her life. She had to decide whether to move across the country and relocate to the West Coast with no firm job leads, or remain on the East Coast with better prospects for employment. "I don't know what I want," she said. "I have a very hard time living my life. In fact, I feel like a stranger in my own life. I can be such a chameleon. I take on the attributes of whomever I'm with, like Woody Allen's Zelig."

Trained since childhood by her well-meaning parents to look to them for how to be—and torn between their diametrically opposed messages of how to do that—it is no wonder that Dani felt deeply at sea about her future.

A friend voiced practical concerns and told her not to move. She decided to remain on the East Coast.

"I won't be dictated to and told what to do. I want to do what I want to do," she explained to another friend.

"Why are you not living the life you want?" the friend asked. "What do you *really* want apart from following—or rebelling against—the advice you frequently solicit?"

A hallmark of authenticity is that our lives are our own—not secondhand copies or imitations of someone else, but an expression of who we are and what we value.

When we have given up being in charge of our own lives, we have effectively abdicated our responsibility to be ourselves by "outsourcing our values," as my self-rebellious client eventually realized. In a democracy, each of us gets one vote. No one has the right to vote for us and it is an evasion of responsibility to give up one's vote. When we fully realize that nobody but us is at the wheel, we can experience a profound transformation. In his thirties, a close friend of mine "fired" his parents as the final authority on his life, as he put it. For several decades, he has lived in a manner that reflects what he truly feels and believes. He is not defined or constrained by social conventions—the expectations of other people or silly platitudes that others have internalized. The last time I visited him he announced in the middle of the evening that he was sorry, but that he felt tired and was going to bed. The next day, he became ill; his fatigue the night before was probably feedback that he was under the weather the previous evening. Many people would have stayed up out of guilt, further compromising their health.

There is an unconscious self-centered bias in the way many of us think about authenticity. We assume, without ever realizing it, that it's the journey of a solitary, isolated, unencumbered individual who operates as a free agent with no ties to anyone else, shakes off the yoke of external dictates, and stands apart from other people and external pressures in the quest to be free. From this perspective, authenticity is essentially both individualistic *and* at odds with the external world.

"There is no such thing as an infant," the psychoanalyst D. W. Winnicott provocatively asserted, by which he meant human beings never exist in isolation and there are always particular parental caregivers that profoundly impact, even cocreate, who the infant is. I am suggesting that we need a relational model of authenticity in which our self-realization occurs through relationships with a larger, shared world. In a radical sense, I can only be—and become—me through you. "i am through you so i," as cummings expressed it. Who I am, in other words, is forged in the crucible of both *your* concern and empathy, and *your* needs and challenges.

Authenticity refers to the process of living one's life according to the needs of one's inner being, rather than the demands of external constraints. But it may also involve values that are socially acceptable or sanctioned—such as selfless generosity—if they are freely chosen and an essential aspect of who we are. We may challenge behavior that is in accord with societal ideals, in other words, and be inauthentic, yet follow specific cultural dictates and be authentic—if we deem them healthy and life-affirming.

Authenticity is priceless. "Men can starve from a lack of self-realization as much as they can from a lack of bread," the novelist Richard Wright wrote. Without a life that is our own we are constrained and impoverished, merely existing and surviving without passion and vital purpose. When we are authentic—when our lives belong to us, are really our own, and provide a home for all of who we are—we put ourselves in the best possible position for healthy intimacy, the final stage and fruition of self-care.

PART

II

═══

CULTIVATING

THE GARDEN

OF LOVE

11

We must love another or die.

—W. H. AUDEN

THE GARDEN OF LOVE

I'm standing on a street corner in San Francisco. It's a beautiful, breezy summer day. An elderly couple walks toward me, arm in arm, their faces suffused with joy and contentment. I am touched and inspired that despite their age, their feelings for each other—and their love—still flourish.

Imagine a world with no human relationships. No friendship, no intimacy, no love.

Human beings need relationships and intimacy. Without connection not only would we soon become extinct, we'd be terribly lonely—devoid of the love that is crucial for us to survive and flourish.

Love is something that most of us seek, but tend to lose; we feel buoyed and sustained when it is present, and deprived and bereft when it is absent.

Love seems to have grown more elusive for many people. Despite its indispensable role in our lives, there is great confusion about what it is and how to sustain it. It is often assumed that love is a feeling that we "fall into" and are helpless to stop. We are ecstatic when it is present; we are heartbroken and lonely when it is absent. From my perspective, besides being a glorious feeling, love is an *environment* that two people create and sustain, or neglect and let go to seed—like a garden.

A garden is a place vitalized by the sun, nurtured by the rain, and cultivated by people. Each garden is unique, from an English cottage plot overflowing with flowers and greenery to a Japanese Zen sanctuary of raked sand and deliberately placed rocks. Relationships, like gardens, are places of growth and decay, majesty and mystery. They require vision and discipline, patience and humor. Continual effort is required to overcome obstacles—from weeds and pests to droughts and storms—and to maintain healthy growth. Relationships and gardens thrive when properly cultivated. And when they flourish—when elements are well tended and harmonious—they offer solace, nourishment, and inspiration.

"In every study in which Americans are asked what they value most in assessing the quality of their lives, marriage comes first—ahead of friends, job, and money," wrote Judith Wallerstein and Sandra Blakeslee in *The Good Marriage: How and Why Love Lasts*. Intimacy can be a haven from the frenzied pace of life and skewed values. It can also lessen the loneliness of the competitive, often isolating workplace, and provide emotional sustenance and refueling. And intimacy is not just a sublime union of souls—as Shakespeare and Milton depicted—that validates our existence. It also helps us see with new eyes and can be enormously liberating.

In this chapter I will focus on how to cultivate the garden of love. Loving well is the most rare and difficult of arts—one that few have mastered, one that our culture hampers.

Consider two very different views on love and its vicissitudes. The first, a romantic ode, was written by Irving Gordon in 1951 and made famous by Nat King Cole:

Unforgettable, That's what you are . . .

The second, a literary portrayal of marriage from *A Wilderness of Mirrors* by novelist Max Frisch in 1964, has a less inspiring view:

Then you live in the everyday again, which is truth, with pyjamas and a toothbrush in your foamy mouth in front of the other, with classical nakedness in the bath that does not excite, intimate, you talk in the bathroom about the guests who have just left, and about the intellectual world that links you. You understand each other, without having to agree . . . you long jointly . . . but not for each other. . . . No one will stop you. You don't need a rope ladder in order to kiss, and no hiding place, and . . . no fear that your amorous sin will be found out. You are approved of. . . . Confession with its joys has been used up, trust is complete, curiosity abandoned. . . . The past is no secret any longer, the present is thin because it is worn out day by day, and the future means growing old.

Many relationships begin with the kind of enthrallment, idealization, and passion depicted in "Unforgettable," and gradually disintegrate into the familiarity and disappointment of the prosaic marriage that Frisch describes. These vignettes, like the many accounts of love that we have encountered or experienced, suggest that most of us could benefit from considering how we might create and tend a relationship in which love flourishes.

Spiritual Views of Love

One way of thinking about love is as always kind and patient, filled with truth and loyalty, devoid of envy and dissembling, and immune to erosion or decay. This picture of love is most famously presented in the first letter of St. Paul to the Corinthians. While not a discourse on the nature of love, it has served, I suspect, as a reference point and standard for many people:

> Love is patient; love is kind; love is not envious or boastful or arrogant or rude. It does not insist on its own way; it is not irritable or resentful; it does not rejoice in wrongdoing, but rejoices in the truth. It bears all things, believes all things, hopes all things, endures all things.
>
> Love never ends. But as for prophecies, they will come to an end; as for tongues, they will cease; as for knowledge, it will come to an end. For we know only in part, and we prophesy only in part . . . now we see in a mirror, dimly, but then we will see face to face.
>
> Now I know only in part; then I will know fully.

Compelling, isn't it? It describes a love that is rock-solid, pure, and perfect.

Paul's words substantiate the picture many of us have of love: the version that we were socialized to hold and that television, movies, and popular songs affirm; the notion that there is one true love that happens immediately, is destined, a perfect union, and secure and everlasting.

If our love doesn't meet this description, does that mean that it isn't real? While Paul presents an inspiring vision of love, it does not jibe completely with our experience, which suggests that love among human beings is not always indestructible, that it is not the solid, unshakable, stable beacon we idealistically long for; but rather, it is fragile and it can erode. If Paul, like us, "sees through a glass darkly," might love not always be kind? Might it harbor resentments and generate disappointment, lead to deprivation, and sometimes even fail?

Psychotherapeutic Visions of Love

Here is another way of thinking about love: many of us tend to choose partners who *psychologically* resemble our parents. We relate to them in old, familiar, and restrictive ways, what Freud called transference, by which he meant, interacting with people in the present as if they were figures from the past. The relationship with our partner contains many of the qualities that constrain the rest of our relationships. Because of how our parents treated us, we may assume that our spouse is criticizing us or rejecting us when he or she may not be feeling that way. Relationships can bring out the worst in us as well as the best. What appears as love can mask pathological submissiveness, and what seems to sustain a couple may restrict them. This sobering picture of love has appeared in psychological texts from Freud to the present.

Psychotherapeutic experience with individuals and couples suggests that the problem with spiritual accounts of love such as Paul's letter to the Corinthians is that too often they present an idealized vision. The picture clashes with our own experiences in relationships, where staleness *and* passion, resentment and romance may sometimes coexist, where love oftentimes fades in spite of starting out with promise. Couples (and their psychotherapists) know the ways that love is not always kind, that it may generate the worst in us, that it may sometimes self-destruct. Psychotherapy does us a great service by presenting a more realistic account of love that confronts rather than evades its idealizations and illusions.

The problem with psychotherapeutic perspectives on love is that they are too often grim and solemn, empty of the joy and intimacy that love engenders. *Spiritual* perspectives hold out the hope that there are possibilities for a love more intimate and ecstatic than psychotherapeutic versions usually describe.

Love, to borrow Pascal's description of human beings, is characterized by grandeur as well as by misery (*misère*), greatness as well as wretchedness. Only a view that embraces both (as well as other apparent oppositions) can illuminate love. By drawing on the fertile resources of therapy—its capacity to illuminate hidden meanings and obstacles—and remaining mindful of and not forsaking the optimistic possibilities for love depicted in spiritual traditions, we can experience a more sustaining and fulfilling intimacy and flourish.

Cultivating the Garden of Love

A man and woman make a garden between them.

—Louis Gluck

Let's return to the garden. There are five steps in creating one:

1. Planning the garden: studying yourself so you know what you want and need and can choose a healthy and compatible partner.
2. Preparing the soil: working on yourself so you are ready for intimacy with another person.
3. Planting and tending the seeds of intimacy: emotionally investing in the relationship.
4. Harvesting the garden of love: appreciating what you have sown.
5. Maintaining the garden of love: composting problems and nurturing and protecting the intimacy that you have created.

Planning the Garden

The first step in building a garden—or a meaningful relationship—is deciding what kind we want. We would choose a different site and proceed in a different way if we were growing vegetables than if we were constructing a Japanese rock garden. A relationship is also shaped by its purpose. Are we hoping for an intimate relationship or a platonic friendship? Are we wishing to deepen a committed relationship or deciding whether we want to continue dating?

Once we decide what kind of garden we want, we must place it in a good site that has the necessary elements—fertile soil, sufficient light and shade, and water—to thrive. Good sunlight and soil are crucial for growing plants. Choosing the right kind of person, with whom we share compatible values and who desires the kind of life we want—our passion, purpose, and ideals—is the best foundation for intimacy. The more we work on self-care, access our passion and purpose, and live authentically, the easier it is to choose a partner who resonates with our values and authentic selves. If we want a life of exploration, growth, and service, for example, we will probably be mismatched with someone whose overriding aim is luxury and comfort. Just as you can't grow strawberries and watermelons in the same patch, it is tough to create a gratifying relationship with a person with whom there is little possibility of developing a friendship.

While love often leads to our greatest joy and insight, it can frequently result in shortsightedness. In *A Midsummer Night's Dream*, Shakespeare wrote, "Love" is "said to be a child, / Because in choice he is so oft beguiled." People commonly choose partners based on superficial qualities such as appearance and status, neglecting what would truly nourish and sustain them over time. Physical beauty, money, and power often seduce us, and shape whom we are attracted to and whether we even consider—and how accurately we perceive—their character. Many men I have treated eventually became bored with women they initially found physically attractive, who, with time, they discovered lacked substance and sensitivity. Many women I have worked with came to feel that they married for money and then felt deprived when their husbands lacked dimension and depth.

A savvy businessman who regularly ended up with physically

alluring but unsuitable women put the brakes on his destructive pattern of dating only after I asked him if he chose business partners based on their appearance without learning what kind of people they were, what they valued, and how they treated him. (While love shouldn't be like a business contract, we do need to go into both with eyes wide open.)

"Virtue has never been as respectable as money," Mark Twain wrote. Physical beauty and wealth alone are not reliable foundations for intimacy. Respect and integrity are critical, which is why not getting seduced by appearance or status is necessary when picking a good "site" for a relationship to flourish.

The second obstacle in choosing the necessary elements for a relationship is that we tend to conceive of intimacy in narrow ways shaped and limited by our past experiences, and we choose partners with whom we may repeat old patterns and problems. People in therapy who complain about feeling emotionally invisible in childhood often are in intimate adult relationships characterized by a struggle to be appreciated and valued. Their parents could be deceased or living on another continent yet they choose partners who treat them the way their parents did. In their choice of mates they neglect themselves in the same demeaning way they were neglected as children. They also inevitably play a similar role to the one they were implicitly or explicitly assigned in childhood; for example, relating to their partner deferentially or distantly, thereby re-creating what they hated in childhood.

Because feelings are often our compass, as was suggested in chapter 5, most of us operate under the seductive principle that "if it feels good (or familiar), do it," which makes established patterns of interaction—even when they are painful or dysfunctional—seem like the only choice. That is why it is often necessary to be psychologically separated from our family and culture of origin—otherwise we may choose partners who emotionally resemble our parents or enact mindless rebellions against them. We may need to "go against the grain" of what we think we want and how we feel, in order to choose partners with whom we can flourish. One concrete way of doing this is to consider a prospective partner's *excellence of character*—what the ancient Greeks thought of as virtue. Is he honest and loyal, compassionate and generous, fair and of sound judgment? Is there a capacity for self-reflection and examining and transforming weaknesses of character? Is he capable of freeing himself from emotional blindness? How does she respond to people under duress, including those who annoy her or who are exploitive?

"Fast openings make fast closings," I once heard Joel Kramer say. He meant relationships, as well as yoga postures. In other words, don't be seduced by that instantaneous ecstasy when you think you've met your soul mate—the vast majority of people who get divorced had that same feeling once and would have bet their lives that it would last forever. Give yourself the space and time to scout and get to know prospective partners. When you take the time to choose your partner carefully you avoid many problems and heartache down the road.

Preparing the Soil

But Love has pitched his mansion in the place of excrement.

—W. B. YEATS

Once we have chosen the type of garden we want and picked a good site, we must prepare the ground. Even fertile soil has rocks. We need to remove obstacles such as stones and debris, rake the dirt, mulch—whatever the soil needs. The soil must be balanced—not too acidic or alkaline. Weeds are inevitable, but we pull them so they won't leach nutrients. In *The Good Marriage: How and Why Love Lasts,* Wallerstein and Blakeslee found that none of the couples in happy and fulfilling long-term marriages they interviewed "denied that there were serious differences—conflict, anger, even some infidelity—along the way. . . . Most regarded frustrations, big and small, as an inevitable aspect of life that would follow them no matter whom they married."

There are many characteristic impediments—or weeds—in relationships. Here are some of the crucial ones that I have observed in many years of working with couples:

- Cultural myths
- Poor self-care
- Childhood fears and conflicts about intimacy
- Fundamental differences about goals and responsibilities

- Lack of empathy
- Longstanding disagreements and simmering resentments
- No reliable method for handling conflicts

Weeds in relationships erode trust, friendship, and passion—the cornerstones of intimacy. Some weeds can be pulled quickly and easily; others need to be dug up by the roots. I'll explore each of them, examining the more stubborn ones in greater depth in the following chapters.

CULTURAL MYTHS

Our culture poses grave threats to intimacy. I am speaking of those forces that collapse inner space—the inhuman pace of life, the bombardment of information, the pollution and colonization of our imaginations. I also mean insane pressures at work; a growing sense of alienation; obsession with appearance and sound bites; skewed values that reward greed; relentless focus on financial measures of success; and cultural myths about love. All of these forces cloud our minds, sap our spirits, and demoralize our souls. And get in the way of intimacy.

Love is arguably the most frequent theme in popular culture. But the "love" presented in romance novels, soap operas, songs, and the lives of celebrities is often completely unrealistic, full of fake romanticism or debilitating cynicism. Because of this, and the cultural pollution we explored in chapter 1, there is a dearth of role models for healthy intimacy.

Almost every Hollywood movie about relationships implies a rosy future of happily-ever-after. But films end where real-life relationships begin. From *Sex and the City* and *Hitch,* to *Pretty Woman* and *Sleepless in Seattle,* romantic comedies focus their attention on the yearning to be connected and finding a knight in shining armor or the woman of one's dreams, not the actual relationship. We never see what happens after the star-crossed lovers hook up—how they navigate real life, which is often populated by rebellious teenagers, spouses who are too tired for sex, job losses, illnesses, and unexpected distresses that challenge even the most robust union.

In inundating us with unrealistic views of intimacy and defective role models, cultural myths about love reinforce our taking relationships for granted and ignoring that they require work. Writing in the

Sunday *New York Times Magazine,* Elizabeth Weil said, "My marriage was good, utterly central to my existence, yet in no other important aspect of my life was I so *laissez-faire.* Like most of my peers, I applied myself to school, friendship, work, health and, ad nauseam, raising my children. But in this critical area, marriage, we had all turned away." She is not alone. I have three plants in my office. I often tell clients that they represent three crucial aspects of a couple: parenting, work and household, and marriage. Most couples water the first two plants and neglect the third—marriage—letting it wilt, wither, and die.

POOR SELF-CARE

Intimacy is frequently compromised and often sabotaged because of lack of self-care, another pernicious weed. This can take many forms, from self-neglectful caretaking and accommodation to the needs of others, to inauthentic behavior because we are living according to someone else's values and ideals. Caretakers (and accommodators) selflessly give to other people and neglect their own needs. Sometimes such selflessness is what life—or a partner—requires, but it often leads to a caretaker suffering from a lack of a sense of deeper purpose or a meaningful contribution. You can't really find your passion and take seriously what inspires you when you are solely devoted to caring for other people. Such behavior may feel so ingrained and inevitable that you can only avoid it if you actively resist it.

Amanda, a very successful political consultant, was in a loving relationship with an interesting and highly competent man she had known for about six months. She had a fulfilling job and a rich network of female friends in Washington, D.C. When her boyfriend took an exciting job in New York, they both left Washington immediately and moved in together in New York. A person with good instincts, Amanda had in the past regularly dismissed them in her relationships with men. Amanda and I eventually realized that she had seamlessly taken on her boyfriend's viewpoint, and didn't even consider how she felt about moving away from work opportunities and friends. In New York she feared that she was digging her own grave, and felt as if she was suffocating. She wanted to be authentic, but she felt guilty because it might challenge—or change—the relationship she had accepted without much forethought.

The expectation of "mind reading"—assuming that your partner can magically know and provide what you need without having to ask her for it, which we'll explore in depth in chapter 14, "Leave the Mind Reading to the Magicians," is another type of self-neglect in intimate relationships. Spouses will inevitably fail and disappoint because, as far as we know, most people are not clairvoyant. When our partners can't read our minds it deepens convictions that we are unloved and unworthy, spurring an ongoing wish for proof of love, leading to further unrealistic expectations, which causes hurt and anger.

Another symptom of lack of self-care is the absence of boundaries or the erection of inordinately rigid ones. Boundaries are crucial in defending and protecting us and creating the possibility of living fulfilling and authentic lives. Without boundaries, we are like cells without membranes, lacking a buffer between the world and us—too exposed and vulnerable. Yet when they are too rigid, we are cut off from other people. In "A Fence around the Garden of Love" we'll examine how to create healthy boundaries.

Poor self-care can also be implicated in wielding power destructively, steamrolling or excessively trying to control our partners, which sets the stage for rebellion or resentful conformity, both of which sabotage intimacy, a topic I'll explore in chapter 17, "After the Bliss . . ."

Inadequate self-care is a breeding ground for deprivation and resentment, causing those afflicted to lash out at their partners. When one lives in a place of *emotional scarcity*—a sense of self-deficiency and an absence of confidence and resources—it is more difficult to access one's passion and purpose and it is hard to be generous of spirit and patient, both invaluable assets in helping couples navigate rocky periods.

CHILDHOOD FEARS AND CONFLICTS

Self-hatred is a huge saboteur of intimacy. Lenore, a middle-aged woman I once knew, was wracked with self-contempt. Any perceived imperfection or any genuine problem she had became automatic proof of her loathsomeness. She saw herself as inadequate. She tortured herself continuously and had a deep conviction that she deserved this torment. She felt so unlovable that when someone adored her she was hostile and tried to sabotage the affection: "If you love me you're a fool," was her unspoken message to potential love interests.

The fear that intimacy equals self-loss is another important barrier to love. When closeness with parents or surrogate parent figures leads a child to feel suffocated, intimacy as an adult can feel terrifying. Barbara, a psychotherapist in her forties, couldn't let her lover, Leah, who was caring and independent, fully into her heart. While Leah knew that Barbara really loved her, Leah couldn't get as close to Barbara as she would have liked. Barbara told me that she feared being engulfed if she lived with Leah, even though she admitted that Leah gave her space. When we explored when and with whom she might have previously felt engulfed, Barbara remembered the ways her mother overwhelmed her. Being in an intimate relationship as an adult raised the specter of "having the life sucked out of me." Because she feared that she couldn't make her life her own when emotionally close to another person, Barbara needed to be somewhat isolated from Leah to feel safe; and hence she never quite committed. Barbara stopped therapy before this could be resolved—an indication of how deep-rooted her fear was.

Children who were abandoned by parents, siblings, or close relatives or friends—whether through divorce or death—may tend as adults to keep potential lovers at arm's length throughout their lives because connection seems dangerous, leading to loss and desertion. Keeping loved ones at a distance can be a dysfunctional way of protecting against greater closeness and the terror of anticipated abandonment.

FUNDAMENTAL DIFFERENCES ABOUT GOALS AND RESPONSIBILITIES

Clashing expectations about what each partner is responsible for and owes the other can be experienced as a huge weed with deep and tenacious roots. Most couples have an implicit—but rarely discussed and thus never agreed-upon—contract of expectations about what they are owed and will provide. And when these expectations clash, as they usually do, misunderstanding and disappointment grow like, well, *weeds*. Rochelle, an Ivy League graduate, enjoyed a successful career as a dentist before she married Harold, an affluent businessman. Raised by parents who shared the burdens of running the home, she assumed that she and her husband would both work collaboratively at home. Harold, who had been spoiled as a child, expected and demanded that Rochelle take full responsibility for their household, which made her feel demeaned, as if she were his maid. Their differing agendas resulted in Rochelle either seeking a partnership and constantly getting disappointed, or conforming to her husband's expectations and resenting him. Both scenarios left her feeling deprived and angry.

LACK OF EMPATHY

The absence of empathy is another weed in the garden of love. Trust in the reality of our experience is one of the bedrocks of our existence. Empathic attunement to our emotional reality from parents and valued friends, family, and colleagues is like psychological oxygen. It fosters belief in ourselves and is vital to flourishing. Lack of empathy makes us feel unseen and unknown and is crippling. When one or both partners are not attuned to the reality of their mate's feelings it undermines the relationship.

LONGSTANDING DISAGREEMENTS AND SIMMERING RESENTMENTS

When couples lack a strategy for resolving—or at least addressing—discord and conflict, they often either fight incessantly, cobble together a makeshift approach to coexisting, or avoid discussing contentious topics. When partners collude in avoiding what troubles them, it may momentarily lessen conflict and disappointment, only to foster chronic disagreements and antipathy. Many couples avoid potential conflict at home by not discussing what is bothering them. There is a hidden wisdom in their strategy, because if they had continuously discussed their conflicts without a constructive method or mediator they would have fought even more. But while such evasion is often a functional strategy, it renders their conflicts more toxic because they are suppressed and they fester. Helen and Marty never fought, yet were on the verge of divorce. As I observed them avoid and bury conflict and dilute and deny seething animosity during our first session, I remember thinking that they fought too little for their own good. In other words, conflict avoidance was both sapping energy from their relationship—creating weeds that leached life from their marriage—and causing emotional minefields that periodically triggered deprivation and rage and led to complete shutting down and withdrawal.

NO RELIABLE METHOD FOR HANDLING CONFLICT

Conflicts over communication—especially the urge to defeat your partner and win—are fundamental obstacles to intimacy. The drive to triumph is natural and inevitable because it fosters survival. In intimate relationships, however, it is disastrous, causing couples to focus on defeating rather than on understanding each other. Once one or both spouses is devoted to winning, it is enormously difficult, if not impossible, to resolve conflicts over power and boundaries, sexuality and money—four crucial areas that interfere with most relationships.

INTERPERSONAL COMPOSTING

Composting, which we explored in chapter 5, is the next aspect of making a garden. The gardener uses organic waste—which most people throw away—to enrich the soil. In *emotional composting*, illuminating difficult or challenging feelings—which we tend to ignore or avoid—helps us increase self-understanding and enrich the self. In *interpersonal composting*, conflicts that arise in a relationship—which most couples neglect or futilely fight over—can deepen intimacy when approached wisely.

Lillian was dumping on Marcus in our therapy session. She was excessively critical and argumentative—and I'm not sure what was really at stake. While the three of us knew that she could become contrary and impatient when she got tired or stressed, this seemed more intense. Marcus was not sure what he had done to trigger his wife of ten years. Neither was I. They were silent for a while. It was tense and quiet, with mutual resentment filling the room.

"I'm sick and tired of your contempt," Marcus said. "It's like you're picking at me, hunting for proof to build a case. I really don't know what I've done to piss you off. And I'm frankly sick of it."

"You've done nothing," she blurted out, "but I'm mad at you for some reason. You put me in a strange position. I don't know what it is you *want* from me, Marcus. Sometimes when we're having these deep discussions that you crave, I feel like we're soul mates and then at other times . . . never mind."

"Stay with it," I said.

"It's all the little things that add up, Marcus," Lillian continued.

"What little things?" he asked.

"The comments when I am putting on makeup, the critical stares when I am getting ready to go out, the impatient pointing at your watch as I am dressing."

"Honey, we're late for everything and you're always in the bathroom looking at the mirror past the time when we need to leave," Marcus replied.

"You really hurt my feelings a few weeks ago when you asked what I was '*doing* up there,' implying that I'm a one-dimensional Barbie. You want a philosopher who is also eye candy. I have to look good for your business dinners and whenever we go out, yet if I spend a long time getting ready or have a massage or a facial and get my hair done regularly, and buy clothes—well I am always having to defend the time I spend and it's driving me crazy!"

"Can we explore this without either of you defending your positions or attacking each other?" I asked.

"I am tired of being dumped on by her," Marcus blurted out.

"No attacking," I said.

"I'm sorry, I'm sorry," Marcus said. "You are my wife, I love you and I'm attracted to you. I love it when you look really good and other men notice you. I didn't think I was giving you such a hard time about the time. I'm sorry that I'm hurting you, but I just don't know what to do about it or even how to think about it."

"Stop making me feel bad, wouldn't be a bad start," Lillian said.

"We are going down the same one-way street," I said.

"I am lost," Lillian said. "So am I," Marcus added.

I explain composting to them and then describe its three stages:

- Opening to and getting curious about what you are experiencing
- Translating its meaning
- Transforming, or deciding what action to take

First I helped Lillian and Marcus slow down and stop defending themselves and attacking each other. Then they could begin to examine the building blocks of their circular fight. We discovered that underneath Lillian's initial anger at Marcus, she was fearful. She had been emotionally beaten down by her father, a former army sergeant and a relentless critic, and unsupported by her mother. All her life she had labored under the fantasy that she was not good enough, not smart enough, not pretty enough. Her irritation with Marcus, we learned, was a result of her fear when he seemed vulnerable. While she liked that he was "more feeling-full" than many of her friends' husbands, as we delved deeper she admitted that she associated sadness with weakness. She realized that when he cried or was down, it made her feel that he couldn't protect her. She was embarrassed to admit that she then felt as if she was a frightened daughter with a weak father. Once she understood that this was an "emotional splint" that interfered with healing her own fear, she gradually relied on herself more. Her trust in her own opinions and ideals slowly grew, and she no longer made Marcus responsible for "healing my own deficits." As she became more comfortable when Marcus was vulnerable—because she wasn't desperately needing him to appear strong so she would feel safe—her sniping decreased.

Marcus had been a shy, vulnerable teenager who dated very little in high school and also felt inadequate. We eventually learned that he was using Lillian to show the world what a successful man he had become. Once Marcus felt more appreciation for himself and his accomplishments, his need for Lillian's appearance to be a reflection of his own worth lessened and he could appreciate her physical vitality and allure without recruiting her to fit into an image designed to prop him up. As Lillian and Marcus stopped needing each other to bolster their own fragile self-esteem, the critical atmosphere receded and their love for each other flowered.

When we compost relational weeds and enrich the soil of intimacy, empathy and mutual respect, trust and safety, can be cultivated.

Planting and Tending the Seeds of Intimacy

Love doesn't just sit there, like a stone, it has to be made . . .
all the time, made new.

—URSULA LE GUIN

Tending a garden involves ongoing care and commitment. After being sowed and planted in fertile soil, everything needs to be cultivated in different ways depending upon its nature—seedlings, for example, must be moist but not wet, otherwise they will rot; developing plants may have to be watered more deeply and less often, to encourage deep root growth.

There are great variations in the path that people travel in order to find love and keep it alive. Historical studies of love suggest that it is protean, taking on various forms.

Not only is there a great deal of evidence that people in the past thought and felt differently about "passionate attachment" than we do, but there has been a profound revolution in marriage in the modern age. "[E]very advice book, every medical treatise, every sermon and religious homily of the sixteenth and seventeenth centuries firmly rejected both romantic passion and lust as suitable bases for marriage," wrote the historian Lawrence Stone in "Passionate Attachments in the West in Historical Perspective."

"Public admiration for marriage-for-love is thus a fairly recent occurrence in Western society . . . only winning general acceptance in the twentieth [century]." It is only in the last two hundred years that "Europeans and Americans begin to see marriage as a personal and private relationship that should fulfill their emotional and sexual desires," noted Stephanie Coontz in *Marriage, a History: How Love Conquered Marriage*. "Once that happened, free choice became the societal norm for mate selection, love became the main reason for marriage, and a successful marriage came to be defined as one that met the needs of its members," according to Coontz.

The qualities that I suggest are essential to a flourishing, loving relationship are shaped by my experiences observing what heals couples in crisis. Care and commitment, empathy and mutual respect, the ability to communicate, idealization and the tolerance of imperfections, acceptance of differences and the capacity to forgive, sexual passion and shared values, are crucial. So is an environment of attunement in which one feels known and cherished, emotionally and physically excited, deeply connected, and enriched and enhanced.

Such an atmosphere is something that must be cocreated by both members of a relationship and must continually be nourished. We must cultivate and tend what we have planted. Time together characterized by care, attentive listening, and emotional responsiveness nurtures the relationship, as does feeling cherished and respecting the character of your partner.

But a singular emphasis on these essential qualities or experiences neglects another crucial facet to sustaining love, namely the creation of what Wilkinson and Gabbard term the experience of a "romantic space" in a relationship which "sustains a feeling of being in love." The notion of romantic space derives from the psychoanalyst D. W. Winnicott's concept of *potential space*—an environment conducive to imagination and creativity that is characterized by openness, playfulness, flexibility, and the capacity to perceive experience and relate to other people in a multitude of ways. To illustrate potential space, consider this: A husband placed two branches he found while walking in the woods into a vase that his wife left near the fireplace in their living room. The wife noticed it and felt that the "Zen sculpture" her husband spontaneously fashioned enhanced the ambience in the living room. Later that day she found another branch and added it to the vase. The husband liked her addition. The "aesthetic jazz" they created—their willingness to play with and beautify their home—was synergistic, enriching both their environment and their relationship.

Romantic space, as I conceive it, is an atmosphere two people create—and need to sustain—in which the couple has *expanded interpersonal space* and there is a more open and spacious atmosphere in the relationship.

Rita and Aaron were locked in a seemingly insoluble fight. He wanted to move back to France, where he was born; she wanted to stay in New York because of family, work, and friends. They had discussed this topic countless times and ended up feeling exhausted and disappointed. I suggested that they discuss the topic by switching perspectives. He would present Rita's viewpoint as sympathetically as possible and she would do the same from his perspective. Aaron had great difficulty entering into Rita's point of view. He could do it intellectually, but not emotionally. I pushed him to stretch himself, telling him that he would grow on a personal level from being able to empathize with another person's point of view. He tried. At first he just halfheartedly repeated the arguments that Rita had presented.

Rita looked at me discouraged.

"Dig deeper," I said to Aaron.

To our surprise—and delight—Aaron said Rita had a powerful desire to be connected to family, fulfilling work, and friends and it would be heartbreaking for her to move.

Rita had been trying to tell him that for months and he had never conveyed any understanding or empathy. Aaron's empathy, emotionality, and expanded inner space brought tears to everyone's eyes. The atmosphere in the room changed—it felt lighter and more spacious— and everyone felt more centered and open.

Aaron and Rita discussed the contentious topic again from their own points of view while trying to stay attuned to their partner's feelings and needs. After quickly finding a creative solution that respected both points of view, they spontaneously kissed. They felt closer than ever.

Romantic space in a relationship is an attitude and a spirit of greater receptivity, centeredness, and clarity that fosters and nourishes each partner's authenticity and aliveness. Each partner is committed to self-care and growth, not simply to comfort. The relationship is a place of vitality rather than stagnancy. Hence it is more passionate.

Ron and Rita, who worked together in a small successful business, felt that their loving relationship of ten years needed rejuvenation. After realizing that having more of a life outside of their union could only enrich it, they actively focused on nurturing other friendships and selected hobbies, which they noticed enlivened the relationship. They also instituted what they called "mystery dates." About once a month, one of them would choose an activity that was either new or they thought their spouse would find gratifying—such as hearing unfamiliar music. One person did the planning and surprised the other. Ron and Rita reported that the relationship had been enhanced.

When there is a romantic space in a relationship, there is a greater willingness and capacity to take seriously your partner's feelings and feedback and learn from each other. There is mutual respect, as well as an awareness of differences. There is also more flexibility and creativity, especially an enhanced capacity to handle conflict skillfully, with the intent to "resolve and evolve." Conflicts from the past, as well relational tensions and weeds in the present, are treated as potential sources of healing and closeness.

Not only is there more vitality and harmony in the relationship, but there's an increased capacity to play and relate to each other in richly varied and textured ways. Experimentation and inventiveness, mutual learning and growth flourish. When both people in a relationship nurture romantic space, there is the emotional safety and encouragement to relate creatively and multidimensionally to expand the couple's personal and relational repertoire.

A partner may be at different times many things: best friend, lover, parent, nurturing maternal presence or a protective paternal one, someone else's best friend, valued coworker. When there is romantic space in a relationship, we see our partners in many ways and no single aspect dominates; we experience our partners in different roles simultaneously. We are comfortable, even energized, when our lovers have many functions or lives. Our partners are sometimes quietly benign presences that allow others in the family to take center stage. Or they play a central role, lending a more directive hand. When we are vulnerable or down, our spouse is nurturing and supportive. At other times, as when we are stuck, our partner is challenging and even confrontational. At still other times, a couple is engaged in an active collaboration.

The capacity to see our spouses as our best friends does not preclude treating them as accomplices engaged in illicit pleasure, as our protectors, or as nurturers. This fosters trust and aliveness, depth and excitement. Something in a relationship may be missing if we see our partners as only maternal or paternal or as simply a nurturer or protector. Many relationships founder because the husband sees himself as a teenager (or a boy) and expects his wife to be a mother figure who cooks and does his laundry, while the wife sees herself as a teenager who needs to be supported and protected by Daddy.

Different types of love flourish in the same relationship when there is expanded interpersonal space. Sometimes there is a carnal fusion in which boundaries between the lovers are crossed and their identities feel merged. Or there is a loving connection between them but also a great deal of psychological separation. At other moments, desire rules and one takes rather than gives. At still other moments there is what Aristotle in the *Nicomachean Ethics* termed a *philia* sort of love—a deep, loving friendship, in which one appreciates rather than desires to possess the other and the lovers are not fused or submerged in each other.

There are many tones and colors in the symphony of love that need to be played in harmony. Most people would agree that connectedness to and engagement with one's partner plays a central role in a loving relationship. Without connectedness a relationship is detached, resembling two parallel but separated and segregated planets each following their own orbit and never touching. But connectedness without autonomy and individuation impedes intimacy, as we've discovered earlier, for the person who is not growing not only brings less to the relationship, but is often deprived and angry, which usually gets dumped onto her partner. And such a person is more prone to drowning or getting swallowed up in the other person, which leads to her feeling as if she is losing herself. As long as Amanda didn't take seriously what she wanted in her relationship, she would feel bereft even if she loved her boyfriend and he loved her. When each partner is not individuated—pursuing his or her authentic life—then the relationship is constrained. But too much autonomy can foster impressive solos in which the other person is a mere accompanist and not a participant in a duet. Crucial to intimacy is the recognition that one's partner is a separate and equivalent center of experience and initiative, a person in his or her own right, not merely an object for the other person's use.

In a romantic space in a passionate relationship, autonomy and connectedness, as well as other apparent oppositions, can be integrated and serve one another because they are not seen as separate or conflicting. One experiences this not by seeking a comfortable middle way, which rejects both extremes of apparent polarities, but by finding an active, vital engagement in which both partners are taken seriously and work together.

Consider loyalty and disloyalty. Loyalty—an unquestioned commitment to one's partner—is essential to a loving relationship. It is the glue that fosters safety and trust. But too much loyalty, as the unquestioned commitment to a partner who is hurting you, can be dangerous. It can breed blind obedience, myopia, and an evasion of ethical responsibility.

Jacqueline was critical of and impatient with her shy and sensitive ten-year-old-son, Peter. Her husband, Ted, was troubled by her behavior, but his loyalty toward his wife prevented him from telling her. His father had been in the same role with an overbearing wife. Instead, Ted said nothing and either coddled his son to make it up to him, or periodically exploded at his wife for something trivial and unrelated to their son, which disturbed and confused her. Meanwhile Peter grew up feeling as if he was a bad boy who was unlovable.

There are individuals in relationships—perhaps even loving ones— who are psychologically restricted and submerged because their devotion to their partner precludes any concern for their own feelings and needs. But there are moments when a relationship is best served by a capacity to question, challenge, and even dissent. Experimenting with "disloyalty" may at times be affirming for both partners and the relationship as a whole. Of course, the healthy proportions of loyalty and disloyalty need to be ascertained on an individual basis. This is true of all of the interlacing qualities that comprise the symphony of intimacy: passion and reflection, security and risk, intimacy and autonomy.

Harvesting the Garden of Love

Harvesting involves reaping what you have sown or appreciating what you have—not allowing it to be compromised by fantasies of a fictional ideal. Being grateful for "volunteers," or the seedlings that appear in a garden without having been planted, is another aspect of harvesting. Volunteers in a relationship are unexpected discoveries or precious moments.

When we tend a relationship well, we create a garden of love in which passion grows over time. The relationship is a *we* that cherishes both *I*'s. In other words, the relationship meets the needs and brings out the best in both people and bridges intimacy and autonomy. Each person can be authentically him- or herself while being connected to and loving a partner—this is a key dimension of flourishing. When we harvest the garden of love, we feel reverence and gratitude for the intimacy that we have cultivated. We let the way love has opened our hearts and eyes wash over us and infuse the rest of our lives. We treat the relationship as a rare and special plant that requires attention. We are grateful for what we sow, commit to sustaining it, and strive to appreciate and renew the relationship for its duration. And we leave room to notice the volunteers—the gifts of unpredictable growth. Tina and Stephen, a couple I once knew, told me that one of the unplanned and unexpected seeds that sprouted in their relationship was her sparkling intelligence, which had grown and fed the relationship over time, but was hidden when they first met because she was very shy and her "voice" had been squashed in childhood by self-involved and negligent parents. As she felt seen and valued by Stephen, it encouraged the emergence of her formidable and quirky intelligence, which lent depth to their relationship.

Maintaining the Garden of Love

Gardens are maintained by *deadheading*—taking off withered blossoms to support flowering or improve the appearance of a plant—as well as watering, feeding, and composting.

Love is never a "final presence," as Ulanov and Ulanov aptly note. The happy couples Wallerstein and Blakeslee interviewed "regarded their marriage as a work in progress that needed continual attention lest it fall into disrepair . . . A good marriage is always being reshaped so that the couple can stay in step with each other and satisfy their changing needs and wishes." We maintain the garden of love when we attend to both what helps it thrive and what doesn't. Continuing self-care and dedication to the health of the relationship are indispensable. Committing to quality time—and leaving space for the timeless time we discussed in chapter 1—as well as dreaming together about a better future, are powerful ways of maintaining the garden of love and helping it flourish.

Thorns in the Rose Garden

The final facet of creating a loving space in a relationship entails learning to work with difficulties, including things that disturb, enrage, or even scare us.

We have a tendency to conceive of intimacy and love in an idealistic way, and our utopian pictures hide the reality of imperfections and fallibility. We often assume that our own or our partner's imperfections, not our ideals, are the culprit. Rather than question those standards, we blame ourselves (or our spouse) for our failure to experience continuous love.

It may be useful to end my examination of love by reflecting on the earthly reality. Creating a loving relationship entails living through and transforming what Thoreau would term the "quiet desperation" that accompanies the journey of most individuals. Many relationships struggle with dashed hopes and failures, unfulfilled ambitions, and even bitter resignation, amid blissful union and joyous discovery. Because reality rarely lives up to our fantasies, working with unloving feelings and thoughts is crucial for sustaining a loving relationship.

There are at least two other ways to take care of the relationships we have created, in addition to ongoing weeding and composting of conflict. Deadheading is a useful method for maintaining a garden. We figure out what doesn't work and needs to be eliminated. For some, this may involve jettisoning activities, stagnant friendships, or behaviors that are harmful or no longer serve our emotional or physical health; others may change the way they relate to or treat their partners. Larry finally realized that his weekend-long golf jaunts were interfering with his relationship with Margaret. And she stopped spending hours on the phone speaking to female friends when he got home from work. They both reported feeling closer and happier.

Sutra 2:16 of the Yoga Sutra suggests another way that we can maintain the garden of love: avoid the trouble that is to come. Ron and Steffi always fought after visiting her parents. He felt that she was too enmeshed with them, sharing private matters such as their financial situation, which embarrassed him and kept her passive and dependent. Steffi felt attacked by Ron and unsupported by him. She also thought that he didn't understand the importance of family and how crucial it was for her. As Steffi and Ron began anticipating the psychological minefields that got triggered when they visited her parents, talked about them respectfully, and prepared accordingly, they worked together so that the tension and conflict no longer divided them.

The Religion of Love

"To fall in love," suggests Jorge Luis Borges, "is to create a religion that has a fallible God."

Love is like religion. It is awesome and majestic and has ultimate significance. It is something we believe in. It requires faith and devotion. And it provides meaning and direction.

The Latin word *religere* means to bind or connect. A loving relationship unites and binds two people, thereby offering connection, solace, and freedom from isolated, encapsulated selfhood. Despite a culture of ever-expanding hedonism and isolation, we yearn for something more sustaining than self-gratification or self-sufficiency. The epidemic of angst—the ubiquitous alienation and the rampant greed and immorality, the cultural pollution and financial stresses on relationships—throws us back on ourselves and we are self-preoccupied and feel empty and lost, accountable only to the dictates of our individual wishes.

The answer to the question asked by the song "Why Do Fools Fall in Love?" is: so they can find meaning and worth outside their indispensable—although egoistic—inner worlds.

Love is a religion with a *fallible* god, because while it has immense power, it is also imperfect and flawed. It needs to be continuously maintained—watered and fed, weeded and composted—and it does not provide certain answers or unerring protection. It does not solve all one's dilemmas. It does not offer insurance against loneliness and suffering and loss. Lovers are still left with heart-wrenching choices and excruciating moral decisions and, in the case of the death of a spouse, cavernous voids.

Each couple—the lover and the beloved—is unique. Since love entails mystery as well as certainty, questions as well as answers, allow my exploration of the psychological ingredients that nourish a loving relationship to stir your passions about the subject and prompt reflections and questions, critique and elaborations.

No Winners, No Losers

Expanding Interpersonal Space

It was a warm spring day, but there was a palpable chill in my office. A very stylishly dressed couple—black on black—sat across from each other. He was in his late forties; she was in her thirties. Something seemed really off about them. I have worked with many couples over the years. Some of them waited too long to come in and ended up negotiating the emotional shoals of divorce in their therapy sessions. Others took a while, but eventually learned to express their hurt and deprivation and began working toward constructive solutions for the relationship. These two did not fit into any obvious category. It wasn't that they seemed angry or even emotionally involved with the issues. They were both utterly cold, silent, and withdrawn. But they were focused, like snipers.

The husband began quietly extinguishing his wife, as if he were listing the faults of a child abuser. She showed no emotion as he slammed her. When it was her turn, she reacted to what he was saying by nailing him right back. Calmly. Coldly.

They were both obviously in pain. Each of them felt misunderstood, frustrated, and deprived. I felt sad for them—two competent and accomplished people, stuck and unhappy about their home life. And angry—very angry.

At first I couldn't figure out what was underneath the barbs and cruelty of what they said. But as I listened to them, I realized that they weren't here to fix anything. It slowly dawned on me that they weren't even assigning me the role of arbiter, trying to get me to side with one of them against the other. Many couples do that, initially; the ones who want to stay together eventually stop. Here, the stakes appeared higher and more devious.

After each finished laying out an articulate and convincing case against the other, we were all silent for about a minute.

"No," I said.

They looked confused.

"No, I won't," I continued.

They looked unsettled.

"I am not going to court for either of you," I said. They fidgeted. "You didn't come here to improve your marriage. Each of you came here to enlist me as a character witness in divorce court, which isn't what I do, or want to do. Under the guise of coming to therapy and working on your marriage, you have each attempted to recruit me for a job whose sole purpose is to destroy your spouse. I try to help couples salvage their relationship or decide that it is unsalvageable, not play an adversarial role in court."

They were each trying to win, which made both of them lose. The surest way to guarantee that a relationship will fail is to try to defeat your partner. Inevitably both of you will be disappointed and deprived.

That same week I heard the raised voices of another couple in the waiting room. By the time I opened the door of my office several minutes later, the couple in their early forties was looking at everything but each other.

I introduced myself and they followed me into my office. Cathy sat on the sofa, and Robert chose a rocking chair. They were both tall and slender and conservatively dressed. They glared at each other. Tension filled the room.

"What brought you here and how can I be of help?" I asked.

"Do you have all day?" Robert mumbled.

Cathy glanced at Robert, rolled her eyes, and began.

"We've been married for eight years and have two kids, a six-year-old boy and a three-year-old girl. We lived together for a while before getting married. It turned out that we actually grew up fairly close to each other, in Ohio, and met while we were both working in the same building in New York."

I learned that Cathy and Robert were brought up as Methodists, and their fathers each owned small businesses that had been in their families for generations. As they got to know each other, they realized that they had very similar ideals. They wanted more opportunities than their midwestern towns offered, but they also both liked the values they were raised with, the friendliness and intimacy of small towns, and the feeling of belonging to a community. The strong physical attraction they felt for each other was only enhanced by what they shared.

"Meeting and getting to know Cathy felt familiar and good," Robert injected. "Like seeing an old friend who you can just be yourself with." Robert had a wistful smile as he spoke.

"It all sounds past tense," I said.

They were quiet and pensive. Cathy was fending off tears and Robert was also close to the edge.

I waited.

"The relationship has slowly evolved—or devolved—into tension and distance," she said. "Like two battling roommates."

Cathy complained that Robert worked all the time and was rarely around. She felt abandoned and lonely, overwhelmed, raising their children alone. She was annoyed with Robert because he constantly nixed almost all her home renovation dreams and plans. Robert complained that Cathy was too critical, cold, and detached. (I wondered if this was code for their having no physical intimacy.) He also felt she was oblivious to money and that he not only carried the financial obligations alone, but her compulsive spending sabotaged his efforts to finally get the family on a more solid economic foundation.

When Robert and Cathy weren't fighting, each pursued his or her own interests: Cathy gardened and did crafts; Robert overworked and watched sports on TV. The kids were the only thing they shared.

At the beginning of the second session, Cathy looked upset and immediately launched into a diatribe about Robert. "You are always working, you don't spend enough time at home. I feel like a work widow."

At first Robert seethed and then he jumped in and lambasted Cathy. "Nothing is ever good enough for you. I'm always working because you are always spending money. I have to work."

"You're a tightwad who pinches pennies," Cathy responded. "And speaking of criticism—you've become very judgmental toward *me*."

Reacting to her anger, he escalated his attack, which only triggered further hostility and rage from her.

Accusations and counterattacks flew back and forth so fast I could hardly understand what was at stake. I tried unsuccessfully to redirect them, but their fighting drowned me out.

I realized that it was premature for us to even work on their problems because there was a reservoir of hurt feelings and anger and no constructive communication between them. They lectured and attacked, avoided and debated.

It was time to intercede.

"Throw me your wallets!" I said.

They looked at each other and then stared at me.

"Throw them to me."

They complied, finally working cooperatively. I took the wallets and placed them on the black ottoman at my feet.

"Do you enjoy throwing your money away?" I asked.

Again they stared at me blankly. "No," they said in unison.

At least there's one thing they agreed on.

I spoke slowly, giving each word emphasis. "If you follow this one principle—which I will try my best to help you to do—you will save yourselves a lot of time, money, and tears," I said. "Be more interested in *understanding* your spouse than in *winning*. Otherwise this process will take longer than it needs to and you'll waste a lot of money trying to win. But you won't win. Ever. It's like going to Las Vegas or Atlantic City—you will always end up losing. And even if you 'win,' you actually lose, because your spouse—who has lost—will be resentful and will pay you back by sniping at you, or withholding sexually or emotionally. And you both will continue to be miserable."

The Quickest Way to Sabotage a Relationship

Negotiating an intimate relationship is one of life's great arts. Couples collide for many reasons: the stresses of balancing work and home life; clashing values; unresolved issues from childhood that interfere with intimacy; lack of adequate role models for healthy communication; and an absence of tools for handling problems and conflict.

But in more than thirty years of working with couples, I've discovered that the biggest source of conflict isn't money or sex, in-laws or different values. It's the urge to *win,* which takes various forms from trying to defeat your partner in an argument, to punishing your spouse by sexually withholding from him when you are mad at him, to doing a task poorly that your partner asked you to do (such as vacuuming or the dishes), to attempting to curry favor with your children during a divorce by spoiling them more than your spouse does. The focus in this chapter is on the first kind of winning, which is the predominant force that undermines relationships.

It's natural to want to win, to be right. It makes us feel strong and secure. It is gratifying. For a moment, at least, we can experience a sense of triumph. Going for the win is a sort of preemptive strike—if we hit first, we believe on some barely conscious level that we'll avoid being bullied, shamed, humiliated. When our pride is injured, we attack in order to protect ourselves, and sometimes to exact revenge. We try to win because we believe it's the only course of action available—we are afraid that unless we dominate, we'll be dominated and not taken into account. We think that our only two options are to conquer or to be a doormat. We are trying to win:

- When the need to be right and justify what we believe is more important than hearing our partner or improving the relationship.
- When we question or deny the feelings and perceptions of our partner, and respond to a sentence that begins "I feel..." with "No you don't..." or "You shouldn't..."
- When conversations feel more like hostile debates than open dialogues.
- When we interrupt each other or when we mentally rehearse what we are going to say while our mate is speaking.
- When we listen for what we already believe instead of listen to what the other person is saying.

Trying to win is always disastrous for cooperative ventures such as relationships. It invalidates your partner's feelings—and sends a message that "I am more important than you," generating a cycle of mutually escalating resentment and hostility. Arguments occur with increasing regularity as each person focuses more on defeating his or her partner than on hearing and understanding what he or she is feeling and trying to express.

Empathic Listening: The Doorway into Intimacy

The key to flourishing as a couple is cultivating understanding through *empathic listening,* a hallmark of good psychotherapy. The concept of empathy means listening *to* what our partner is really saying and feeling from his or her perspective, rather than listening *for* what we already believe he or she is going to say, and then dismissing it. It was a cornerstone of the writings of Carl Rogers, a humanistic psychologist who wrote *On Becoming a Person* and created client-centered therapy, and Heinz Kohut, who authored *The Restoration of the Self* and developed psychoanalytic self-psychology. A story I once heard about Rogers paints a vivid picture of empathy. A colleague referred a friend to Rogers. The friend loved fishing. Several months into treatment Rogers' friend said to him: "I didn't know you knew so much about fishing." "I never fished, and I don't know anything about it," Rogers responded. He so empathized with his patient that the patient was certain Rogers was an experienced fisherman.

In *Getting the Love You Want* and *Keeping the Love You Find,* Harville Hendrix, a marital therapist and pastoral counselor, later ingeniously applied this powerful and easily teachable skill into work with couples—an approach he called *intentional dialogue*—training them to be empathic toward each other.

In empathic or compassionate listening, we may not always agree with our partners' words, but we strive to understand the logic and value of what they think and feel. When each person is committed to understanding the other's point of view, an atmosphere of trust and safety develops and both feel heard and respected—an intentional dialogue. This state of being makes it infinitely easier to tackle difficult conversations and topics.

Before I taught Robert and Cathy how to become empathic listeners, I asked them to think about what set off the other and to avoid doing so. These triggers (for example, "You're just like your mother/father," or, "Even your sister agrees that you are too...") create a volatile psychological minefield. Communicating without setting off any explosives is a powerful and immediate way of making the environment safer and more constructive.

Then I instructed each of them to speak about one difficult issue, focusing on their feelings—speaking in the first person ("I feel sad/mad/hurt/scared")—without attacking the other person. The idea was for them to express authentic emotions without judging or sparking resentment or shame in their partner. The partner was asked to listen without trying to win, focusing on hearing the deepest meaning behind the words; empathizing with, rather than criticizing or arguing about, the validity of what their partner said. The listener's job was to repeat back what he or she heard and ask the speaker if he or she felt heard. They continued this process until the speaker felt understood. And then they reversed roles and repeated the process.

This isn't always easy in the beginning. It takes patience and practice. When something one partner says triggers anger or irritation, we can remind ourselves that we don't have to agree. We don't even have to solve this problem. *All we have to do is listen and understand what our partner is thinking, feeling, and saying.* When our emotional reaction interferes with empathic listening we can also use the yogic breathing and meditation we practiced in earlier chapters. Close your mouth and inhale and exhale gently and easily through your nose, staying grounded in the present moment, instead of getting emotionally hijacked by your reactions. Or focus on the body sensations of the disturbing emotions. Both techniques create internal space and provide perspective. This allows us to hear what our partner is expressing without distortion, and that makes him or her more willing *and able* to listen to us.

Robert told Cathy that he was concerned about money. I heard both vulnerability and fear in his voice.

"So am I," said Cathy defensively.

"When Robert is finished, you can speak, Cathy."

"I'm scared," Robert admitted. "Everything feels like a house of cards."

I could see that Cathy was quieter, sitting still, listening intensely to her husband. Gradually, her face softened. Eager to heal the breach, and obviously grasping the principle of compassionate listening, Cathy empathized with Robert. "You're really feeling pressure, aren't you," she said.

"That's what I've been trying to tell you for several years," Robert said.

"I always felt that you were attacking me," Cathy replied.

"It's about *me,* not *you,*" he said. "I am fearful about money and the future."

"Now I really want to know what that pressure is like for you," she said.

"I'm really worried about our future," Robert continued. "I feel we need to live on a smaller scale and have more of a safety net to protect us in case something happens to me. My father died at my age, you know."

Cathy was leaning toward Robert, listening attentively.

"I would like to spend more time with you and the kids," Robert continued, "but in order to do that, I have to work less, and one way of doing that is to downscale and lower our expenses."

"You are worried about money and our financial future. You feel great pressure and you would like us to downscale, spend less, and have more quality time with family," Cathy said softly. She looked right at Robert. "Do you feel that I'm hearing you?"

"For the first time."

I looked at Cathy. I shared the sting of his accusation.

"*Understanding,* not winning," I reminded him.

Robert took a deep breath. "Yes, I do feel you heard me, Cathy. Thank you," he said quietly. There were tears in his eyes, and in hers. Much of the hostility had evaporated. There were small and tentative smiles. They both sounded lighter. I saw some hope.

When we listen empathically and engage in an intentional dialogue we expand interpersonal space and the atmosphere of the relationship radically changes. Both people are more open-minded and centered, listening to each other without an agenda; hearing on deeper levels and in an increasingly intuitive and creative way. Each partner feels validated and taken more seriously. A mutually reinforcing circle of goodwill is created. Each person feels as if the other is really hearing what he or she is saying and is thus more willing to reciprocate. When Cathy debated with Robert in the past, he felt like a failure for not being able to meet all her financial needs. He also secretly felt shame that she was mocking his anxiety about money, and so he would react in anger. Part of this reaction came from his experience with his overly critical parents, who made him feel humiliated for his vulnerabilities, and Cathy had been reinforcing Robert's experience in his family with her critical and impatient attitude. Cathy, who came from a family where her needs were often overlooked or denigrated, took Robert's hostility as evidence that he didn't care about her feelings. She would either withdraw, refusing to communicate any further, or treat Robert with contempt, which deepened his feelings of shame. By listening to Robert's concerns, Cathy helped him express his underlying anxiety. Now he felt more willing to hear Cathy's feelings.

Cathy told Robert that she felt really isolated and burdened, running the household and caring for their two children alone, prevented from working more than part-time because of her responsibilities to the family. She also wanted to make their home warm and nurturing. As we neared the end of the session, Robert said that he had really heard her feelings of frustration and isolation. Cathy felt that for the first time he was taking her seriously.

As the therapy progressed, both Cathy and Robert were able to share even more deeply. Cathy missed the self-esteem and sense of accomplishment she had received from her full-time position as a nursing administrator. And Robert was finally able to say that he feared that he would turn out to be like his father, who was not a great provider.

When Robert and Cathy began listening *to* each other, instead of trying to defeat each other, a spirit of mutual respect and cooperation replaced the contentious atmosphere that haunted their relationship. Their capacity to meet each other's needs increased and the problems that divided them shrank. Cathy realized she was spending excessively in an attempt to make up for feeling deprived by Robert's absence, and she decided to economize. Robert recognized that the family wasn't in as precarious a financial position as he believed. He began leaving work earlier—no longer dawdling to avoid Cathy. And he encouraged Cathy to resume work during the daytime. Robert and Cathy began spending more time together—walking several evenings a week after dinner and pursuing a mutual passion, dancing. Their practice of listening *to* each other had brought them closer and made them both stronger.

Empathic listening also freed Kenny and Marlene from the suffocating grip of a longstanding stalemate. For many years they had been struggling with Marlene's difficulty taking care of herself. Ironically Marlene, who was an emergency room nurse, took lousy care of herself—grossly overeating, gaining a huge amount of weight, and when not at the hospital leading a very sedentary lifestyle. Even after several health scares, nothing Kenny tried—being patient, conveying concern, confronting Marlene about his feelings—seemed to have any effect. By the time they came for therapy, Kenny was very frustrated and angry. After teaching them the process of empathic listening, they seemed open to trying it.

KENNY: I'd like to talk with you about something that I've been struggling with.

MARLENE: Okay, let's hear it.

KENNY: I would love it if you would commit to take better care of yourself physically. I am concerned about your health; I'm scared that you are potentially endangering yourself; I feel you'd be happier and more vital and energetic, which would enrich our relationship. My being in this position—the overseer of your health—also repeats my role in my family of origin, being made to feel hyperresponsible for my troubled sister.

MARLENE: I hear that you are worried about me and that you want me to be happier. Is that right?

KENNY: Yes, and there's a little more.

MARLENE: Go on.

KENNY: Your taking better care of yourself would help us, as well as you, and the role I'm in—caring more about your welfare than you do—throws me back to a painful and destructive role of caretaker.

MARLENE: I hear you saying that my taking better care of myself will help both of us and get you out of the harmful position of being responsible for someone else who is neglecting themselves. Is that right? Is there anything else?

KENNY: *(Tears in his eyes)* I'm afraid you'll die prematurely.

MARLENE: *(Tears in her eyes)* You are afraid for, and concerned about me, not criticizing me. Do you feel heard?

KENNY: I do. Thanks.

MARLENE: I can understand that you are worried about me—I'm worried about myself. It's a big struggle for me to break old habits and establish new ones, so I can just imagine how you are feeling, watching me struggle and fail. And I don't want to be in a position where you have to take care of me—that would feel terrible, even though I know you'd do a good job. But I don't want to put you in that position.

As a result of engaging in intentional dialogue and not focusing on winning, Kenny and Marlene both reported that a barrier between them had dissolved and a doorway into deeper intimacy had opened, and that they felt deeper understanding and closeness.

Empathic Listening at Home

How can you work on this in your own relationship?

You can practice compassionate listening at home. First expand personal and interpersonal space by slowing down, lessening distractions, and concentrating on your relationship. Engage in whatever practices or rituals will help you be focused and receptive, from walking or listening to music, to meditation or yoga. Set aside a block of uninterrupted time to talk on a regular basis—once or twice a week or whenever one of you requests time. Turn off the TV and cellphones and let the answering machine pick up calls. Lowering the lights can be helpful. Some people might like to be physically close; others feel safer if they're not looking directly at each other. Speak in a heartfelt and gentle manner with sensitivity to tone and timing. Consciously think about how to talk about your concerns and your needs without triggering or hurting your partner. Practice listening *to* what your partner is saying in an effort to build understanding and fresh solutions, instead of waiting for evidence to build a case.

Fear and pride are two of the main obstacles to practicing empathic listening. Many people are afraid that they will be at a disadvantage, even lose themselves if they empathize with their partners. But trying to win doesn't really protect them. In fact, it increases the chances that they will get wounded in an acrimonious battle. Empathizing with your partner is the quickest way to deescalate conflict and increase the chances for understanding and goodwill to prevail.

A sign that you are shifting from winning to understanding comes when you learn something new about your partner or yourself. For example, a couple I know fought regularly about time. Barbara's family visited every few months on a Saturday afternoon. Ted wanted to know when they would be arriving, which Barbara could never specify because they were unclear. Ted came from a highly punctual family, but struggled himself not to be late. He wanted to know their estimated arrival time so that he could both work out before they came and get home before they got there. Barbara kept telling Ted to come home whenever he was finished and not worry about it. Sometimes he got home after his in-laws had arrived and felt guilty he had not been there to greet them. As Ted practiced empathic listening with Barbara, he learned that she knew Ted valued timeless time—which is based, as I suggested in chapter 1, on putting away watches and schedules, living in the moment, having fewer planned activities, and not rushing to get somewhere. Ted was highly scheduled during the week, and needed to have more free time at night and on the weekends. She also convinced him that her family felt the same way about being too tightly scheduled and did not care if Ted came home after they arrived.

Empathic listening taught Ted something new—that Barbara was attempting to give him a gift by encouraging him to be timeless on the weekends—which brought him closer to her.

Couples can respond more skillfully to triggers, weeds, and relational minefields, and surmount seemingly intractable problems when they confront them cooperatively with an urge to understand each other. When each person strives to empathize instead of to defeat his or her partner, couples can expand interpersonal space and more readily access clarity and creativity, which exponentially increases the chances of approaching stubborn problems in fresh ways. *When no one loses in a relationship, each person wins.*

Empathic listening is a wonderful tool for enriching intimacy, but

in my clinical experience, many couples discover that they need something else too—otherwise, they have greater understanding of their
conflicts, but change eludes them. In the next chapter, we'll build on
what we learned about handling challenging emotions in chapter 5, so
we can *compost* several characteristic interpersonal conflicts.

13

> Becoming "awake" involves seeing our
> confusion more clearly.
>
> —CHOGYAM TRUNGPA

COMPOSTING INTERPERSONAL CONFLICT

"We are celebrating twelve years of strife next month," Larry, an earnest and hardworking architect announced when speaking of his marriage to Monica, a talented photographer, who refused to come in with him for therapy. "My wife has a tremendous temper and is prone to scary, angry behavior. Screaming. Breaking dishes. You get the picture."

"What do you do when she acts that way?" I asked.

"I tried the intentional dialogue approach with her, which we learned in our previous therapy—empathizing with her rather than taking her denunciations personally. Regardless of what she said—no matter how critical, demeaning, or judgmental—I reflected back her needs and feelings."

"What happened?" I asked.

"It was helpful. She started out being furious and then became less aggressive and dissatisfied. She even told me for the first time that she'd had a very neglected childhood. She also told me that having someone listen helped a lot."

"That is not easy to do," I said. "It is difficult to empathize and not react in the face of strong emotion."

"But there's still a big problem," Larry said. "She has a lot of trouble with money—managing it and discussing it. She spends compulsively and has no sense of limits. She earns twenty percent of our income and spends eighty percent of it. While I believe that it relates in some way to her traumatic past, I'm having sleepless nights because of the financial hole she's put us in. I've cut the babysitter, let go of my administrative assistant, but nothing stops her. Perhaps the worst thing is that she refuses to talk about her spending, creating a budget, or having any limits, which are treated by her as a punishment."

It sounded like a train wreck waiting to happen. "Empathy is not enough," I said to Larry. "Imagine a leaky bucket. Until the holes are fixed, no matter how much water is poured in, it will never get filled. Your empathy helps, but it is insufficient. Lack of empathy would make things worse, but it doesn't repair the fault line from her past."

I have to admit that I was not totally surprised. Empathizing does make things better—and without Larry's devotion to really listening to Monica, their relationship would undoubtedly have been worse—but something more was needed. She was still out of control and behaving in a way that was destructive to her and their relationship. Whether I was correct or not in my private speculation that Monica's compulsive spending was a way of attempting to manage unbearable emotions, from years of clinical experience I was certain of one thing: that her behavior would ultimately bleed them dry unless she dealt with her underlying feelings. Sometimes we need to go beyond listening empathically in order to heal longstanding, entrenched feelings and trauma.

Empathy Is Not Enough

From the humanist psychologist Carl Rogers to Heinz Kohut, the founder of psychoanalytic self-psychology, empathy has enjoyed a highly valued status in Western psychology. Empathy, like health or peace, seems an unqualified virtue. When partners in a relationship are empathic to each other, they can build bridges of emotional understanding across the chasms that ordinarily separate people. When empathy is absent, potential misunderstanding, prejudices, and even oppression can dominate a relationship.

Empathy has been important to me personally and professionally— opening up deeper understanding and connections with friends, family, and patients. It is also vital to couples and intimacy; enabling spouses to enter the differently organized and sometimes foreign psychological worlds of their partners, which fosters the development of a more meaningful bond between them. As spouses feel emotionally understood by their partners they increasingly trust that their vulnerabilities and needs will be treated with respect and care, which encourages the sharing of formerly hidden and shameful experiences. Each spouse gradually internalizes his or her mate's empathic stance and is able to view his or her own experience with greater understanding and acceptance. The capacity for empathic self-observation can actually *replace* the conditional acceptances of those people in a person's past that have been misattuned and hurt them.

Empathy is an essential, although incomplete, facet of the process of change in both psychotherapy and intimate relationships. It is essential because it fosters a safe, trusting environment and opens up the possibility of deeper levels of understanding and compassion between patient and therapist, or husband and wife. It is incomplete because it omits certain vital elements of the therapeutic process, particularly what I called in chapter 10 a person's ongoing efforts at *self-creation*. Self-creation has two dimensions: our responsibility for caring for ourselves and relating to other people in a healthier way; and fashioning a meaningful and fulfilling life based on our unique values and ideals. It is often assumed that patients in therapy will automatically grow and flourish when they are heard, but the way empathy is often perceived can lead to an evasion of responsibility. In order to change, we need to stop perpetuating the problems from the past in the present, while actualizing a more self-respectful and authentic existence.

The limitations of empathy became clearer in my work with Larry and Monica. Empathic listening alone failed to mobilize Monica and lead to meaningful change. Months later, even after Larry continued to try to empathize with her, she still struggled with taking care of herself, out-of-control rages, and expenditures. And she devoted much of her time with Larry to either attacking him or detailing how she had been wronged by a variety of people (never her parents) and why things could not/would not change. No attention was ever focused on what she might do to live a fulfilling life and how she was contributing to her feelings of despondency.

I realized that while Monica was helped by Larry's empathic stance toward her anger in the present and her raw deal in the past—it validated her experience, made her feel understood, and soothed her—it could not overcome her own self-sabotaging behavior and emotional stalemate with Larry. Seeing someone as a fragile and helpless victim in need of empathic support can be a wonderful, compassionate beginning, but it can also ignore a person's unconscious contribution to keeping him- or herself stuck. Far from being a helpless victim, Monica was highly skilled, albeit unconsciously, at fashioning a particular life involving shabby self-care, restrictive relationships, and a great deal of personal deprivation and suffering, all of which unwittingly repeated her experience of a childhood of misery and deprivation.

While Larry and Monica's home life was dominated by Monica's litany of injustices and deprivations, I was convinced that until she addressed her unconscious role in cocreating her suffering, she would remain miserable and continue to undermine her marriage.

One day, several months into treatment, I greeted Larry in my waiting room. He got up and came into my office with a woman who had been sitting a few seats away from him. Monica had finally come to a session.

I learned, as I listened to Monica's description of her life, that the needs of others took precedence over her own best interests, except when she spent money on herself. She left herself out of the equation in every other area. She illustrated the profound psychological cost of self-neglect that I explored in the first half of this book. Monica could not have enriching relationships with others or feel personal contentment as long as she focused solely on what she could give *to* others to the exclusion of what she needed and wanted *from* them.

For Monica to have a life that might feel like her own, being understood wasn't enough. She also needed to take responsibility for changing the direction of her life, and for forging new ways of treating herself and relating to others. She did not really change until she understood and challenged old and restrictive behaviors and attitudes. And this did not happen until she recognized the ways she unwittingly collaborated in, as well as was the victim of, her own suffering. Only then did Monica begin to mourn and work through how she treated herself and had been treated. This was the catalyst for helping her pursue new ways of living. In order to do this she needed to understand more of her impact

on others, including Larry; especially the way she organized relationships so that other people could rescue her from the degraded state
she was immersed in. If I had encouraged Larry to just empathize with
her experience we wouldn't have gotten to the root of the problem, but
rather would have ultimately reinforced her self-centeredness and sense
of entitlement.

Monica began coming to therapy with her husband and we explored
the possibility that she was evading responsibility for the quality of
her life. She examined her own role in perpetuating her suffering. She
noticed, for example, how her lifelong focus on being treated badly by
other people obscured her responsibility for the way she unconsciously
attempted to remain linked to her parents by putting herself last. This
led to an exploration of why on some level she was invested in holding
onto a "snapshot" of her childhood emotional pain so it might finally
be witnessed and validated by someone. (One reason that people hold
onto symptoms is that they are waiting for their suffering to finally be
recognized by the inflictors of that pain.) She unconsciously equated
living a more fulfilling life with letting go of the grievances of the past,
which in turn would mean she'd be forgiving her parents. Letting go of
the past also meant giving up hope that the injuries of the past would
ever be seen and acknowledged by her parents.

As she became more interested in having a life in the present rather
than commemorating her pain from the past, Monica opened up in new
and fulfilling ways. She joined a triathlon club that held weekly training
sessions. She started participating in longer workouts, reading about
nutrition, and losing weight. She got into excellent physical shape. She
began relating to her parents in a more authentic and self-respecting
manner. She did not let them walk all over her and she felt comfortable setting limits with them. She felt that her life was finally her own.
Monica's performance at work also reflected the change; as her competence emerged she took risks and obtained a fulfilling job. She became
sensitive to the financial pressure on Larry, and she did not feel so compelled to spend money heedlessly.

Larry began to get curious about why he had accommodated Monica
and failed to set limits. As he became clearer about how he attempted
to stay connected to his narcissistic mother by being the sort of person

that she wanted him to be, he was able to be more authentic and strong-willed with his wife. She initially fought it, but eventually felt safer when he was straightforward and powerful.

Empathy is central to the therapeutic process, and to intimacy, but an exclusive focus on understanding can end in the neglect of other crucial facets that foster change such as helping us confront our self-deceptions and dysfunctional strategies of self-protection and enhancing our capacity for self-responsibility, self-care, and new ways of relating to other people and ourselves.

Interpersonal Composting

Empathic listening is wonderful, but when you find, as Larry and Monica did, that it is not enough because certain conflicts remain unresolved, there's an approach we can apply to these situations. *Interpersonal composting* builds on the insights of emotional flourishing and applies them to relationships instead of individual transformation. Meditative therapy provides the foundation for interpersonal composting, which has three elements:

1. The teachings on meditative awareness of Jiddu Krishnamurti and Joel Kramer.
2. Psychoanalytic attention to the importance of discovering the meaning of people's experiences and actions and Carl Jung's recognition that these often have a double significance—they harken back to old, unfinished conflict and conditioning (e.g., earlier traumas, wounds, and conflicts) and can be harbingers of new, untapped potentials.
3. Behaviorism's understanding that action is a crucial aspect of change.

Combining these three perspectives offers a potent brew—a realistic and concrete way of bringing change to lives and relationships.

Meditation the way Krishnamurti and Kramer depict it in *Freedom from the Known* and *The Passionate Mind*, respectively, means something entirely different from the traditional understanding of it. Meditation is not a particular system or method to control or shape the mind, or to deliberately attain a specific goal or state. It is a *special quality of non-judgmental alertness* in which we examine what we are experiencing—a feeling, an old troubling conflict, something we fear—with whole-hearted attention and without an agenda to change, deny, or justify it. In an interview, Kramer described how to practice the yoga of mind:

> I can observe that when you hurt me, I automatically want to hurt back. If I can just observe this automatic, conditioned response without judging it, I can see my conditioning. And that seeing frees me from having to react to you in an automatic way. In order to do that, though, I have to be willing to look. . . . Many traditions touch on this—Vipassana, certain Hindu techniques, Taoist traditions. They are all describing a quality of awareness that does nothing but observe. You observe the movement of thought within yourself; you don't try to silence it or make it go away.

This quality of attention that Kramer discusses—I think of it as an innocent and allowing mind—is simple, but not always easy to access because of our powerful, lifelong conditioning to judge and justify, which causes us to try to get rid of (or suppress) what we discover instead of simply seeing what is truly going on. Many couples rationalize away conflict and discontent—or blame it on their partner (or themselves)—instead of becoming curious about what it means and what they could learn from it.

When we meditate we intimately engage what we encounter, without translating it into what we already believe, so we can discover what we don't yet know. Such awareness is focused on seeing what is, which not only affords an unusual clarity and objectivity but has an uncanny capacity to reveal, in an instant, whole configurations of hidden meaning. We have all experienced it—walking, swimming, showering—when we suddenly realize the answer to a conflict that had been troubling us.

We need to become curious about whatever we are struggling with—from emotional deprivation and hostility to conflicts over power and control—translate what it means, and decide what action to take.

As Monica correctly decoded her frivolous spending—she was treating herself in the same depriving way her parents did, as well as attempting to nurture herself with cotton-candy self-care—she felt sad and bereft. This inspired her to heal her earlier trauma in a healthier way and seek genuine nourishment. When Larry realized that he was conforming to his wife in the same way that he had to his mother, he was able to be more decisive and set more constructive boundaries in his marriage.

Interpersonal composting helped Marlene and Kenny—whom we met in the last chapter—deepen their relationship by accessing a level of intimacy that wasn't possible through empathic listening alone.

"I think I'd like to define where I am having trouble and enlist your help in working on those areas," Marlene said to Kenny during a session.

"Maybe there are things you are doing and not doing that can help me get clarity and get over this hump," Marlene continued. "And maybe you could help me get insight."

"What I hear," said Kenny, "is that you'd like to figure out where you are struggling and work together with me on remedying it—and that might include those things I am doing that could help you get clear about what is going on and begin to initiate changes. Do you feel heard Marlene?"

"Yes," she replied.

"Is there more?" Kenny asked.

"Two things," said Marlene. "First, physical impediments; second, when I get really worried—always financial—it kills my ability to engage in self-care. Self-care feels frivolous; maybe I feel unworthy. The panic is so huge. I am not sure if it's self-loathing or I don't feel deserving. Something happens so fast that I can't feel it. It makes me feel so bad that I have to distract myself—like read mysteries, watch TV, eat something. It is a terrible state to be in and it feels physically destructive to stay in it. I feel bad that I didn't walk or read an interesting book. Anything that 'stirs me up,' like exercise or reading a serious book, is upsetting. It feels like PTSD. I freeze so that I don't breathe. Walking, exercise, dancing feel like I'd wake up too much and it would magnify the terrible feeling. I wish I could turn that around. I wish I could do something physically that would counteract it. I feel that I couldn't survive feeling any worse."

"There are two aspects," Kenny said. "Something is getting in the way and when you get very anxious and worried—usually about financial matters—it sabotages your ability to take care of yourself. Self-care feels frivolous and perhaps you feel undeserving. You also feel it happens so fast or is unconscious and you can't see it. And you feel very bad that you watch TV, read books unworthy of your intelligence, or eat something to distract yourself."

"You got it," Marlene said.

"Is there more?" Kenny asked.

"That's pretty much it," Marlene replied.

"Is it okay if I tell you how I'm doing?" Kenny asked.

"Sure."

"I feel neglected by you . . . and robbed. Even your brother agrees you could do more with your life."

"Even your parents think you are not ambitious enough," she retorted.

"Can we leave your families at home?" I said.

"I am sorry," Kenny said. "That was a low blow."

Tears slowly rolled down Marlene's face.

"What I realized tonight," Kenny said, "is that you are not trying to rob me, but trying to regulate yourself. If you didn't do that you would feel horrible and overwhelmed, so you frequently keep yourself in a self-induced coma. But that is killing you, not healing you."

"Say more about feeling robbed," Marlene said. What is it you feel I'm taking away from you? I hear it, but don't feel it yet."

"I accommodate to your shut down state by trying to make you feel better, but that narrows my own horizon of possibility. I'll sit with you when you watch TV so you won't be lonely, but I might feel more turned on and alive by connecting or doing something stimulating. When I join you in the shut-down state, there isn't much life there."

"You'd rather do things more stimulating so that we can both grow," Marlene said. "And when I'm shut down, it's really boring for you, so you have to do stuff that is stimulating otherwise you feel deprived, which triggers the role you were in childhood, taking care of a difficult younger sister."

As I listened to Marlene and Kenny I heard several key themes, in addition to Kenny's deprivation and Marlene's coma. Kenny's remark about Marlene's brother signaled *contempt,* one of the most destructive emotions to a marriage. The marital therapist and researcher John Gottman notes in *The Seven Principles for Making Marriage Work*:

> Sarcasm and cynicism are types of contempt. So are name-calling, eye rolling, sneering, mockery, and hostile humor. In whatever form, contempt . . . is poisonous to a relationship because it conveys disgust. It's virtually impossible to resolve a problem when your partner is getting the message you're disgusted with him or her. Inevitably, contempt leads to more conflict rather than to reconciliation.

Marlene's sleepwalking through life was a great danger to the relationship, as well as to her own well-being.

As we composed Kenny's "low blow" remark by becoming curious about what it meant, we learned that he was "calling in the troops," relying on people outside their relationship to fortify his position and validate his feelings, which he felt weren't being taken seriously by his wife. Reference to outside authorities was an attempt to buttress his argument.

Marlene looked relieved.

"I don't think I help," she said. "When I live in a coma-world much of the time, you can't feel seen or heard by me. I'll make you a deal," Marlene said. "I'll work on hearing you and trying to make our relationship more alive and less depriving, and you don't 'call in the troops.'"

"Deal."

Kenny and Marlene composed their recurrent conflict by opening to their destructive patterns, deciphering the meaning beneath their behavior, and fashioning a mutually satisfying solution.

Next they each had to address the core traumas shaping their own behaviors. They needed to take off the emotional splints they employed to cope with childhood conflicts beyond their resources, and heal them properly. Marlene, like Monica, had to work on the terror that initiated her strategy of self-protection. As she began to experience unwanted feelings and realized how they grew from the soil of a neglected and deprived childhood, she mourned what she had never been able to put into words until then.

Sedating herself numbed joy as well as agony. As Marlene no longer lived in a frozen state she slowly began to notice what made her feel more delighted and alive—writing and photography, gardening and playtime with their granddaughter. She began to value herself and learned healthier methods of self-soothing such as walking in nature, playing with her granddaughter, and dancing to her favorite music. And her burgeoning happiness delighted Kenny.

As Kenny understood how he was repeating with Marlene what he experienced with his younger sister, he became increasingly disenchanted with the role of savior. He practiced nurturing himself instead of automatically attending to the needs of other people.

Composting the thorniest weeds in their relationship—childhood conflicts and poor self-care, lack of empathy and simmering resentments—helped Marlene and Kenny's relationship thrive.

We can compost our relationships by becoming curious about knotty problems or conflicts instead of blaming our partners and trying to win. The emphasis in meditative therapy on cultivating heightened attention and focus and then translating the meaning of what we discover is indispensable. Before engaging in composting, each partner can engage in an awareness practice—from listening to favorite music to meditating or doing some yogic breathing—which will expand inner space and cultivate focus and equanimity.

Marlene and Kenny found a yoga practice that worked for them, especially when they were composting interpersonal conflict at home. The renowned twentieth-century yoga teacher Krishnamacharya taught: "Inhale, raise arms slowly overhead. Exhale, lower the arms with a hissing sound in the throat. The hands should touch your sides as you complete the exhalation." When we link movement with breath we expand inner—and interpersonal—space. Interpersonal space grows when each partner expands inner space; then partners are less defensive and more generous of spirit. Subsequent conversations will be infinitely more constructive, flexible, and creative. In other words, we can be more respectful and take our partners more seriously; we will also devise solutions that are innovative.

In the second stage of interpersonal composting we need to ask what an argument *means.* To do this both partners must be open to feedback. Kenny's hostile low blow, for example, was a sign that he was hurt and angry. Sometimes the meaning is more indirect. In such cases it can be clarifying to explore whether there is an advantage in the apparently negative or destructive behavior—what Freud called "the secondary gain," by which he meant the benefit from the ailment. Marlene's self-anesthetizing dulled her pain. Larry's feeling of being exploited allowed him to maintain a self-image of a superior person who was not being treated fairly.

It is vital that we approach what arises as having validity to our partner, even if we don't agree with or like it. Kenny "called in the troops" because he felt powerless about getting through to Marlene, who was not very empathic to his experience because she had shut down to protect herself from her own painful feelings. We need to discover the logic underneath what our partners and we say and feel. What was Kenny feeling underneath the surface of his hostile gesture of recruiting evidence for his viewpoint? Meditative focus on the texture of the emotion and psychotherapeutic emphasis on translating what it means are invaluable.

Then we should try to understand what we are unconsciously trying to accomplish. Monica's excessive spending was an attempt to feel less deprived; Kenny's savior role made him feel like a "good boy" who was worthy of being loved.

If we can't figure out what a feeling or interaction means, it is sometimes helpful, as I suggested in the last chapter, to switch roles and present our partner's point of view as sympathetically as is possible, staying alert to how his or her perspective makes sense and what it feels like. We can strive to understand our partner's point of view, including feelings and values, ideals and beliefs. This can cultivate seeing with opposite eyes, an insight from the Yoga Sutra I discussed in chapter 3. After doing this, we can share what we have learned and have the discussion again, trying not to trigger our partner, and incorporating our new understanding of our spouse into our own point of view. Clues that we are on the correct track are if we have learned something new, the discussion seems like a collaborative enterprise rather than an adversarial discussion, or we feel closer.

If the conflict is not resolved, be patient and try to not allow it to infiltrate and sabotage other areas of life. Still take that walk or go to the movies even when the conflict is not resolved. Agree to revisit the disagreement at another time. It is crucial that we not give up, and that we protect the rest of the relationship, a topic we'll discuss in detail in chapter 19, "Scorched-Earth Moments: Surviving Hateful Feelings."

Once we are clearer about what the conflict means, the next stage of composting—what to do about it—often arises spontaneously. Once Marlene understood her role in Kenny's resentment and her need to not be blindsided by him, she suggested a solution that was creative and mutually agreeable. If no solution emerges and we are not sure what to do, strategize with your partner about a new way to move through and beyond disagreements in a way that honors what each of you needs as well as both of your vulnerabilities. For example, Marlene committed to being more attuned to Kenny and asked him to refrain from shaming her.

While the relationship between Marlene and Kenny is not perfect, they are closer than ever before. They not only handle conflict more immediately and skillfully, they feel more intimacy and joy.

Interpersonal composting can be a powerful way to nourish the garden of love. Once we develop faith and trust in our collective capacity to compost weeds, our courage to face more insidious forces that undermine our relationships deepens. Challenges to our relationships are viewed as opportunities to remove obstacles leaching life from intimacy, rather than as roadblocks that must be avoided, and together we flourish.

14

"You can read minds?"

—Ben Stiller as Derek Zoolander

Leave the Mind Reading
to the Magicians

Learning to Ask for What You Need

Of all the living creatures on the planet Earth, human beings alone have the ability to speak, write, and think in rich and eloquent language. Yet when it comes to expressing our own needs—a central ingredient in healthy relationships—we often forget we have this power. Instead we rely on a riskier, unproven method of communicating with our nearest and dearest: we expect them to read our minds. This is a highly ineffective form of communication, a pernicious weed in relationships, and a sure recipe for disappointment, deprivation, and eventual bitterness.

An exploration of what mind reading is and why we expect our partners to do it can give us tremendous insights into how to resolve it.

Carol loved getting flowers. Every birthday, a bouquet, sometimes two, arrived from her mother and sisters. She often bought herself flowers. The delicate and fragrant blooms made her feel gracious and feminine. Her husband, Jim, a loving and supportive man, always noticed and admired the bouquets; but after twelve years of marriage, he had yet to buy her a single rose.

Carol did everything she could to let Jim know that she would like to get flowers from *him*. "Oh, aren't these flowers pretty? Jim, you have to smell these lilies. They make me feel so good. What a great present!" Carol believed she was being perfectly clear.

Jim never took the hint. Yet Carol kept hoping that somehow he could—and should—read her mind. When he didn't, she continued to believe, without any concrete evidence, that one day he magically would.

She was not only setting herself up for disappointment, but by waiting for Jim to divine her wishes Carol put herself into a position where she did not have to take seriously what she wanted and her expectations would never be met. She believed that asking for anything for herself was selfish and that other people should come first. Although Jim was a loving and attentive husband, Carol felt hurt that he simply did not see what was so obvious to her.

Expectations of mind reading also occur in the bedroom, where many people find it difficult to speak directly about what they desire. Bob was frustrated. He had been married to Wendy for five years. Although she had always been quiet and shy, Bob thought he should have broken through her reserve by now. He didn't understand why she sometimes moved away from his embraces or kept her emotional distance when they were making love. He didn't believe that she was having an affair, and he couldn't figure out what he had done to push her away. He asked her if anything was the matter and when she said there wasn't, he didn't quite believe her.

Wendy felt as if Bob didn't understand her needs. She wanted him to slow down and be romantic—touch her in a certain way, say how much he loved her. She wanted to feel connected and safe within his arms, but Wendy wasn't telling Bob any of these things. Instead, she thought that he should know what to do without her having to say it. After all, she had demonstrated that she could anticipate *his* needs and fulfill them. She believed that his failure to do the same for her communicated that he wasn't really trying.

This conviction also allowed Wendy to not risk burdening Bob with her needs, a habit she developed growing up with a depressed and vulnerable mother, who was constantly exhausted, overwhelmed, and incapable of being there for her three children.

Without feedback or direction from Wendy, Bob didn't know to change his attitude or rhythm. Instead, he felt rebuffed and thought Wendy was stalling because she didn't want him or she didn't like sex anymore.

Eventually Bob stopped trying to have sex with Wendy as often. She was hurt and felt he did not find her as attractive as he used to. There was a conspiracy of silence; neither Bob nor Wendy would actually bring up the topic with the other. Each of them thought this was what eventually happened in marriage, so they tried to remain cordial and act as if everything was fine.

Beyond the bedroom, there are many situations where couples confront the hope of being clairvoyantly understood. Cynthia, an executive coach and mother of two elementary-school-age boys, was disgruntled with her partner, Alan, a documentary filmmaker. Her dissatisfaction manifested as a lot of criticism and digs as well as a growing distrust. The source was not immediately clear. Cynthia felt overwhelmed by parenting and working. "There are not enough hours in the day to get everything done," she explained. Cynthia was constantly juggling multiple tasks and responsibilities—driving her sons to athletic events and music lessons, going food shopping, straightening the house and cooking—all while feeling dissatisfied with her efforts. Alan, who also worked very hard, balanced a high-pressure job with spending time with his active boys and paying the bills, babysitting, and doing his share of housework. He felt controlled and devalued by his wife of ten years. At the end of their first session with me Cynthia realized that underneath her impatience and huffiness she was "drowning" in her busy life and wished she had a "wife" at home. She recognized, with a lot of sadness, that she had been beating Alan up and nagging because she assumed he knew that she expected him to be an executive assistant, a wife who would feel responsible for and oversee running their lives. She was hurt that he had failed to fulfill the "contract that we never signed."

In therapy Cynthia realized that her mother had been highly devoted to her. Throughout her life, her mother focused more on her only daughter than on herself or her husband. Cynthia assumed that her husband would relate to her in a similar way. She also had no example of an adult who directly asked for what he or she needed.

The Psychology of Mind Reading

Why do we want other people to read our minds? Why don't we just speak up?

Because of the cultural taboo against selfishness that I discussed in chapter 8, many of us have a great deal of trouble thinking about—let alone asking for—what we need. Like Carol, we falsely equate focus on ourselves with pathological self-centeredness—so we embrace selfless-ness, something most spiritual traditions reward. Is it so surprising that after carefully practicing selfless thinking and behavior we find it difficult to know what we want or need and end up feeling deprived and uncared for?

Another reason people such as Wendy have great difficulty express-ing their wishes is because they fear burdening other people. They have learned that it is emotionally safer—although often more of a depri-vation—to push their needs away. They are afraid of how it will feel to ask for what they want, and silence becomes a protective mechanism against disappointment when their needs are not met. Because they may dread being dependent on other people and being let down, they become hyper-self-sufficient and try never to communicate any needs.

We usually come by our feelings of nonentitlement and fears of being rebuffed honestly. We learn very early on, and through subse-quent experience, that our needs are not acceptable to our caregivers. And we tragically mistranslate *their* self-centeredness, preoccupation, and misattunement as proof that we are not entitled to what we want, and that we are *bad* even for asking. We feel greedy and selfish and we learn to strive never to be humiliated again. We bury our needs. And we rely on unrealistic modes of communication such as mind reading so we don't have to ask for what we want and we can bypass potential vulnerability and disappointment.

And then there are those people such as Cynthia who never learned how to ask for anything because they never had parental role models— they never saw such behavior modeled when they were growing up and they have never tried it themselves. They expect that other people will be magically attuned to them as their mothers were. The psychoanalyst D. W. Winnicott argues in his seminal 1956 paper, "Primary Maternal Preoccupation," that mothers of infants are in a highly attuned, altered state of consciousness in which they can sense on a profound level subtleties of their babies' experience. Many mothers of infants intuit, for example, subtle shifts in breathing, smell, and mood. This highly responsive state is extremely functional; it helps mothers tune in to their infants' needs even though the infant doesn't have the capacity to put them into words. Mothers of infants must determine what is happening with their children without the infant's assistance—the child's survival depends on it.

In focusing on being responsive to a child's needs, parenting, like falling in love—the time when we are obsessed and utterly attuned to the object of our affection—sometimes has a side effect that few people consider. This depth of being attuned to trains certain people to expect their spouses to know what they need, without their having to ask for it. When one's partner fails, as will often happen, it is erroneously presumed that it's a sign of not caring. What it is, however, is proof of the problems that ensue when we expect the other to clairvoyantly know what we need.

The ability to read minds is often used as a loyalty test: *If you really love/value/care about me, you'll know what I need, even without me asking. If you don't know what I need—even when I don't tell you—then you don't really love me.* Trying to read another's mind is an impossible test. It not only leads to hurt, deprivation, and painful misunderstanding, it often triggers renewed expectations of superhuman understanding as well as ongoing "loyalty tests" and forms of passive-aggressive behavior that undermine and erode intimacy. Certain people may expect mind reading because they are setting their partner up to fail—looking for their spouse to be in the wrong. This can be motivated by all sorts of things, from trying to make them feel inadequate, to wanting to punish them, to trying to get their partner to reject them.

Bart and Serena were locked in a long-term power struggle. Each one had a great deal of difficulty asking for what he or she wanted and used mind reading as a viable communication tool. As each partner inevitably failed the other, they became more withholding and contemptuous, which poisoned the relationship. They were so hurt and angry by the time they sought therapy that they had already decided to get divorced. They were using therapy to build a case against each other instead of trying to improve their marriage.

Avoiding Mind Reading

There is a better way to get your needs met than by expressing them obliquely. The trick is to know what you need, and to feel entitled to it, state it in plain language that does not trigger or alienate your partner, and guide your partner toward being attuned to you. All of this requires self-awareness and emotional self-acceptance, compassionate communication, and empathy.

Psychoanalysis, Buddhism, and yoga can provide the necessary tools to facilitate doing this, as they each give us ways to cultivate the qualities we need to communicate in a more direct and healthy way. Expanding inner space, slowing down, detecting what we truly feel, composting challenging emotions, developing a sense of purpose, and living authentically are huge boons to getting in touch with and expressing our genuine needs and deepening empathy.

Psychoanalysis sheds light on some of the psychological reasons why people deprive and sabotage themselves. They maintain emotional allegiances to self-centered and unloving parents, attempt to do "penance" for imagined crimes, and reenact childhood scenarios of deprivation in an attempt to finally master them. More specifically, therapy helped Carol realize *why* she didn't feel entitled—she unconsciously blamed herself for her beloved mother's premature death when she was fourteen. In addition, it helped her recognize that putting herself last was a way of attempting to stay connected to her mother, a devout woman who valued "spiritual selflessness."

In our work together Carol learned to say to Jim: "I love flowers and I promise I will never refuse any that you bring me." And when Carol found it difficult to verbalize this, Jim was able to explain: "I can't read minds, Carol. I will inevitably fail in knowing what you want and need unless you actually tell me, and we'll both feel bad. It would be much easier for me and much better for you if you tried to let me know more directly what you want or need from me. I'd be happy to do what you ask of me." Therapy helped Jim realize that his failure to get flowers was unconsciously a way of paying Carol back for expecting that he read her mind in other areas. Once she validated how she made him feel inadequate, his generosity was no longer blocked and Carol was inundated with flowers.

Therapy also helped Wendy realize that her mom's struggles were not because Wendy was too demanding, and that Bob was not as fragile as her besieged mother. This enabled Wendy to learn to rely on Bob. She learned to say "Bob, I like sex, and I want to have it with you. Could we try a couple of things that would make it better for me?" Bob was very happy to accommodate Wendy, and she learned that it was less dangerous to plainly state what she wanted than to expect her partner to read her mind.

Cultivating Empathy

Wendy and Bob also needed to deepen their capacity for empathy. Empathy is not a fixed trait, but a quality that can be cultivated. In *Emotional Awareness,* a dialogue between the Dalai Lama and Paul Ekman, a world-renowned expert in the experimental study of emotions, Ekman suggests that empathy has several components, including emotional recognition, emotional resonance, and compassion.

I taught Bob an empathy-training exercise from another of Paul Ekman's books—*Emotions Revealed*—during which he visualized a time in his life when he experienced what Wendy told him she was going through. As Bob attempted to notice any feelings or images that arose, he realized that Wendy felt unwanted and uncared for, which helped him to be more responsive to Wendy's needs. Wendy's trust deepened and she was able to speak more directly about what she wanted.

Once Jim recognized Carol's disappointment and resonated with her subsequent pain, he felt compassion for her. He realized that he had buried resentment about her occasional snotty behavior. His resentment faded when he told her that she had hurt his feelings, and so did his withholding of affection. This led to breaking through his resistance to empathy.

Not only can your partner try to be more empathic, both spouses can be more attentive to signs of disappointment, which sometimes signal the unstated desire for mind reading.

Alan practiced Buddhist *metta* meditation, a practice focused on cultivating loving-kindness toward other people and oneself. The meditator wishes herself and other people well-being and freedom from suffering: "May all beings be free from enmity, affliction, and anxiety, and live happily," says the Buddhist Khuddaka Nikaya's Patisambhidam-agga. Next one sends loving-kindness to friends, a neutral person, and a difficult person. Eventually one wishes boundless happiness on all beings. Metta meditation can be used to calm a distressed mind and act as a potent antidote to anger. The continual practice of sending loving thoughts and feelings toward other people and oneself can soften rigidly held critical beliefs, as well as foster greater compassion and self-acceptance. Recent neurological studies by Dr. Richard Davidson and Antoine Lutz of the University of Wisconsin at Madison suggest that such a practice can increase one's capacity for empathy by altering activity in brain areas such as the cerebral cortex, as well as enhance a person's capacity to understand the emotional state of other people.

As a result of his meditation practice, Alan became more forgiving of and patient toward Cynthia. The practice of Zen meditation helped Cynthia to remain grounded in the present moment, to not rush ahead of herself, and to catch herself whenever she was expecting Alan to be as selflessly devoted as her mother. It enabled her to challenge familiar—and familial—experiences about automatic attunement and have more realistic expectations.

In addition to these meditative techniques, there are various yogic breathing practices that can help us to realize the expectation of mind-reading. Here is one that worked for Bob:

- Turn off your cellphone.
- Sit upright in a chair.
- Since you will be breathing through your nose, close your mouth.
- Breathe freely on the inhale as your stomach expands.
- Briefly hold the breath, and then let go of everything as you exhale.
- Pause.
- Begin again.
- Do this for several breaths.

You may notice that you both let go of whatever you were holding on to and clean the mental/emotional slate so that you can approach your partner in a fresh and open way.

Bob credited his yoga practice with helping him become attuned to his feelings—especially the times when he felt passion and then stifled it. This helped him speak more directly with Wendy about their sex life.

While it often feels very good to have someone anticipate our needs without us having to ask, *we should take those instances as the rare gifts they truly are.* In real life, the people who care about us often need us to tell them what we want. Leave mind reading to the magicians; simply asking for what you want and expanding your empathy for your partner is the best way to get it.

15

Let there be spaces in your togetherness.
—KAHLIL GIBRAN

A FENCE AROUND THE GARDEN OF LOVE

Setting Healthy Boundaries

A few years ago a close friend of mine, an avid gardener, became increasingly disenchanted with the herd of deer using her property as a feeding station and in the process destroying her beloved flowers. She bought Milorganite, an organic fertilizer that was supposed to repel deer, planted shrubs that deer are said to not touch (the experts were wrong), and finally "joined" the deer (an attempt at mental jujitsu) by feeding them. Nothing worked. So she put up a fence around her property. Her flower garden flourished.

Fences protect intimate relationships as well as gardens and neighbors.

Human beings are both remarkably receptive to the world—several of our senses open directly to the universe—and heavily fortified from it by protective physical boundaries—membranes and tissues of various degrees of thickness and permeability.

Boundaries are crucial to intimacy and flourishing, as well as survival. They protect us emotionally and physically by creating a sanctuary from external impingements, which fosters the development of inner space, and the quietude and privacy necessary to think and feel, both of which are foundations for couples creating romantic space. Without boundaries we are more vulnerable, like cells without membranes. And when we have protective borders and are comfortable establishing them when necessary, not only are we safer, we are even more receptive to other people and the world.

Because of the forces we've already explored that collapse inner space—from bombardment of information to cultural pollution—the individuals and couples I counsel are increasingly harried and reactive, demonstrating that healthy boundaries are more crucial than ever before.

Problems with boundaries are tenacious weeds in the garden of love. They manifest in many ways: an inability to set them at all; disrespect or disregard for our partner's boundaries; limits that are set too prematurely; and boundaries that are too rigid or unmovable. The absence of boundaries leaves us unprotected and deprived of the space we need to consider what we feel and need and to live authentically—a breeding ground for resentment. Ignoring or overriding someone else's boundaries can cause depletion and anger. Boundaries that are too hastily or rigidly built can cut us off from positive relationships and intimacy.

Yes People: The Absence of Boundaries

Los Angeles bank employee Carl Allen (played by Jim Carrey in *The Yes Man*) was depressed and withdrawn after his divorce. He spent his spare time watching movies alone in his apartment and wallowing in negativity. After reluctantly attending a motivational seminar, he vowed to stop being a "No Man" and made a covenant with himself to say "Yes!" to every situation regardless of how it felt.

Saying yes opened up new worlds—he learned Korean and the guitar, and was exposed to all sorts of new experiences. But it also left him without boundaries because he couldn't refuse any request no matter how he felt about it—from organizing his best friend's fiancée's bridal shower, to shutting down the bank branch where he worked, to moving in with a woman he had just met. There was no Carl Allen without boundaries—only a selfless granter of whatever request he encountered. If you cannot sometimes say no, your yeses have significantly less meaning.

A Kiss Is Not Just a Kiss:
Premature Boundaries

Deanna set premature boundaries with her husband, Harry. When I met them they had been married for five years and had an eight-month-old baby. They sat apart from each other on a long sofa in my office and were obviously tense. Deanna began speaking in a low voice. She was very tired and had not slept well the night before. She described Harry's unprovoked hostility, his coldness. She said the baby had been even more fretful than usual, and she attributed it to the tension between Harry and herself.

When Deanna finally stopped and looked down, Harry said, "I came home last night a little earlier than usual, and I was really happy to see you. You were standing at the counter and when I went to kiss you, you turned and gave me your cheek. You do that a lot. I'm tired of approaching you and getting a cold shoulder. I don't deserve it. I feel like I hardly know you anymore. I feel guilty, like I did something wrong . . . and I don't know what I did."

Harry was getting upset as he spoke. "I know she doesn't love me," he said with tears in his eyes. "When I come home from work at night, you don't even want to give me a kiss."

"We kiss," Deanna answered.

"No, you turn away and give me your cheek. You act like my sister."

"I don't know what you want from me."

"I just want a kiss, Deanna—a kiss between a husband and wife, on the lips."

"That's not all you want," she said.

"Is that a crime? Would you be happy if I wasn't interested in you that way?"

"No . . . it isn't because I don't love you. You aren't the problem."

"Of course I am," Harry said. "It's me you don't want to kiss."

"How do you feel when Harry walks in the door?" I asked Deanna.

"Excited to see him," she said. "I look forward to his coming home."

"And then what?"

"I just seem to shut down," she said. "He stands there and I think he wants something more from me and it feels like too much."

"How do you respond?" I asked.

"I avoid kissing him. And the tragedy is, he's a great kisser, which was one of the original turn-ons in our relationship."

Harry looked pleased. But the compliment was tempered by the sadness of remembering how distant he was from Deanna.

Before exploring how Deanna and Harry resolved their conflict over boundaries, consider Lily and Jim's quarrel at bedtime.

Not Being a Captive Audience

Lily and Jim, a couple in their late thirties, illustrated another problem with boundaries, namely disrespecting them. They came to therapy because of escalating tension. Lily felt that Jim had been distant and she was worried that they were growing apart. Jim was a hardworking executive with a lot of responsibilities and pressures. Lily worked part-time at the local public library and had a busy and full life, balancing her job with taking care of their three children.

"I feel abandoned by him," Lily said. "He is going to bed later and later, sometimes after I have fallen asleep. We have always been close. But now he's been dawdling in the bathroom, puttering around on the computer, and watching the late news, which he's never been really interested in. He seems to be avoiding me. He isn't getting enough sleep, and he's tired during the day and has circles under his eyes."

"Nighttime is a nightmare," Jim said. "What you call 'talking' is really just me being a sitting duck for your nonstop harangues, just when I want to relax at the end of the day. Your anxious monologues juice me up and keep me awake for hours."

"But there's never a good time to get into this stuff during the day," Lily said to Jim, "and I feel deeply frustrated that I can't talk to you about the things we need to talk about. You're supposed to be my partner and I can never talk to you about things that need to be addressed."

"How would you like it if, just as you were finally leaving the day behind to crawl between the cool sheets, you were assaulted and confronted by your spouse, who felt that it was a fine time to discuss family finances, new construction projects, in-laws' visits, or worse, core differences in parenting styles?" Jim asked wearily.

"But when are we going to talk about things?" Lily spoke plaintively. "The morning is a rush hour, and you don't want to talk when you get home. On the weekends you don't want to think about anything that you have to use your brain for. Bedtime is the only time you're available!"

"But I can't handle the heaviness before bed, honey," Jim said, more vulnerably. "I just want to go to sleep, maybe cuddle a little first, but nothing mentally heavy. I've been thinking and planning all day. I'm tired, unfocused, and I don't have good energy. I've started to dread the end of the day."

Before discussing how Lily and Jim solved their apparent impasse, consider Amanda and Ron, who had a different disagreement over boundaries.

"I Avoid You So I Don't Drown": Rigid Boundaries

The bane of Amanda and Ron's existence was not conflict over what happened in the bedroom but parents—specifically Amanda's mother, Rosalind, a cultured woman in her eighties who never met a person she didn't try to make feel guilty and responsible for her pervasive unhappiness. Rosalind nearly drove both Amanda and Ron out of their minds. What troubled Amanda most was Rosalind's refusal of all constructive assistance. It seemed to Amanda that when she offered her mother a banquet of opportunities, Rosalind acted as if the refrigerator was empty—as if she were a hostile teenager.

In our first session I learned that Amanda's mother moved in with them after Amanda's father, Rosalind's husband, died some years ago. Nothing was ever good enough for Rosalind, and Amanda was overwhelmed by her mother's self-centeredness and neediness. Amanda understood that her mother was depressed over losing her spouse of many years, but resented that her mother relentlessly pushed away all her efforts to support her feeling good about her life. In fact, Amanda began to realize that her mother unconsciously kept herself miserable in order to make everyone—especially her only child—feel responsible for her misery. Amanda and I eventually realized that Amanda stayed distant from her mother—setting a rigid boundary—to protect against "drowning." "Getting close to her means I disappear," she frequently said to me.

Healthy Boundaries

There is more to boundaries than spending quiet time alone by going for a walk or taking a bath or not answering a phone call when you are depleted or in the middle of a conversation with your partner or child. And there are many types of boundaries—from the freedom to pursue what is important to you regardless of societal or familial approval, to space from extended family.

In order to illuminate healthy boundaries let's return to Deanna and Harry: "Do you feel pressure from Harry when you turn your cheek away?" I asked Deanna.

"Yes!"

"What's the pressure?"

"Having to perform—having to be physical, no matter how I feel," she replied.

"Great," Harry said. "Just great. It's inspiring to know your wife is so excited about seeing you."

"Deanna's refusal of a kiss sounds like a form of self-protection," I said to Harry.

"Against what?" Harry asked.

"A kiss from her will not just be a kiss to you, Harry; and she is afraid you'll want more, which Deanna may not be able to give at that time."

Deanna was nodding. "I've been so tired. And when we get into bed, I really just need to sleep. If I say no to making love," she added, "I'll hurt your feelings, so I just don't even want to start. So I avoid you sexually."

"Don't *not* give him a kiss, if you really want to," I said to Deanna. Harry leaned forward, listening carefully, watching his wife's face. He looked victorious.

"And you," I said to Harry, "don't go any further than a kiss, unless

Deanna gives you a go-ahead signal. If Deanna knows that you are satisfied with a kiss, she can be in charge. Then she can express the physical affection she actually feels toward you without withdrawing. Until Deanna tells you differently, Harry, a kiss is just a kiss. And maybe you can work on getting some time away together, even an afternoon, when you can get a sitter and take a break from the baby and get to know each other again."

Deanna moved closer to Harry and grabbed his hand and they both smiled. "Is this permission to go ahead?" Harry asked. Deanna kissed him flirtatiously . . . on the lips. We all laughed.

Deanna and Harry's story illustrates a universal human tendency: in trying to cure or avoid one problem, she actually created a worse one. Her pleasure in kissing her husband got sabotaged by her fear of where it would lead.

When I recognized that *not* kissing Harry was a *misguided cure and a premature boundary*—the right impulse but the wrong solution—I helped Deanna and Harry devise a resolution that respected their needs for closeness and space without generating another problem that hurt and deprived each of them.

The next week I learned that Deanna no longer turned her cheek, and Harry didn't ask for more.

Lily and Jim were also able to skillfully and quickly resolve their dispute when we understood the fear that Lily's boundary crossing with her husband was attempting to manage.

Lily had a constructive urge—to connect with her husband—but the incorrect approach. She confronted him when he was relatively defenseless.

"You need to respect Jim's boundary at night before he goes to sleep and pick better times to talk," I said. "There's a great temptation to discuss all your concerns and unfinished business as you're going to bed, because you finally have a captive audience, but it's not a good time for Jim. And it's not good for you either, because he's still not hearing you if he's tired and resentful."

Jim looked relieved, but Lily seemed frustrated.

"Jim, for Lily to back off and respect your need for quiet time before bed, you have to show her good faith. Prove to her that you will take her concerns more seriously at another time, so she doesn't feel that bed-time is the only time she'll get your attention."

Jim also had the correct impulse—to protect his sleep—but the wrong response. He avoided Lily—and getting the sleep he needed—in order to thwart her and protect himself.

Amanda fell into a similar trap. She gradually learned how to be con-nected to her mother—which made Rosalind feel less desperate and alone—without feeling responsible for her happiness.

"I think you may keep your mother at a distance so you don't lose yourself," I said. "The dilemma is: either you try to connect with her and feel smothered and threatened, or you hold back and she feels abandoned."

"You mean there's another option?"

"What if you connected without trying to get through to her or change her?" I suggested. "You can be close to Mom, be there for her, without trying to get rid of her unhappiness or stop her from being negativistic."

"That feels right, but how do I do it?" Amanda asked.

"Well, first you have to accept that when you offer advice, it's just an *offering* and you can't be attached to whether or not she takes it. Your job is to offer it. Hers is to make the decision. You can also say to her, 'We have a dilemma: if I try to connect with you, you either push me away or drown me and if I remain distant you feel more lonely and bereft. What do you think we should do?'"

"I think saying that will definitely help," said Amanda, "because it respects my boundaries, and it gives her a choice. But I have to be will-ing to accept whatever she says."

Amanda came in two weeks later to report that her mother was okay and they had had a lovely discussion. "I didn't feel responsible for mak-ing her happy or getting through to her and purposely stayed within range yet protected. It still doesn't feel easy, but I'm getting the hang of it. I have to let her know I'm there while protecting my space."

Amanda's attempt to protect herself from her perceived loss of free-dom and self-sufficiency caused her to close herself off from someone she loved at a critical time in both of their lives.

Healthy Interpersonal Negotiation

Deanna, Jim, and Amanda each had the *right impulse,* but the *wrong solution,* which created unnecessary problems in their lives. In their efforts to guard themselves in emotionally difficult situations, they set boundaries in indirect and inappropriate places. Good boundaries can protect us; bad ones can constrict us. Once we have better boundaries, we can actually be more open to ourselves and other people. Once Deanna could regulate her physical intimacy with Harry, she was more able to be close and affectionate with him, without feeling so vulnerable. Jim stopped avoiding Lily in the evenings once he knew that Lily respected his need for peace and sleep. And Amanda spent more quality time with her mother.

For Deanna, Jim, and Amanda to set better boundaries, they each had to learn how to handle conflict constructively by engaging in *healthy interpersonal negotiation.*

There are four stages to this process:

1. Figure out the true nature of the conflict.
2. Express needs clearly and directly, without blame or rancor.
3. Understand the validity of each person's feelings and needs.
4. Work cooperatively to find a creative solution to the dilemma.

The first step is figuring out the true nature of the conflict underneath the mutually reinforcing and escalating cycle of fear and withdrawal, hurt and hostility. Ordinarily the negative interaction happens so quickly that it is difficult to determine who is doing what to whom. Deanna's dread of sexual pressure from Harry operated so automatically that she instantaneously withdrew from the physical affection that she actually enjoyed. Harry's hurt from being rebuffed by Deanna happened so rapidly that he attacked her without recognizing that he felt rejected and deprived.

Psychotherapy, meditation, and yoga are immensely helpful in opening up inner space, slowing down our reactions, and creating an opportunity to get in touch with, reflect upon, and sometimes compost our feelings. They also increase our capacity for empathy, as I've suggested earlier, as well as making wise decisions.

Each person has to figure out what they feel and need and how they react to their partner. This is where one needs to practice emotional composting. Opening to the conflict and our feelings about it, translating what they mean, and deciding what to do is invaluable in handling the barriers to communication. Lily had to recognize that she pressured Jim to talk at bedtime because she needed quality time to connect and feared he would never discuss important matters with her at any other time. Jim needed to realize that he was avoiding Lily at bedtime so he could have a peaceful sleep. And Amanda had to recognize that she avoided her mother to protect herself.

Many people think they are only entitled to their feelings when they are in crisis mode, such as during a physical illness or an emotional meltdown. Only then does it feel acceptable to take oneself seriously. Working on self-care—discovering and taking seriously what inspires us, living our purpose and values—helps us cherish and take care of ourselves. Jim didn't have to wait until he became sick or exhausted from lack of sleep to speak to Lily about her timing. Harry didn't have to be on the verge of divorcing Deanna out of sexual frustration to discuss his wish to be closer to her. And Amanda could speak honestly to her mother instead of precipitously withdrawing from her.

Our feelings are not facts, as I suggested in chapter 5. They are sometimes skewed by earlier experiences, and often distort our judgment and decisions. But they are an important part of our reality and must be taken seriously—at least as a starting point for our experience. Neither you nor the person you're in conflict with is inherently wrong for feeling the way you do, and each individual must reflect on the validity of his or her feelings to determine if they are a window into what is truly occurring rather than an absolute authority. Deanna didn't have to feel in the mood the moment Harry walked in the door. And Harry wasn't bad because he wanted to be physically intimate with his wife when he first saw her after a long day at work. When each person pays attention to self-care, listens empathically, expands inner and interpersonal space, and composts conflicts, relationships become a place in which each partner's day-to-day reality can be respected and taken more seriously.

We must express our needs clearly and directly, without blame or rancor. This is the second step of interpersonal negotiation. Amanda said to Rosalind, "I want to be closer to you," not, "You are a cold fish."

Once we share our feelings, it is essential that we understand—and take seriously—our partner's feelings. There is a danger in assuming that our needs are superior. Understanding the validity of each person's feelings and needs is the third step of the process. Continual practice of empathic listening greatly aids us. Rosalind recognized that while she wanted to be closer to Amanda, connectedness for her daughter raised the specter of feeling suffocated and losing herself. Harry had to respect that although he wanted more physical intimacy with Deanna, she could only get so close to him when she was tired and cranky. None of these people were inherently wrong for feeling the way they did.

Taking another person's feelings seriously does not mean that we always agree with or automatically accommodate them, but rather that we respect and understand their perspective. This may take time, patience, and flexibility. Listening compassionately—trying to empathize rather than trying to win—will make your partner feel heard and encourage him or her, in turn, to listen compassionately to you.

Once each person understands the other's feelings, it is time to revisit the original conflict. For change to happen, both partners need to work cooperatively to find a creative solution to the dilemma—one that not only respects the feelings of each person but that is mutually satisfying. Our attitude should be: here's what I need, tell me what you need, and let's figure out how we can both feel respected and nurtured without either of us stepping over the other person's boundaries or disrespecting the other's wishes and feelings. Deanna and Harry could have more physical intimacy, but only when they were both relaxed and willing. Jim could agree to talk more with Lily, but not while they were winding down for the evening in bed. Amanda could reach out to her mother, but only if she respected her daughter.

Couples who find mutually gratifying solutions to their conflicts—instead of patchwork ones that create additional problems in their wake—discover possibilities for intimacy and closeness that they never imagined, and free up hidden reservoirs of energy that enable them to live with greater creativity and passion, and to flourish.

16

> **You must attain liberation without avoiding the passions that rule the world.**
>
> —VIMALAKIRTI   ·

THE YOGA OF SEXUALITY

Reinvigorating Passion

On the train several years ago during my morning commute, I ran into a former high school classmate. Larry had been a senior when I was a freshman, but we knew each other from the track team, where he was a shot-putter. He was still warm and gregarious, and we launched into an animated conversation on the ride into New York City. I was interested to learn of his huge successes in the advertising industry; he was intrigued by my studies of Eastern thought and the book I was writing. We both lost track of time and enjoyed reconnecting.

At the end of our trip as we walked into the main concourse of Grand Central Station he asked, "What's the title of the book you're working on?"

"*The Good Life*," I replied.

Larry shook his head like a CEO nixing a foolish idea. "The title of your book should be *How Yoga Helps Your Sex Life*."

"But that's not the point of it."

"It doesn't matter. By the time they've bought the book it's too late for them to know."

While yoga can help your sex life—the practice of asanas and yogic breathing cultivate heightened awareness and physical flexibility, strength and vitality—couples that are passionate about each other don't need gimmicks. When idealization and sexual ardor predominate in the romantic phase of a relationship, passion is like an emotional credit card with no limit and instant access. Sex does not take any effort when romance is in full bloom. It's the first step in a relationship before familiarity, comfort, and complacency can settle in.

What most couples experience is that passion fades over time. Fatigue and habit, neglected conflict, and buried deprivations sabotage even the most fervid romances. Home life can begin to feel routine, stifling, or worse, like prison. Domesticity and parenthood often deflate eroticism. Sensuality becomes suffocated under dirty laundry, endless errands, and sharing war stories about work. Can a working mom who each morning packs lunchboxes while simultaneously doing a load of laundry and checking homework and email be a vixen at night? Can a husband who admits fears about losing his job still turn his wife on?

Not if she feels, as many women do, that a sexy man is one who is master of his universe and impervious to fears and self-doubts. Numerous men complain that women say that they want their partners to be open yet invulnerable, in touch with their feelings but not emotionally weak. But when men discard the emotional armor they have often been raised to employ, in the face of certain difficult life situations they will experience a fuller range of feelings, including ones that women have to learn to accept without devaluing—emotions such as self-doubt, fear, and sorrow.

Although emotional intimacy is a foundation of physical intimacy, in some cases it can inhibit erotic desire. In his essay "On the Universal Tendency to Debasement in the Sphere of Love," Freud noted the pervasive difficulty most people have integrating "affectionate" and "sensual" feelings. Such people, according to Freud, rarely experience physical passion with those individuals they feel the most emotional tenderness toward.

In previous chapters we've seen how certain weeds—from lack of empathy and hidden resentments to poor self-care and premature or nonexistent boundaries—erode passion, but there are several other obstacles in the garden of love: information overload, fatigue, betrayal, and severed trust. Principles and practices of meditative psychotherapy—cultivating heightened attentiveness and decoding meaning—are powerful tools that we can use to reinvigorate passion, a central—although not sole—ingredient of a loving relationship.

Too Much Information

"TMI!" a teenager yelled out several years ago in a therapy session when her parents alluded that their relationship was not simply platonic. Everyone burst out laughing. But too much information—and the unending pressure to keep up and stay connected via email and texts—is exhausting couples and disrupting their sex lives. There is a decline in Eros, notes Esther Perel, couples therapist and author of *Mating in Captivity: Reconciling the Erotic and the Domestic*. We are "too busy, too stressed, too involved in child-rearing, and too tired. . . ."

When we are desperately struggling not to drown amid the minutiae of the daily grind, exhausted and depleted, we do not have fallow time to recharge, and this basic need leaves us seeking disconnection. We zone out on TV or mindless Web surfing, which leads to isolation, not to intimacy. How often have you fantasized early in the day about having a romantic evening, only to get home and want to veg out, too tired for anything except solitude, television, and comfort food? Such "cotton-candy" efforts at self-care leave us starved for vital emotional nutrients and devoid of nourishing intimacy.

Communing with another person in real-life intimacy can often be just too much work at the end of an exhausting day. We'd rather be alone, or with virtual reality, because we are depleted and feel that we don't have anything left to give. This behavior is a pale substitute for being emotionally or physically intimate with another human being. Each day blends into the next, more and more time passes between sexual encounters, and while we are affectionate toward each other, passion and good sex become less frequent.

As with self-care, *couples-care* requires that we build in what nurtures us—and guard not just our own inner space but the interpersonal space of our relationships as well. Closed inner or interpersonal space is a mood-killer. Passion needs a protected environment—and the safety, security, and time—to grow and flourish.

In chapters 1 and 2 we explored various ways to protect and expand inner spaciousness—techniques ranging from yoga and meditation to listening to favorite music and appreciating beauty. Couples can also work on removing the emotional obstacles between them. While we often attribute our difficulties to being tired and overwhelmed, there are sometimes deeper causes including buried resentment and simmering antagonisms. We need to practice empathic listening and emotional composting as regular disciplines so when we face challenges in our relationships—hurt and anger, resentment and jealousy—we will be able to use these tools to deepen emotional intimacy. They provide feedback that feelings need to be explored and understood. When we fail to empathize with our partner's experiences and to compost what emotionally stands between us, we shrink and sometimes eradicate both inner and interpersonal space. Empathy and composting can also help us handle the burdens that most couples confront, including a new baby, illness, financial struggles, and conflicting schedules.

> *I love mistrustfully.*
>
> —ADAM ZAGAJEWSKI

Trust and safety are hugely important in expanding interpersonal space, and both are threatened by buried conflict—something we've already explored in earlier chapters—as well as by betrayals, including, but not limited to, affairs.

When I met Nick he was devastated—and gun-shy—after finding out about his wife, Caroline's brief affair. At first he had been hurt and enraged, but gradually, as Caroline empathized with his humiliation, his self-protective distance lessened and he came back to the "land of the living."

Eventually Nick and Caroline explored the context leading up to the betrayal. While she loved being a mom, she wondered if there wasn't more to life than taking children to the dentist, endlessly cooking meals, and listening to other parents swap stories at soccer games about topics that rarely inspired her. She felt deadened, which she linked to being stuck in a life that she never expected when she was an academically ambitious undergraduate at an Ivy League university. Her deadness caused Nick to feel rejected and he shut down to protect himself, which made Caroline feel abandoned in her terrifying numbness. Nick learned that Caroline felt so lifeless that she was willing to risk everything for a few exciting moments of pleasure.

Caroline and Nick both wanted to try to salvage their marriage. After many months of individual therapy they began to trust each other again, but there was still little passion between them.

"How do I turn up the heat?" Nick asked me.

I remained silent, not sure where he was going.

"Caroline is warmer now," Nick continued. "Not only that, she recovers more quickly when she is upset. But there is still no physical intimacy. I'm not sure if she is interested. And we don't even talk about it. Is there a necessary stage in regaining passion and getting closer—enjoying each other, having fun, that might be needed?" he asked. "I have this nagging feeling that I have to do more—turn up the heat in the kitchen. I think I need to tell her what I want."

"And how do you imagine she'll react?"

"She'll get defensive and withdraw."

Nick and Caroline had struggled for emotional intimacy in the preceding months with no sexual contact, but over the past few weeks Nick had been reporting that he and his wife were finally connecting more deeply and consistently emotionally. He now wanted to approach her and perhaps break the ice. But how?

Nick struggled with passivity, and had tended for many years to observe life from a distance, to be a spectator. We both felt he "lost points" with Caroline because of this.

Assistance came from an unexpected source—yoga, the heart of which is the exploration and transformation of the mind, which aided him in rebuilding shattered trust.

There are 195 sutras, or short, terse passages in the Yoga Sutra—the foundational text of yoga compiled about 200 B.C.E. These range from ethical teachings to descriptions of meditative states of consciousness. Even though they contain several equally important components—personal and social ethics, physical postures, regulated breathing, controlled use of the senses, and meditation—the predominant emphasis in most yoga classes in the United States is physical flexibility and dexterity, the asanas. The other elements of yoga tend to receive much less attention. And yet, only three sutras are about asanas. The Yoga Sutra is primarily focused on mental transformation. A core teaching is that yoga is a state of mind—not an activity. According to sutra 1:2: "Sustained and total attention in a direction of our choosing" is the essence of yoga. We are experiencing yoga when we are fully and wholeheartedly immersed in an activity that we have chosen—playing with our child, listening to our spouse, or making love.

As Nick described his wish, and fear, of approaching Caroline, one of the three yoga sutras (2:46) having to do with asanas came to my mind: *"Sthira sukham asanam,"* which means, "alertness and ease makes an asana." If there is focus yet struggle it's not an asana. If there is comfort but distraction that is not an asana. When *sthira* and *sukham* are in balance there is "alertness without tension and relaxation without dullness or heaviness," writes T. K. V. Desikachar in *Reflections on the Yoga Sutras*.

Nick was a student of yoga so I sensed he'd understand. "It's only an asana when there is both attention and ease," I said. "What if you approached Caroline sexually with alertness and ease?" I asked. "Focus will reveal how to approach her safely, which will make both your vulnerabilities and hers easier to handle. And ease will give each of you veto power and a sense of control. That will make it safer to grow reacclimated to each other and play, risk, and explore."

Weeks later, after approaching Caroline "yogically," Nick sounded like an advertisement for my friend Larry's book title. "Yoga has put the X in my sex life," Nick reported.

Unlike Caroline and Nick, the erotic spark in Amanda and Jerry's marriage had been dulled from a betrayal in the past that was not of their making, but they had to resolve it, nevertheless, for intimacy to flourish. From the outside they had what looked like a perfect marriage. They were kind and supportive toward each other, shared similar values and compatible neuroses, had fun, and were raising two contented and self-confident teenage daughters.

But there was an absence of passion, which had slowly diminished over the twenty years of their marriage. There were a variety of reasons—from making their children the center of their lives to not building in enough timeless time and not taking care of themselves physically. Amanda complained of a lack of intimacy with Jerry, which he at first ignored because he felt that she pushed *him* away. While she knew he loved her, he was not very demonstrative and spent a lot of time doing solitary activities such as fly-fishing and stamp collecting. But as he heard her desperation at home, Jerry felt bad that he had hurt his wife and damaged the relationship. As he made a concerted effort to connect with Amanda and be more affectionate—telling her he loved her, holding and hugging her—she pulled away. The more loving he became, the quicker she withdrew.

As Amanda composed her withdrawal by reflecting on what it meant that she rebuffed Jerry's advances, she remembered something she overheard her mother yell at her father when she was a child: that he neglected his family and was nice only when he wanted sex from his wife. Amanda linked lust with betrayal, felt a loyalty toward her deprived mother, and rebuffed Jerry's advances. As Amanda realized how she had traded passion for security and had been "erecting road-blocks that interfered with erections," she began seeing Jerry with more amorous eyes. Not only did her affection for him deepen, it ignited passion that had been absent for many years.

The Mind Betraying the Body

Some couples are betrayed from within themselves. This can lead to dating—or even marrying—someone we are mismatched with, or unconsciously or willingly sabotaging ourselves in intimate relationships. There are couples that get married even though only one of them wants to.

Mike felt betrayed, not by his wife, Edie, who did not have an affair, and in fact loved him deeply and passionately, but by his own body. While he still felt genuine affection for his wife, he was consistently impotent. After medical tests came back negative and we determined that he loved Edie without ambivalence, we realized that he was being betrayed by his mind.

The culprit? Excessive self-consciousness. Mike looked at himself as if through a microscope—every flaw was magnified. He found the ways he thought and spoke, looked and acted all loathsome in the skewed light of his all-condemning gaze. It was not surprising that Mike had a great deal of trouble immersing himself in anything he did, since he consistently observed himself with a critical and condemning eye. His nitpicking made him feel demoralized and unhappy. And as anyone who has ever felt uncomfortable about how he or she looks or feels knows, nothing is a greater saboteur of passion and eroticism than self-consciousness. When we watch ourselves perform, we not only create a divided self—a judging spectator and a condemned performer—but we observe the performance instead of being immersed in it. "I can't think and hit at the same time," Yogi Berra famously said. Neither can we be passionate or erotic when we are self-conscious or judging ourselves.

Mike remedied his affliction by practicing yoga. He found that beginning his day paying attention to his breath and body as he gently stretched taught him how to more fully engage whatever he was doing without judging his performance. Over time this capacity transferred into his sexual relationship with Edie. She remarked several months later that he seemed more fully engaged, physically relaxed, and without an agenda when they made out and made love. They both agreed that the absence of pressure and the greater presence of playfulness added spice to their love life.

The Yoga of Sexuality

Change base lust into refined love and
it is worth more than a mountain of gold.

—Ikkyū

The foundation of the yoga of sexuality is the state of being fully and wholeheartedly immersed in and unself-conscious about the dance of intimacy. We dance best when we are not concentrating on the steps. Both partners have receptive minds and bodies when there is nothing else but the unself-conscious movement of their erotic encounter. They don't rate their own or their partner's performances or wonder if they are inadequate. Both people are unhurried, not focused on getting anywhere. The physical intimacy is playful and directionless, unpredictable and at times thrilling. Because there is no agenda, there are greater possibilities for exploration and adventure. Since neither partner quite knows what might happen, the erotic encounter can be more liberating and exciting.

One of the saddest consequences of Hollywood portrayals of intimacy is that they give us distorted images of and expectations for relationships. When all of the movies about relationships focus on exhilarating romances and passionate trysts between people with perfect bodies, as if that were the totality of relationships, we can be severely disillusioned when our own relationships contain disappointment and disillusionment. When the honeymoon phase ends in real life some people assume that it's a death knell. Movies gloss over the truth that our relationships begin where most films about relationships end. Perhaps if more people realized that marriage is a *starting point,* not a finish line, we'd make more of an effort to take care of ourselves and commit to exciting and wooing our partners. Divorce lawyers would earn significantly less. Too many people are lost in an unconscious hunt-and-chase game, in which playing hard-to-get raises their perceived worth, and being available devalues it, as Joel Kramer and Diana Alstad note in "Transforming Sexuality: Changing the Context of Conquest." Conquering the person we are hunting or chasing becomes more important than making the relationship work.

Once a couple is invested in their relationship, it is easier to interest them in nurturing and protecting erotic space. Aware of the way security and familiarity seem to breed lack of sensuality, many self-help books stress mystery and tension to enrich erotic intensity. What I have observed clinically is how often emotional intimacy, especially sharing one's deepest hopes and dreams, which can only occur when there is safety and trust, is a powerful aphrodisiac. As Caroline shed her feeling of deadness, she became more alert to what inspired her. When she started to grow more passionate about her life and shared this passion with Nick, their physical intimacy deepened dramatically.

Expanding Erotic Space

Yoga and meditation can help us expand erotic space by teaching ways to engage the world with fewer expectations and agendas. This eliminates clutter from our minds and leaves more room to access imagination and fantasy. It also helps us to be engaged in intimate encounters without rushing or losing focus.

Since domesticity and work erode passion, many couples find it crucial to step outside the domestic role of caretaker, breadwinner, and protector, and change channels by engaging in or discussing a mutual passion. The purpose is to create safe zones, to cordon off erotic encounters from parenting, work, and domestic concerns. That makes it easier to access erotic space and connect with and expand our imaginations. While erotic intensity can be difficult to sustain, building in opportunities for sexual ardor to emerge on a regular basis, as well as leaving room for spontaneous encounters, helps a couple keep passion alive over time.

In chapter 9 we explored the ways our lives are greatly enriched when we can play a variety of instruments of our being—including nurturing our talents and following our inspiration, cultivating our skills and living our values—in harmony. Another crucial aspect of expanding erotic space is practicing the symphony of our emotional and sexual selves by integrating instruments of our being that are normally segregated, such as passion and friendship, aggression and empathy. We need to play several key "instruments"—including creating emotional stability and erotic intensity, as well as meeting and eliciting the desire of our partners without forgetting our own. Because of the cultural admonitions and prohibitions that we discussed earlier involving selflessness and self-sacrifice, many people—especially women but also men—stifle their aggression and neglect self-care. The challenge in erotic encounters is to play the two seemingly discordant instruments we have explored throughout this book, namely altruism and self-care. Too much focus on yourself may feel depriving and frustrating to your partner. Too much attention on the other person may inhibit your own self-assertion and pleasure.

Mike's self-consciousness extended to how his wife was feeling while they made love. On the one hand, his sensitivity enriched her experience; but it also inhibited him, leaving him feeling cheated and resentful. As he became less self-conscious and self-critical, he found it easier—and immensely enjoyable—to shift back and forth between focusing on Caroline's fulfillment and his own. The erotic intensity and ecstasy increased for both of them.

When a couple expands erotic space within and between them, becomes one with the dance of eroticism, and harmonizes altruism and self-care, their garden of love flourishes.

But as we'll see, honeymoons never last forever. Conflicts over power and control challenge even the happiest union.

No matter how extraordinary any single experience
may be, there's always the morning after—after
mystical experiences, after making love . . .

—JAMES OGILVY

. . . the homicidal bitchin' that goes down in
every kitchen.

—LEONARD COHEN

AFTER THE BLISS, THE DISHES (AND ONLY I KNOW HOW TO LOAD THEM)

Negotiating Power and Control

You feel radiant, transported to another realm. All that exists after making love with your partner is the transcendent glow of her presence. You are happy to be alive.

You walk into the kitchen, wanting to be helpful, and load the dishwasher. Several minutes later, your wife comes in, opens the dishwasher to include one last fork, and proceeds to restack everything you put in. Then she turns to you and says, for the umpteenth time, "There is a better way to do this." You are annoyed. You were her hero a short time ago; now you have been reduced to the status of a not-too-bright loser. Your reaction is out of proportion, and you're hurt that she is no longer feeling loving and sweet and has destroyed your ecstasy by being irritated and dismissive—only she seems to know The Right Way to Do Things. You bark something snarky, which shocks her, and causes her to counterattack. Suddenly you are in the midst of a full-blown argument, and the closeness you've just shared evaporates.

Or . . . you say nothing about her holier-than-thou stance and silently decide to avoid household chores, permanently. But down the road, your wife is annoyed that you do so little to share the domestic burden, even the tasks you used to do willingly, and more regularly. She's also offended.

After making love, she feels touched by her husband's sweetness and tenderness and unusually close to him. But when she sees him cramming plates into the dishwasher her postcoital bliss is immediately dissipated, burned off by annoyance. All she can think is: "Why doesn't he get it? I've told him a million times! If he just stacks them haphazardly they won't fit and certainly won't get clean. And I'll have to do two loads—useless work that I don't have time for. If he doesn't remember, he doesn't respect me!"

And so blooms another potentially noxious weed in the garden of love: *power.* "When one speaks of power," noted the French philosopher Michel Foucault, "people immediately think of a political structure, a government, a dominant social class, the master and the slave." But power—the ability to wield control over a situation or get what one wants by exerting influence over another person's values, feelings, or actions—is present in intimate relationships and friendships, as well as in families and parent-child interactions.

Power lunches. Power walks. Power drinks. Power naps. Power is everywhere. Power shapes human relationships and has been studied and illuminated by political theorists and feminists, family therapists and sociologists, but its place in intimate relationships remains a neglected topic that is incompletely understood—especially by couples.

In our world, power, which is expressed directly through physical domination or bullying, indirectly through emotional manipulation or withholding, is often a dirty word. It tends to be either hungered for and abused—think of politicians, CEOs, and gurus run amok—or rightfully viewed with cynicism and mistrust. Power is often used to coerce, dominate, and oppress, as in the sickening cases of rape, sexual trafficking, and child pornography. Power wielded without compassion and purpose results in recklessness and exploitation. It can send a destructive message in an intimate relationship: *My needs are greater, and more important, than yours.* Because the exercise of power usually leads to a disabling inequality, it can be a huge barrier to intimacy.

Power operates in all relationships. It can't be eliminated, but it doesn't have to have harmful consequences. The wish to control is natural, inevitable, and evolutionarily necessary. Our survival has been based in part on getting what we need from the environment, from basic resources to complex emotional nourishment, including being seen and valued by other people.

It is important to note that depending on how consciously power is employed and toward what ends, it can have a constructive or destructive role in a relationship. Wielding power unmindfully—for example, excessively trying to control or harm your partner—sets the stage for masochistic surrender, resentful conformity, or hostile rebellion. The intelligent and responsible use of power, on the other hand, can be an antidote to drifting or staleness; moving a relationship out of enervating patterns and ruts; opening up new worlds and experiences. When used with awareness, power—what we might think of as *constructive influence*—can be a spur to action leading relationships in healthy and novel directions.

We live in historically unprecedented times in which questions of power and decision making are treated in a more egalitarian manner yet more confusing than ever before. Before the 1960s, marriage was a largely contractual arrangement composed of set roles and rules, unequal distribution of power favoring men's needs, and idealistic vows. The social ferment of that tumultuous and transformative time—the women's and human potential movements, the struggle for civil rights, and the sexual revolution—created a counterreaction against restrictive traditional roles and the lack of power of women. Increasing numbers of women and men are now questioning and challenging inherited conceptions of power and control in intimate relationships. Not only do women feel less locked into unhappy marriages, but male privilege and power inequalities are increasingly viewed as socially constructed and unjustified. The numbers of women who are seeking an equitable role in shaping values and decisions in their primary relationships—thereby exerting power constructively—continue to grow.

The sharing of work, child rearing, and running the home has made marriages more equitable, often brought greater emotional intimacy and fulfillment, *and* made questions about power and responsibility in relationships infinitely more important and complicated. Who attends to your infant in the middle of the night when both parents have crucial meetings the next morning and are exhausted? Who shops for essentials on the weekends when the husband wants to recharge his batteries and loaf, and the wife has a list and also needs to recover from a brutal week at work herself? Can veto power over sex be overturned? It's not always clear how to weigh competing needs and demands in an increasingly complex and frantically fast-paced world.

In order to use power wisely we need to reckon with its shadow side, namely *forms of domination,* which are a key aspect of its misuse.

Forms of Domination

"[T]he legal subordination of one sex to another—is wrong in itself, and now one of the chief hindrances to human improvement . . . it ought to be replaced by a principle of perfect equality, admitting no power or privilege on the one side, nor disability on the other."

—JOHN STUART MILL

Jim dominated Carol. Even his friends were uneasy about the way he demeaned and controlled her. He constantly judged and corrected her, treating her as if she was a misguided child. Carol felt sad, but oddly comfortable in the role she had been assigned. A lawyer and a competent mom, Carol grew up with an autocratic father who dominated her mother, a skilled social worker. In the face of Jim's emotional abuse Carol shut down and said nothing, but she seemed crushed. And powerless.

After a while, Jim's more discerning friends noticed that he was changing in ways that diminished him as a person. He was more rigid and impatient, closed to feedback, and increasingly isolated from other people.

After two years of marriage Carol couldn't take it any longer, contacted a lawyer, and initiated a divorce. Jim was shocked and lost; he could not imagine living without his wife.

Leslie and Roger, who loved each other and were very supportive of each other's careers, were also locked in a power struggle. While she reported that he was the one in the driver's seat in the relationship, he felt powerless to stop her from doing things that were eroding his trust in her and sabotaging the marriage.

Leslie regularly spoke to Roger in a stern and disrespectful tone of voice with little awareness of how impatient she sounded. He felt demeaned and shamed. When he tried to tell her, she laughed it off saying he was too sensitive or she was just kidding. She also failed to take care of herself—a continuing source of frustration and resentment for Roger—and created huge clutter in their home. No matter what Roger said about how disturbed he felt about her lack of self-care or the shambles in the house, Leslie didn't change. Not only was Roger losing hope that she'd ever take his concerns seriously, but he was withdrawing from the relationship.

There was a pattern here: when Roger was growing up, nobody in his family took him seriously or struggled to get to know who he was. He felt invisible with his wife in the same way he had with his parents and sister.

Most children learn the dynamics of power and control from their parents. While "the family, justly constituted, would be the real school of the virtues of freedom," as John Stuart Mill wrote in *The Subjection of Women,* it is often the place where we are taught subtle and overt lessons about power and control. Children are small, innocent, vulnerable creatures in a big, confusing, and scary world. They witness parents, siblings, and teachers dominating or submitting to those in power. They observe—or are the victims of—adults or peers who sometimes undermine those with more power by passive-aggressive or obstructionist behavior. Children demand and are thwarted, they bargain and resist, and sometimes manipulate or surrender. They learn to withhold—or submit—to get what they want.

In general, boys and girls tend to have radically different experiences from each other around power as they are growing up. Boys learn to assume privilege and use power directly and assertively; girls are taught deference and learn to wield power indirectly. It is here that the seeds of domination and resistance are planted.

Power imbalances can cripple relationships. What I have often observed clinically is that either one partner dominates the other and loses his or her own humanity, rendering the other subjugated and voiceless—like Roger—or the person being dominated tries to rebel or turn the tables on the dominator by sabotaging him or her through obstructionist maneuvers. In both cases the relationship suffers and a great deal of valuable energy is bound up in essentially disruptive and unproductive battles.

The Power of the Powerless

The apparently powerless often wield a great deal of power through outright deception, purposeful obstruction, and strategic refusal. Resisting power in an intimate relationship can take many forms including violence or divorce, masochistic submission or conscious sabotage, sexual withholding or reckless spending, or any other way of passively defying, disrupting, or sabotaging what is important to one's partner. People without overt power use these strategies to level the playing field or restore a measure of personal pride, dignity, and autonomy. Before she filed for divorce, Carol fought Jim's attempts at domination by closing down and becoming mute when he was verbally abusive, because she knew her protests would lead nowhere and she had learned in childhood that it was safer to be invisible and "off Father's radar" than assertive and conspicuous.

Manu and Jaga painfully illustrated a pattern of wielding power in the face of powerlessness that many couples have experienced. Manu didn't feel respected, especially when his wife, Jaga, barked orders and tried to dictate how he spent his free time. "She is so critical and demanding," he said. "She even blamed me because I didn't make her do yoga. Life with her is like being in the military. I don't have any power." Jaga, on the other hand, complained that Manu eternally frustrated her by failing to do the numerous tasks she assigned him—balking, for example, when she asked him to fill out her insurance forms, do research for their next vacation, or remind her to practice yoga, which she demanded that he "make me do." Jaga presented a compelling case that she had to have a firm hand with Manu, which often included criticizing him, because she shouldered the bulk of the burden of running the house and family, while also working at a highly competitive and pressure-filled job in the financial sector. But when Manu described that he also had a difficult job and was very engaged with their three children, and that Jaga asked him to fill out the forms at midnight on a Sunday evening, when he wanted to rest, treated him in a demeaning manner, and made him responsible for pushing her to overcome her resistance to yoga, it's understandable why they were in a stalemate. Actually a power struggle.

When she dominated him, she had the power. But when he resisted her, he regained it because she wanted something from him that he wouldn't provide and this made her feel powerless. When she stonewalled him after he resisted, she had the power, and he again felt powerless.

Roger illustrated another kind of resistance to power. He glorified his deprivation and treated it as a badge of honor—what Nietzsche called the "ascetic ideal." (I'm better than you because I have less than you.) In his masochistic surrender to Leslie he simultaneously elevated himself and tried to turn the tables on her by presenting himself to other people as a victim whom his wife had exploited. Gatherings with extended family, for example, became occasions in which he would snipe at Leslie, which caught her off guard and stung her deeply.

Several months after Seth married Marnie, a talented graphic artist, she went on "strike" and refused to have sex with her husband unless he would let her quit her job. He informed her that they needed both incomes. Marnie was the center of her unhappily married father's emotional world. Her father had never denied her what she wanted— including a new car when she crashed hers after being drunk—and she felt entitled to do whatever she felt like and ignored Seth's reasoning. Her rationale—"That's just who I am"—was an abuse of power, controlling her partner through apparent powerlessness—something that occurs in different forms in many relationships from refusing to try to change to obstructing our partner's wishes and needs. Since Seth couldn't prevent Marnie's sexual withdrawal, he felt powerless.

What is crucial, when we consider resisting power in a relationship, is whether the struggle against it is actually hurting the one who is rebelling—like Roger—or striving toward something constructive. Roger's frustration with his powerlessness with Leslie, for example, took the form of mechanical rebellion against her wishes in many realms of life, from being habitually late to dropping his laundry on the floor of the bedroom, rather than a direct confrontation of his frustration or a constructive challenge to her imposition of power.

Seth's eventual response to Marnie's sexual withholding illustrated two other pathological forms of resistance, namely sniping and being sneaky. As his sexual frustration increased, he began attacking and bad-mouthing her parenting to both sets of in-laws and her friends, as well as engaging in phone sex with a stranger. None of this behavior dealt directly with the problem between them. In fact, it replicated Seth's "henpecked" father's difficulty handling his own disappointments and aggression and Marnie's indirect reaction to her own frustration with Seth.

Carol's third relationship after her divorce illustrated a *healthy resistance to power.* Tony, her new boyfriend, had been steamrolled in his first marriage. Working long hours to support his first wife's expensive tastes, he spent less time with the kids than she did and gradually felt as if he was "on the outside of the family looking in." He didn't like what he saw. As he slowly awakened to the way his wife ran the show, making most of the decisions about the kids and their social life, he tried to talk with her. A highly controlling father had bullied her, so in her marriage she enjoyed wielding the power in her home as a form of self-protection. When she wouldn't budge, Tony eventually got a divorce.

Because Tony was afraid of being controlled by Carol, he initially related to her in a domineering manner. Since Carol sensed that Tony was a person of good character and they had the potential to create a great relationship, she didn't bail. Instead, she proactively stood up for herself with him, made her needs and wishes known, and engaged in weekly discussions about whatever had to be negotiated—from social plans to dreams about the kind of life they wanted. Decisions were made by considering both partner's needs and the impact their choices would have on the relationship.

Giving Up Our Power

There are several ways that people give up their power. Carol and Roger and Jaga and Manu had great difficulty allowing themselves to feel, think, or act independently of their partners. Instead, they tended to allow their partners to run their lives. Carol, for example, never even thought about what she wanted to do on Mother's Day, while Manu passively let Jaga make their social plans and then complained. Jaga took lousy care of herself physically and tried to make Manu responsible for her body and health. Most people who give up their power not only let their partners make important decisions, they don't speak up, like Manu or Carol, when they are hurt or disappointed.

Giving up your power is a sure step to deprivation and bitterness. Such people often "pay back" their partners by undermining them in other ways or lashing out about unrelated issues, creating an environment of anger and hostility. Harsh digs that seemingly come out of nowhere are often a sign that a partner is suppressing a lot of suffering and animosity.

Signs of Power Imbalances

There are several signs that power is operating destructively in a relationship: keeping score, calling in the troops, and turning the tables. If a situation feels unfair, one partner might tend to measure and compare who does what. When we measure, or keep score—"I did more chores than you"—this can provide feedback that there's a perceived imbalance in the relationship. Keeping score can take various forms from "I love you more than you love me," to "We spend more time with your family than mine," to "I work harder than you do."

We often "call in the troops" and cite other people's ideas and views to buttress our own, as I discussed in chapter 13. In the face of feeling dominated by Jim and not being able to get through to him, Carol blurted out, "Even your sister agrees that you can be a tyrant." By quoting Jim's sister, Carol hoped to strengthen her own fragile standing in the marriage.

Turning the tables on our partners is a way of subverting their power. One form this takes is stonewalling them by consciously blocking them, as Manu and Jaga illustrated. While often submissive to Jim, in certain areas Carol operated like a "brick wall" and didn't do what he wanted, such as making travel plans in a timely manner.

Negotiating the New Uncertainty

Power and inequality, as I suggested earlier, cannot be eliminated from relationships or from life itself. But not all power differentials are negative and not all power is necessarily harmful, so it's important to be able to distinguish between the different manifestations of power. One partner may be more efficient at cleaning up the kitchen; the other partner may be better at grocery shopping. Destructive power has at least two elements: the people who wield it—whether a ruthless dictator or a spouse—are closed to feedback, and those without power have no impact on the power wielders, as Kramer and Alstad suggested in *The Guru Papers*. There is a vast difference between using power in a self-serving way that hurts the relationship, and employing it to empower the person with less authority or bring the couple closer. In *Man for Himself*, the psychoanalyst and social critic Erich Fromm differentiated between "rational authority" and "irrational authority." An individual exercises rational authority with superior knowledge (and expertise) for the purpose of aiding the less powerful one in the relationship; irrational authority is employed for the purpose of perpetuating inequality.

When power imbalances are longstanding and rigidly held in place, this inequality closes down interpersonal space, and couples can't resolve conflicts or creatively respond to the inevitable challenges that they confront in their day-to-day lives. Such relationships are in dire trouble. Carol was crushed and disempowered, and Jim, who had power without accountability, was also dehumanized and demeaned. The master, as the German philosopher Georg Hegel aptly noted, is alienated from his own fullest humanity when he oppresses the slave.

Couples need to struggle against forms of power that are *malignant*, that control or silence their partners and interfere with the kind of *mutuality* that fosters a loving relationship.

They also need to strive for equality and respect even as they realize the inevitability of power and inequality. When we neither indulge the power we inevitably wield nor attempt to deny it, we can more readily ascertain its impact on our partners.

There are a few things couples can do to address destructive inequalities in power:

- They can pinpoint examples of misuse of power within their relationship.
- Those with power can struggle to use it with greater self-awareness, sensitivity, and flexibility.
- The powerful one can aid the partner with less power in having a greater voice and using power constructively.

When Tony looked at his behavior toward Carol, he realized that he had to examine every place in their relationship where he wielded power. He not only committed to using it to enrich the relationship rather than protect himself by simply fulfilling his own needs, he also helped Carol to gain more power. He made sure that he practiced empathic listening and focused on making Carol feel understood, rather than first advocating for his agendas. He readily admitted his fallibility and let Carol know when he wasn't clear about the best course of action. And he deferred when she had more experience or an intuition that a different course of action than what *he* might choose would be the best one.

Manu and Jaga also worked with their imbalances in power. First they attempted to detect the ways they destructively tried to dominate or subvert each other. Next they strove to both avoid power grabs and power plays—trying to control or sabotage the other person—and use the power they had constructively. Manu offered to split the work at home without resentment and do tasks Jaga despised—such as changing the cat litter—and to try to be more proactive and assertive. Jaga practiced asking for what she needed instead of domineering or criticizing him.

Power as a Detonator

Relationships are a domain where we can always expect to find discord, conflicts, and oppositions—competing ideas about how to live and what to do. Once power is no longer a dirty word, we can more easily focus on trying to harness it constructively. Power is often a mighty detonator, which can take various forms including breaking a spouse—or a relationship—out of destructive patterns, jolting couples out of years of complacency, and reinvigorating a marriage that is languishing.

Leslie and Roger visited friends who lived in a pristinely kept house. On the ride home, Roger felt sad when he considered returning to his messy and chaotic domicile. Not only did the disarray at home disturb him, he felt powerless to change it. In the car Roger mentioned to Leslie that he'd love it if they could make some changes and create a more orderly and "Zen-like" ambience together.

"I'd love that too," she said. "But there is no place to put things."

As she launched into her familiar litany of explanations and excuses, he tuned her out and shut down. Because he had been meditating regularly his awareness was clearer and crisper. He quickly noticed that he had repeated a pattern that had occurred for many years, namely that he had caved in to Leslie's rationalizations.

He remained silent for the rest of the trip, letting himself feel his reaction to this pattern of powerlessness in their marriage. He soon realized that her circular logic—"We have no place for the overflow of things so we can't put them away"—would always create disorder in their home and leave him disturbed. As he sat silently in the car and mulled this over he suddenly got an insight and decided to make a change himself, without waiting for Leslie's agreement or blocking maneuvers. He created two "crazy rooms," one designated space for each of them in their small home that were not in shared places such as the kitchen or bedroom, where they could "dump their crap" without disturbing their partner.

Constructive Use of Power

The constructive use of power has a variety of elements. Ideally, both partners must realize:

- ➣ Power is unavoidable and can be useful.
- ➣ Power is fluid, rather than static.
- ➣ Power must be negotiated continually and in a mutually beneficial way.
- ➣ Power needs to be handled with awareness and compassion

through a responsive dialogue in which each person is aware of, and sensitive to, his or her partner's wishes and needs.

- Power should be employed to improve the relationship, rather than to simply benefit the individual wielding it at the expense of his or her partner.
- Couples need to be open to feedback and modification based on the impact of power on each spouse and the relationship.

To do these things, it is helpful for couples to draw on the resources discussed in previous chapters:

- Stop trying to win, because when one partner "wins"—even the one with more power—both lose.
- Harmonize two "instruments" of one's being—self-care (the quest for nourishing oneself, living authentically, and experiencing personal fulfillment) and altruism, or care for the other.
- Compost the underlying personal or interpersonal conflict.
- Connect with what originally inspired us about our partners.
- Dream together about the kind of life we wish to have.

Seth used power constructively when he told Marnie he loved her, wanted to salvage their relationship, and insisted that their marriage would fall apart if they both didn't participate in psychotherapy. She agreed, and at the end of about a year of treatment, she had learned a great deal about two genuine sources of her discontent: she had not followed her passion to teach, and had instead focused on empty substitutes such as fancy dinners and clothes. (Remember cotton-candy self-care?) These made her life look good from the outside but left her feeling empty and hungering for more sustaining sources of emotional nourishment. She had pushed Seth away because she projected *her* self-loathing onto *him,* and therefore believed that he found her despicable. Marnie was grateful to Seth for insisting that she go to therapy, which gave her the impetus to deal with her personal demons and frustrations with Seth more directly and constructively. As she confronted Seth about the ways he rejected her through objectifying her and being addicted to sex on the Internet, which he agreed to examine in psychotherapy, her bitterness and withdrawal lifted and their passion blossomed.

They also found an intriguing way of constructively working out their conflicts over power—tango dancing. A noncompetitive social dance that is extremely intimate, nuanced, and sensuous, it offered them the opportunity of learning to lead and follow and let go of trying to control or subvert each other. And when even dancing didn't resolve every conflict, they chose to give the weaker person veto power, negotiate in a mutually respectful way, and sometimes compromise, as long as neither felt demeaned or resentful.

Katie and Ron were therapists who had both been intruded on and emotionally violated in childhood by highly critical and interfering parents. They eventually realized that they were so busy trying to not impose their will on each other that they missed vital opportunities to constructively influence each other. As each of them worked out their feelings of self-doubt and inadequacy, they slowly became more comfortable trying to advocate for what they felt was healthy for the relationship, such as spending more quality time together and getting on an eating and fitness regime. "By pushing each other in directions we believed in, we rekindled some of the passion we originally had together before we obscured it by falling into the stultifying routines of everyday life," Katie said.

In relationships where power is more balanced, control is wielded more flexibly, and each person's needs and wishes are taken more seriously, both spouses feel safer, and passion and love can more easily flourish. These relationships tend to be shaped less by the force of one partner's will and consequently both individuals feel more personally empowered.

Sometimes, despite our best efforts, power struggles can't be eliminated, and often subtly return and operate secretly and destructively in the form of oppositionality. In the next chapter we'll explore why people are oppositional and how to handle this more skillfully.

18

I would prefer not to.

—HERMAN MELVILLE

TORN CHECKS AND

CHINESE DOCTORS

Skillfully Handling Oppositionality

Cynthia was ready to leave for an after-hours work function and her husband, Albert, was dawdling, making her late yet again, something her hyperpunctual boss did not appreciate. Albert's passive-aggressive behavior caused Cynthia other problems as well: if she hurried him, he'd stonewall her; if she said nothing, she'd seethe. Either way her evening was ruined. All because of Albert's oppositionality.

Did you ever encounter a person with whom you felt relentlessly checkmated—someone who frequently opposed and undermined you? Welcome to the maddening world of interacting with a person who is oppositional.

Oppositionality is a pernicious weed in the garden of love that creates animosity in those who are victimized by it. When we try to get through to an oppositional person, he or she stymies us. If we attempt to confront the person directly we create a mutually escalating cycle of resentment and contempt that sabotages intimacy. This behavior doesn't just undermine relationships, it harms the oppositionalist, interfering with achieving his or her own goals and dreams. In this chapter we'll explore why people are oppositional and how to skillfully respond.

They were on the verge of divorce. Ellen, a small woman with a loud voice, was fed up with Gus, her husband, a burly, quiet man. With unconcealed hostility, Ellen told me that Gus refused to talk about what was bothering him, drank too much, and worked long hours at a job with poor compensation. Ellen wanted her husband to move out of their home, but he refused.

They had been married for several years and had two young children. While there was evidently some affection between them, the problems that brought Gus and Ellen into therapy had been there from the beginning of the relationship.

As is often the case, their issues mirrored the difficulties Gus' and Ellen's parents experienced. Ellen's mother and father divorced when she was young. Her father drank too much; he cared about his family, but was overly judgmental of Ellen and her mother and emotionally distant. Gus' parents were still together, but his father was a highly critical man who verbally beat down his son, drank too much, and was withdrawn from his wife. Gus' besieged mother passively endured her husband's behavior and failed to protect or support her son. Gus grew up feeling devalued and deprived. He had to bury his anger; to express it would have incurred his father's wrath.

In the first several sessions, we only touched upon the couple's issues, the fear, mistrust, and self-protectiveness. Building trust with each of them took time and patience. Once they both felt safer, we explored more deeply. Eventually we uncovered the core challenges that were troubling them, from Gus' oppositionality to Ellen's contemptuousness.

Actually, as therapy progressed, they felt worse—raw and more vulnerable. Would I be able to help them? Would they stay stuck in the misery that had brought them to me? Would they each be able to make the necessary changes? What if it turned out that their hope of escaping the prison and pain of their families of origin was merely a pipe dream?

Like many couples, at this point they pulled back, dug in, and reverted to old, dysfunctional coping strategies—Ellen sniped at Gus and he passively resisted her expectations—to protect themselves against the breakthroughs they simultaneously hungered for and feared.

In the next few sessions, we deepened our exploration of the themes that had surfaced in the first session. Ellen felt deprived and harbored a lot of resentment, which she wasn't shy about expressing. Gus experienced her as angry and hostile—"ranting and raving"—which caused him to shut down, dive into work—the one area of his life that offered any satisfaction—and anaesthetize his pain with alcohol. This only exacerbated Ellen's annoyance and intensified her attacks. But underneath Ellen's anger with Gus—for working at a dead-end job, drinking, and being absent from home—was love, and a wish that someone could get through his nearly impenetrable wall.

Of course, the problems were more complex than that. Gus was too passive, detached, and afraid he'd get torn down if he engaged directly and wholeheartedly. As a result, he sleepwalked through his days, failing to take care of basic responsibilities. Ellen's criticisms of him, which he partially provoked by being irresponsible and emotionally unavailable, only confirmed his belief that he was ultimately unlovable and inadequate. And his distance, which Ellen triggered by her impatience and hostility, corroborated her conviction that men would always disappoint her.

One particular session, several months into treatment, was a nightmare. Gus had no interest in psychotherapy. He silently glared at Ellen, who desperately wanted to get through the wall he continually erected. I sensed that she longed to be closer to her angry and withdrawn husband. Softness and kindness, exasperation and impatience; she had tried them all. None of these responses had made a dent in her husband's armor.

The session resembled a traffic jam—heavy doses of congestion, gridlock, and simmering rage. Gus spent our entire time together quietly sabotaging any efforts to break through the distance between his wife and himself. He successfully stymied both her and my best efforts at improving their rocky relationship. They were frustrated. So was I.

Gus abruptly stood up at the end of the session and handed me a check. *For what?* I remember thinking. *Nothing constructive happened in the session.* I don't know what came over me, but I tore the check in half and threw the pieces in the air. They fluttered down and landed on the floor between us. Gus stared at me, ready to escalate. I didn't blame him. Perhaps I had gone too far.

"I've been told that in ancient China, a doctor got paid only when he helped his patient," I said. "We got nowhere during this session, because you interfered with me doing my job. So I can't in good conscience accept your check. It would be immoral."

Gus glared at me, turned, and left my office without a word.

I can't remember if he ever replaced the check, but the next week, he came back with Ellen—which surprised me—and dove into the session, which shocked me. He took an active role, shared his feelings—including what Ellen did that hurt him—and was clearly working to understand his life and marriage. He was less hostile and more responsive.

Gus and Ellen's unspoken pact was revealed. While they wanted to improve their relationship, they also didn't really believe it was possible. So they had settled for a coexistence that protected them against feeling vulnerable or rejected, but that avoided deeper intimacy. In fact, they had given up on the possibility of a closer relationship, settling for whatever emotional scraps they could get.

In the following sessions, they both began seeing patterns from the past that interfered with intimacy. Ellen realized that she was criticizing Gus the way her father had picked her apart and her mother had put down her father. Gus acknowledged that he was passively resisting Ellen the way his father had opposed his mother. Gus and Ellen also became more sensitive to dysfunctional patterns in the present. Ellen recognized how her criticism and impatience contributed to Gus being angry and withdrawn. Gus realized how his passivity made Ellen feel as if she didn't have a partner.

Over time, their relationship improved. Conflict didn't disappear, but they handled it much more constructively—listening to and respecting each other, as well as composting what they quarreled about. Ellen practiced treating Gus with patience and kindness. Gus worked on not drinking. He learned to express his hurt and anger more directly and to respond to Ellen's efforts to connect. She acknowledged how difficult this was for him and recognized that it was not always her fault when he failed. They each forgave mistakes, dropped grudges, and even compromised. And when that didn't work, a dose of humor helped them ride the waves of the difficult times. They started having more fun together, appreciating their differences.

Pulling the Weed of Oppositionality

I don't normally make a practice of tearing up checks, but if I had approached Gus' rage and obstructionist behavior even more directly,

I suspect that he would have reacted with denial or argued with me, and I—like Ellen—would have been stymied.

Before exploring how to handle a stubborn, obstructionist partner, let's examine the psychology of oppositionality by reconsidering Albert and Cynthia, the chronically late, stonewalling husband, and his frustrated, punctual wife. While Albert's behavior enraged Cynthia—and would undoubtedly disturb most of us—that missed the point of what he was striving to do. Cynthia grew up in a home in which her mother was treated like a princess and her father was submissive and demoralized. Cynthia was not shy about taking center stage in their marriage, with Albert playing second fiddle. This was an eminently familiar role to Albert, whose father was a career military man and an autocrat who ran his family as if it were a platoon. Albert was crushed by his father and had little belief in his own right to flourish. Through a lot of therapy he had slowly become aware of, and disturbed by, his marginal place in his own life. Misguided as it might seem to us, opposing his wife's wishes was not only a vital effort to resist getting steamrolled, it represented the first faint pulsing of a life that was his own. Albert, like Gus, was resisting letting someone else run his life, and both men were striving to retain their autonomy and self-respect.

The two questions to ask in the face of oppositional behavior are: "What is it trying to *oppose*?" and "What is it trying to *preserve*?" Once these questions are illuminated it becomes easier for people who are oppositional to explore other ways of being authentic and retaining freedom without sabotaging their relationships or themselves.

There is no single way to get through to difficult or hostile people. Empathy sometimes makes them feel understood and validated, melting their anger and antagonism. At other times, they may want to hold on to—rather than resolve or give up—their anger. Conflict can be a way of protesting against, sabotaging, or seeking revenge against those who disappoint us. It can also be a barrier against intimacy when one is frightened by closeness. For many people, hostility makes them feel stronger and less vulnerable.

When a person is attached to anger or revenge, empathy or understanding might not be helpful. When we deal with a difficult person who is invested in punishing us, we are not playing on a level field.

Resolving sticky issues is often not a high priority for them. They can't always be approached rationally or logically. When we try to do so, we are thwarted. Cynthia had repeatedly asked Albert in a civil way to be on time, because punctuality at work functions was important to her and her career. Albert either took offense and was late, or agreed with her and was late.

It is generally accepted among psychotherapists of different theoretical orientations—from classical psychoanalysis to object-relations theory to interpersonal psychoanalysis—that *action* is an important medium through which clients communicate with their therapists. Clients not only anticipate that the therapist will react to them and treat them as significant people in their pasts did, they often unwittingly *do* things to elicit similar responses. For example, Gus not only assumed that Ellen would criticize him, the way his father did, he provoked her into acting like the nag he detested. Albert was not only certain that Cynthia would take over his life, he allowed her to, and then protested.

What has been less recognized is that a therapist's actions in therapy—or a spouse's at home—are often a powerful means for communication and change. It's a therapeutic truism that the therapist's verbal interpretations or explanations—linking the client's hidden thoughts, feelings, or fantasies in the past to his or her behavior in the present—fuel change. What the torn check illustrates is that *interventions*—what the therapist *does*—can sometimes be as effective as what he or she *says*. Interventions—conveyed through facial expressions and tone of voice, humor, and laughter—may communicate to the client what might not be expressible through words alone. And they often break through an emotional logjam and bypass a person's resistance, as they did with Gus. Tearing up Gus' check was an intervention that communicated something vital about my understanding of him and his relationship with Ellen.

When a partner is oppositional, we need to approach him or her strategically. Otherwise the person will undermine our efforts. Using humor and taking the power out of his or her hands are two effective means of accomplishing this. Cynthia decided not to be held captive by Albert's schedule. "I'm leaving at five-thirty. If you're ready, great. If not, I'll see you when I get home."

At first Cynthia felt guilty when she left without Albert, but she later became comfortable with following through on what she said she would do.

Behavioral Buddhism—the approach of systematically cultivating greater equanimity that we explored in chapter 5—helped Albert transform his oppositionality. He had been a musician in his youth, and sound was a thoroughly comfortable realm for him. He began by listening to his favorite music—*Madame Butterfly*—on a daily basis. When he had little trouble remaining focused and engaged, which happened relatively quickly, he listened to a compilation of hard rock and practiced hearing it, despite his dislike of it. When this was relatively easy, he listened to rap, his least favorite music. When he could listen to it without tightening or overreacting, he meditated on rebellious feelings, which were easy for him. Next he focused on opening to guilt, especially hurting other people by his oppositionality. When this was tolerable, he focused on vulnerable feelings—such as his fear of being controlled. After some practice this wasn't so difficult.

As Albert realized that he was undermining *himself* when he engaged in oppositional behavior and no longer felt so vulnerable to being shamed or controlled, much of his rebelliousness dropped away and he became more focused on what he *wanted* for his life rather than on what he *opposed*.

When an oppositional person isn't as self-reflective or receptive as Albert, which is usually the case, sometimes mental judo, a kind of turning things upside down so the difficult person gets a completely different picture of what he or she is doing, may be necessary. This often wakes these people up and points toward a way out of the state they are stuck in. Words were worthless currency to Gus—he was skilled at parrying or ignoring them. Tearing up the check was a more effective way of holding up a mirror to his anger and oppositional behavior than *talking* about it. The torn check showed him that he was not getting what he was paying for, the failure of the process was his responsibility, and only he could change it.

Many years after our sessions, I heard from Ellen. Their son was thriving and applying to college. Gus had been sober for years and had changed jobs. He liked his new career and had a retirement and health plan. Ellen felt fulfilled in her work and her life, and she and Gus really enjoyed each other. They hardly ever fought and when they did, they quickly resolved their issue.

"Everyone said we'd never make it," she told me. "If not for you, we wouldn't have."

I was silent and pleased, having never fully realized the impact our work had had on them.

"When we first came for therapy, I wanted a divorce and I wanted you to tell him to leave," Ellen said. "I'm glad you didn't. And I'm glad Gus stuck with me. Now we are the happiest and most in love we have ever been."

Oppositional behavior will never be removed from human relationships. We've all had to deal with it at one time or another, and will have to in the future, but when we learn to respond strategically and playfully, unexpected possibilities for intimacy sometimes emerge.

In the next chapter we'll explore what to do in those horrific moments in a relationship when disappointment, rage, and hate overwhelm our best efforts to create a garden of love.

19

SCORCHED-EARTH MOMENTS

Surviving Hateful Feelings

"I hate you, I hope you die," Rhonda, a forty-something woman said to her husband, Richard, after finding out that he slept with her best friend. How could you do this to me . . . to us?" Before Richard could respond she added: "I am so enraged with you that I don't even want to look at you right now. You nauseate me."

"I hate the way you undermine me in front of the kids," Melissa said to her husband, Ethan. "I feel annihilated and humiliated."

"All you need is love," sang the Beatles, but partners in intimate relationships know that sometimes all we feel, or receive, is hate. For a moment, or an hour, or a day, we despise, detest, and loathe our partners or they feel that way toward us. Does the existence of hate mean the certain demise of a bond? Or is hate, like love, part of the symphony of feelings that coexist in an intimate relationship?

There's a harmful myth afoot that a "good marriage is conflict-free and that good communication can avoid anger," claimed Wallerstein and Blakeslee in *The Good Marriage*. But there is no way for a couple to avoid conflict, anger, or hate when they are forced to balance supporting their partner and the relationship without neglecting their own needs.

Navigating minefields such as sex, whether to take a job offer and move the family across the country, setting limits with teenagers when each parent has an opposing philosophy about accountability, and dividing household chores when both partners work can strain even the most stable relationship.

One of the nine crucial "life challenges" or "psychological tasks" for happy marriages, according to Wallerstein and Blakeslee, is to "create a safe haven for the expression of differences, anger, and conflict." Problems—weeds, pests, drought—have an impact on every gardener. To create a garden of love we need to contain—because we can't eliminate— certain destructive forces such as hate, which enters every relationship. No matter how much we love our spouses, we cannot avoid sometimes hating them, and this is profoundly confusing and unsettling, because the person we momentarily despise may also be our best friend. The more we acknowledge and understand these moments of hatred, the less power they have to ruin a relationship. In this chapter we'll explore what to do in those scorched-earth moments when rage, loathing, and misery seem to obliterate love.

Rage, Hate, and Other Virulent Pests

Pain sure brings out the best in people, doesn't it?

—Bob Dylan

S teve and Yvonne couldn't find a way to resolve their differences. While they obviously cared for each other a great deal and had built a meaningful life together, they also reported animosity and moments of white-hot rage. Yvonne felt like a failure because she had never reached her goals or lived her dreams or created the life she wanted. She projected her self-loathing onto Steve, convincing herself that he was eventually going to leave her. While they had been married for many years, *she* didn't realize that she had already left *him* when she sabotaged their intimacy by creating an impenetrable wall between them. Steve loved his wife, yet he was periodically enraged with her. He found her self-destructive ways maddening and periodically wanted to "strangle" her.

Throughout her childhood, Tracy was encouraged by her mother to put everyone else first. Whenever anything went wrong, she assumed that it was her fault and she felt guilt. Her husband, Martin, was taught by his parents to equate love with being served by a woman, which fit perfectly, and disastrously, with Tracy's own selfless attitude and behavior, but eroded her trust in him and caused her to be contemptuous. Tracy had severe—and unrealistic—expectations about perfect and pure behavior. She followed abstract moral rules in a self-righteous way. For example, she would never drive above the speed limit, and she categorically rejected any excuses anyone ever had for being late. As a result, Martin always felt deficient and it nearly drove him crazy, and periodically resulted in hate-filled diatribes against his wife.

Ronnie was rushed to the hospital after intentionally cutting herself. In a therapy session soon afterward, her husband, Al, listened as Ronnie bitterly described her rage when, at a family gathering, his parents had embarrassed her and Al had done nothing to defend her. She admitted that she then turned her rage against Al for not protecting her from his parents. Her self-mutilation expressed her feeling of having been lacerated by her husband and his parents.

The Anatomy of Hate

Hate, along with greed and delusion, is one of the three "poisons" in Buddhism. It has the power to harm both the person who feels it and the people toward whom it is directed. Hate is not a unitary phenomena; it exists in different degrees of intensity and can take many forms—from fury in the face of insult or disrespect, to meanness and contempt after disappointment or betrayal, to revenge-seeking following shameful submission to a degrading experience.

Those who hate usually come by it honestly. They were exploited, abused, or humiliated, and—perhaps most important—were unable to express their emotions or have anyone witness their shame. Is it any wonder that their feelings festered and became rage?

Hate arises for various reasons, from being vulnerable and scared to enduring disillusionment and betrayal. "The earliest function of rage," wrote the psychoanalyst Otto Kernberg, "is the effort to eliminate a source of irritation or pain. . . . The second function of rage is to eliminate an object or barrier to a fantasied or real source of gratification." Hate can also be triggered when one's quest to be linked to a powerful, idealized figure is stymied, noted the psychoanalyst Heinz Kohut. Tracy idealized selfless, spiritual people like her minister's wife, Maryanne, who had supported Tracy and built up her esteem at a vulnerable time during college. When a boyfriend suddenly dumped Tracy during midterms and Maryanne was not there, Tracy felt demoralized and then enraged.

A person who acts hatefully may be reacting to a fundamental betrayal—such as a woman whose boyfriend violated her child. Hate can also occur when someone projects his or her own self-loathing onto a spouse or reexperiences and then reenacts earlier trauma, treating the victimized the way he or she was treated—what the psychoanalyst Sandor Ferenczi calls "identification with the aggressor." Severe cases of hate may lead to "vengeful acts" or "cunningly plotted vendettas," as Kohut wrote.

Contemporary psychoanalytic understanding of hate emphasizes its contextual nature. Increasing numbers of therapists dispute the view that hate is rooted in our psychobiological makeup and results from our reptilian brain. The view that there is an inherent human tendency toward combativeness protects us against the troubling realization that hate has a context and a cause outside of ourselves. But while we cannot escape our biological characteristics, there are nonetheless causes for bigotry, persecution, and warfare that lie outside of us. Hate, from this perspective, is a learned behavior, not an innate aspect of the human personality. Once we realize that hate is not a given, but a reaction to particular and troubling circumstances—such as being bullied, abandoned, or shamed—we can view hate differently. A contextual theory of hate opens up the possibility that we can illuminate the disturbing circumstances that triggered it—the soil that nourished it.

Faced with rage or hate, we have a tendency to deny it or panic because we are fearful about its implications. At other times, we may retaliate.

Hate is never healed by hate, as noted in the *Dhammapada,* a core ethical text of Buddhism, but hate doesn't always have to destroy a relationship.

Hatred Doesn't Have to Be a Deal-Breaker

"**W**e need to get divorced," Tom, who was thirty-five, said in his first couple's session. His language struck me. He could have said, "We *are* getting divorced."

"Why do you *need* to?" I asked.

"We had a fight—actually a pretty hate-filled one. I overheard my wife talking about me to her sisters at a family cookout; how I loaf around on the weekends. I was humiliated. I feel like she doesn't know me at all. And I thought we had agreed to not put each other down in front of family."

"I'm confused," I said.

"I never saw my parents fighting when I was growing up." So when my wife and I disagreed, I assumed it meant that we had a terrible problem and would have to get divorced."

"Do you want to get divorced?" I asked.

"Hell, no," he replied.

Conflict—even hate—alone does not have to wreck a marriage. In *The Good Marriage,* Wallerstein and Blakeslee discovered that "all close relationships involve love and anger, connectedness and disruption. The task is to find ways to resolve the differences, without exploiting each other, being violent, or giving away one's heart's desire."

While contempt, a form of hatred, is one of the four forces—along with criticism, defensiveness, and stonewalling—that predict divorce, according to John Gottman's extensive studies of successful relationships, hatred doesn't have to be a deal-breaker. It's essential that the feelings are not denied; only in this way can they eventually be understood and transformed.

Hate shouldn't always be endured and explored. Sometimes it is feedback that it is time to move on. In such a case, part of flourishing might entail ending a relationship. Hate is a deal-breaker when it harms either person emotionally or physically and can't be repaired because neither the partner who feels hateful nor the one who may have provoked it (if it was "co-created") will look at their contribution.

When we have decided to try to resolve a hateful situation, rather than leave it, we need to resist avoiding or feeding it. It is more constructive to contain hatred so that it doesn't grow, and simultaneously develop inner and interpersonal awareness (emotional composting) and foster a wise response. In other words, couples in the thrall of hate need to open to its presence without defensiveness, discover what it means, and decide what to do.

Transforming Hate

When your spouse is hateful toward you, it is very difficult to cope. Feeling hated triggers a tidal wave of emotion that is scary and sometimes even demoralizing—especially if we personalize it, which we often do. But while you can make hate worse by meeting your spouse's rage directly with a counterattack, you probably won't be able to reduce it.

How does a couple curb rage? Some try to use suppression; others use humor and deflection. It's crucial to establish a "safety zone," in which rage can be expressed without harm or danger, so that no one is hurt or abandoned.

Meditation and yogic breathing, as I suggested earlier, teach us how to respond to difficult feelings without panicking, retaliating, or fleeing, and are invaluable tools in dealing with hatred. While sitting through the hurricane can prevent further escalation and damage, in cases of abuse or endangerment it is best to remove oneself immediately and seek safety. There is no virtue in sitting still when you are being demeaned or abused, shamed or crushed.

I suggested that Tracy and Martin, Steve and Yvonne, and Ronnie and Al create a "Hate Club." Once a week they gave themselves permission to speak of their hate for fifteen minutes each. They could bring up hurts and grievances, and even express rage and contempt, but they had to do so without heat or rancor. They each did their best to hear their partners, using empathic listening. When they felt heard, they "composted" whatever had arisen. While most people might assume that eventually rage will subside, time *doesn't* heal all wounds, as Martin Luther King, Jr., recognized. Hate is feedback that there is either something disturbing occurring in the relationship or the enraged person feels endangered. The Hate Club provides a safe means of expressing rage and disappointment, so that the feelings are contained but not neglected. Once the rage is expressed both partners need to compost it.

Tracy was sick and tired of settling for a diminished life. Like Peter Finch in *Network,* she was "mad as hell" and "not going to take it anymore." Her husband's entitled stance was only foiling her desire to lead an authentic and nurturing life in the context of an intimate relationship. As she and Martin composted their conflict, what emerged was that she needed to take better care of herself and not be so self-denying. Martin realized that he was perpetuating Tracy's sense of deprivation by expecting her to center her life around him. I suggested to Martin that love often means having to say you are sorry—and then adjusting one's behavior. Martin apologized to Tracy and committed to change. "I have treated you unfairly, I'm really sorry, and I will figure out why that happened and work on it," he said.

As Martin validated Tracy's feelings and took responsibility for the harm he had inflicted upon her, Tracy's contemptuousness lessened. She realized that her moral rigidity and indignation was a way of identifying with—and staying connected to—her father, who was dogmatic, demanding, and unforgiving. It was a way of desperately trying to mold herself into a perfect person so that he might finally love her. And it was also a way of unconsciously punishing Martin.

Yvonne's efforts to compost her self-sabotaging rage taught her that she blamed herself for her parents' divorce and felt unlovable. By maintaining emotional distance from Steve, she protected herself against being devastated by what she anticipated—being abandoned. Sadly, this threatened her marriage, ironically creating the very situation she dreaded but unconsciously felt she deserved.

Steve realized that he was trying to save Yvonne the way he had been recruited by his parents to rescue his wayward, drug-addicted younger sister, instead of fully engaging in his own life.

As Al recognized he needed to separate from his parents and make Ronnie more important than them, her hate evaporated because she felt more valued and protected by her husband.

We have seen that hate is inevitable but doesn't have to destroy a relationship. Like everything else that threatens the garden of intimacy—from poor self-care and impaired empathy to lack of boundaries and imbalances of power—hate needs to be acknowledged and addressed. When we approach it nondefensively, figure out what it means, and wisely respond, hate becomes an intense, but not unharmonious, instrument in the symphony of intimacy.

Sometimes hate—and other troubling emotions—can accumulate and threaten a relationship. Next we'll explore what it means when an intimate relationship seems to be over—and what to do about it.

20

They never saw what they were not used to seeing.
—PABLO NERUDA

WHEN IT'S NOT REALLY OVER

Recognizing the Green Shoots in a Withered Garden

One of the saddest and most heart-wrenching parts of my work are those times when a couple breaks up and I watch the ensuing emotional devastation and there is no way to stop it.

Hearing the phrase "It's over" is one of life's great emotional tsunamis. The ramifications cascade outward from children who feel lost and bereft and blame themselves, to demoralized adults whose lives are devastated, to friends of the former couple who are distressed. We all know of or have lived through war stories from the battlefields of divorce.

What does it mean when a relationship seems over and what can we do about it? And how should a couple respond when all hope seems lost, but a spark of connectedness still flickers even if it is not immediately obvious?

Couples and therapists face this question with ever-increasing frequency. The historically recent expectation of marrying for love and leaving marriages when we fall out of love, and the greater freedom that couples have had since the 1960s, has come with a steep price: a greater vulnerability to divorce. As Stephanie Coontz argues in *Marriage, A History,* "Over the past century, marriage has steadily become more fair, more fulfilling, and more effective in fostering the well-being of both adults and children than ever before in human history. It has also become more optional and more fragile." When the glue that holds a marriage together weakens, when spouses can dissolve a union relatively quickly, when it is no longer socially prohibited to divorce, then both partners are infinitely more challenged and vulnerable, and less motivated to work through their issues.

A year after I challenged their attempts to recruit me as a character witness in court, the cold and very stylishly dressed couple we met in chapter 12 that used their therapy session to skewer each other, came in for an appointment. While it may seem strange that they hadn't gotten a divorce, they, like many couples, stayed together and tortured each other rather than either resolving what haunted them or leaving. And perhaps they returned to me because they were not used to not getting their way and maybe they felt they could still convince me to do their bidding in court. They traded vicious attacks for the bulk of the session. Toward the end, the husband erupted. "It's over," he said, and soon after they rapidly sought divorce.

There are many reasons to decide that a marriage is over based on the obstacles to intimacy I have discussed in previous chapters, from poor self-care and an absence of empathy, to weak or rigid boundaries and harmful imbalances in power. Tragedies and losses, infidelities and illnesses, mismatches and financial disasters—each of these can also sabotage a relationship.

When a relationship is destructive and over, part of flourishing is the ability to know when it's time to bail. Several years ago a former client called and told me that she was very grateful I advised her that there was usually no virtue in staying on a sinking ship. She left a bad marriage "before drowning" and is now happily remarried.

The Bitter End

Several fairly consistent signs indicate that a relationship has run its course. As I've mentioned, John Gottman's research on couples demonstrates that criticalness, contempt, defensiveness, and stonewalling destroy relationships. While all couples probably experience these, what is crucial is whether attempts to repair the damage and reconnect are successful. But when criticalness, contempt, defensiveness, and stonewalling aren't addressed, a vicious cycle ensues that interferes with repairing the harm: "The more contemptuous and defensive the couple is with each other, the more flooding occurs, and the harder it is to hear and respond to a repair. And since the repair is not heard, the contempt and defensiveness just get heightened, making flooding more pronounced, which makes it more difficult to hear the next repair attempt, until finally one partner withdraws."

Relationships are in danger, adds Gottman, when one or both partners view their problems as severe, talking about them seems useless, they try to solve the problems on their own, they each begin leading parallel lives, and both feel lonely.

Brad and Cynthia gamely tried to make their relationship work because divorce was frowned upon in their families of origin and their church. Couples' counseling and relationship intensives sponsored by their church had taught them that their style of fighting was harmful and demoralizing. They decided to get divorced after they realized they had married for the wrong reasons—because of loneliness and fear. They couldn't remember what attracted them to each other, weren't able to name what they shared, and were negativistic toward each other. Once they felt more entitled to be happy, instead of living like "battling roommates," they knew their end was in sight. They are now in more stable relationships that seem headed toward marriage.

Other danger signs that a relationship is over include anger and bitterness, emotional distance, deprivation. The key indicator is that no matter what we do, our partners have moved on—their hearts have closed to us. If one partner is not willing to work on the relationship, it can't be repaired. Any attempts to resolve differences, heal old wounds, or lessen the distance within a couple will be futile unless both are committed to working together.

But there are times when a relationship that seems past salvation can and should be saved.

"It's over," Lois, a defeated-looking middle-aged woman announced to me in the middle of a session several years ago. She was more angry than sad. Her husband, Tim, was clearly crestfallen. The air in my small office was thick with tension.

I was not convinced.

We had been meeting for several weeks, and as I thought about the work we had done together I realized at that moment how scared Lois was of having her hopes shattered by her husband yet again. I said, "I think there are two kinds of 'It's over.' In the first, it *is* over—one or both people have given up on the relationship and it is not salvageable. One partner feels so alienated and betrayed that he or she no longer has feelings for the other—or the feeling is one of murderous rage. All bridges to reconciliation have been burned and hopelessness leeches any wish to preserve the relationship."

Tim looked even more devastated.

"But there's a second kind of 'It's over,'" I continued.

"One or both of you are scared of hoping, letting your guard down, and being devastated again. It's not really over, and the person who says it is doesn't want it to be, but he or she is so afraid of getting burned again that hopelessness is a preemptive strike against additional suffering."

The wife gently nodded her head.

"Which is it?" her husband asked.

"The second," she said.

Barry and Michael were also at the edge. Barry had found out about Michael's yearlong string of affairs with several men and was hurt and devastated. While Michael focused on rebuilding the shattered trust, Barry alternated between rage and sadness. For several months it was unclear whether they would make it. When Barry declared, "We're done" to Michael, I was not totally convinced. I still thought that there was some life in their union. As we worked to help Michael figure out why he had been unfaithful, it became obvious that neither he nor Barry wanted the relationship to end. Almost breaking up had shown both of them how much they mattered to each other. Eventually Michael recommitted to the relationship and gradually healed the breach that he had created in Barry's trust. Barry felt safe enough to risk being vulnerable again, and their relationship became close and vibrant.

One of my own happiest "It's not really over" stories occurred when the implementation of the concepts of flourishing that we explored in the first half of the book saved a couple.

"It's over," Stephanie said to Martin, a practical, nose-to-the-grindstone type of guy.

"I know it's bad, and I don't know how to fix it—and you know I pride myself on problem solving," Martin replied. "But I love you, and the girls will be crushed, and so will I. I will do anything to salvage this," Martin said. "Please give me one more chance."

Stephanie was shocked. She never knew that he really cared so much about the family. She thought his job was his first love and they all came second. She agreed to work on the marriage, but insisted that Martin begin individual therapy. The question: "How might I flourish and save my marriage?" was a constant refrain for several months. He focused on where his life was viable and what needed to change.

On the advice of a friend who said Martin needed to "go Eastern," he began meditating and keeping a journal, trying to record what he felt and what inspired him. At first, intense self-examination left him feeling lost and disoriented. He was flooded with emotions he had not felt in years. But gradually he began discovering what moved him and the kind of life he truly wanted. He realized that he acted like a drone because it was all he knew. His father, who had died when he was fourteen, told him to watch over his mother and sister. A dutiful son, he complied. When he got married, his first priority was financially taking care of his family. As a result of what he learned about himself in therapy, Martin left the financial service sector and began teaching and coaching sports at a local private school.

Several months later Stephanie called me and confirmed what Martin had been reporting, that they were spending more quality time together, were having fun, fighting less and more constructively, and feeling closer than ever.

Declaring that the relationship is over serves various functions. Sometimes it means just what it says—the relationship, like a plant that hasn't been tended, has withered and cannot be resuscitated. Sometimes it really is over.

At other times, the pessimism of this declaration protects a spouse against reinjury, hurt, and pain, even though it simultaneously cuts him or her off from trying to salvage the relationship. It can be a self-protective strategy that lessens the likelihood of shock and devastation—by bracing for defeat—which hides the deeper connection between the couple that still exists beneath the hurt and fear. Seeing this can restore unexpected hope.

Maggie and Arthur, for example, made saving their marriage the center of their lives when they realized that they were hedging on their commitment to each other because they each feared that the other would eventually leave—the way their parents had divorced. They generated a tremendous amount of constructive energy by diving into making the relationship flourish. They rediscovered the shared values for social justice and music and art that had initially attracted them and over several months they created a wonderful bond.

What to Do When You Want to Stay

I t is terrifying to be in a relationship at the precipice. When couples in this situation ask me why they feel so confused, scared, and unsettled, I sometimes say that they are on the verge of a triple death: they are at risk of losing not just a person they once loved, but a world that provided them with meaning and security, as well as a fantasy of the future that they would share together.

The typical reaction when a relationship is at or near the breaking point is anger, panic, or denial. While denial may temporarily push problems out of sight, they often resurface with greater intensity, in a shocking and disturbing way. For example, Morty and Renee, a couple I saw many years ago, had a horrible physical fight when the pent-up suffering of denied and repressed marital tension overwhelmed their capacity to push it away.

Another common tendency when a relationship is endangered is to blame the other partner. In times of personal distress, making someone else responsible for our dissatisfaction offers the comforting illusion that if our spouse would just change his or her behavior or feelings, then our problems would be solved and our fears would subside. This strategy is ultimately ineffective, since in the end it changes nothing and we usually find ourselves exactly where we began: in the midst of trouble that must be addressed.

Some couples fly apart as soon as the going gets tough; they solve their problems by getting divorced. Others try to rebuild the relationship on the ashes of the old one—an understandable yet flawed strategy—since their former ways of relating are precisely what led to the current crisis. Holding on to a fantasy past—the good old days that never were, before children and mortgages—only forestalls the inevitable. But there's a better path to take—building the relationship on a more solid foundation.

When a relationship is in danger, it is crucial to understand several things: Are the conflicts a symptom that it really is over, or are they just waves to be ridden? Are pessimism and hopelessness indicative that the relationship is breaking apart, or are they situational? Can the relationship be repaired and is it worth trying?

There are two key signs of life:

1. Green shoots are evident—fondness and affection, shared values, and buried love.
2. Each person wants to try.

When I am counseling a couple and the demise of their partnership seems imminent, I usually ask: "Do you really want to work on it?" Inevitably they will each express pessimism about salvaging their union and launch into a description of the other's faults to explain why the relationship *can't* work. "That's not what I asked," I usually reply. "I don't expect either of you to have much hope. That's why you are here. How could you be hopeful? The situation is dire. I asked if you *wanted to try*. If one or both of you don't want to work on it, then there's no point in coming to see me, because I can't be of much help."

When a relationship is threatened, instead of running away or desperately trying to rebuild the old, flawed foundation, it is more constructive to treat what is happening as crucial feedback that the old ways of relating are bankrupt, and radical change—on the part of both members of the couple—is necessary. Otherwise the relationship probably isn't going to survive.

Lois and Tim, the fifty-something couple that prematurely decided "It's over," had slowly grown apart over the years because they each focused more on work and parenting than on each other, and took their relationship for granted. They had gone through all of the stages that most couples experience under duress—fantasies of leaving, blaming each other, and nostalgia for the past—before we began working together in psychotherapy. At first, they slowly grew apart and began bickering with greater frequency. While they were sad and confused, neither of them said—or even thought—that their connection was eroding and their relationship was dying. They were each invested in denying that their relationship was falling apart, because of fear and a need for financial and emotional security. When they sensed that they had grown estranged, they desperately tried to re-create parts of their old relationship—rekindling their sexual life; taking long, meandering walks; antiquing; trying new ethnic restaurants—to regain their former spark.

But negative patterns persisted—Lois neglected herself to take care of Tim, while Tim focused on his job more than on their relationship—and none of these temporary efforts stemmed the growing alienation they felt from and toward each other. They both secretly hated themselves—each one thinking he or she was the sole cause of the problem. This in turn led to feelings of guilt, which were intolerable, and they both reacted by insisting that all of the problems must instead be the fault of the other person.

Transformation beckoned from another direction—their problems were feedback that old patterns of relating were not effective and needed to change, or the relationship would die.

I encouraged Lois and Tim to work on four levels:

- Self-care
- Pulling weeds
- Accessing shared meaning
- Dreaming together about a better future

We started with *genuine self-care,* rather than the cotton-candy variety that they had used for years—watching too much TV and spending more time on their PDAs than talking to each other. Lois also began to rein in her out-of-control spending and curtail her time on the phone with female friends when Tim was home—admitting that it was a way of "punishing" him, as well as connecting with people she cared about. Tim put away his gadgets, was more attentive to Lois, helped around the house—instead of viewing it as "her job," which he admitted was his way of seeking revenge on her for ignoring him at home—and stopped escaping for whole weekends at a time on golf junkets and bike rides.

We then began pulling the weeds that were leaching life from their relationship. First we focused on teaching Tim to recognize when he was distancing himself from Lois. He needed to understand what purpose it served and that he was not being smothered by his mother and would not lose himself when he was close to his wife. He also had to uncover what precipitated these feelings. Once he realized that when he had an agonizing day at work he just wanted to isolate, he was able to loosen his boundaries so he was more emotionally available to Lois. When he experimented with this on several occasions, he realized that instead of tiring him further, being connected to Lois made him feel better.

Lois had to develop a stronger sense of what she wanted and needed as well as the self-trust to advocate for herself when she and Tim collided. By protecting what she valued, she was less resentful of her husband. They forged better boundaries, detected imbalances in power, enriched their sexual union, and built space to house the hate that periodically arose. I encouraged them to reconnect with what brought them together and what they now shared and to dream together about the kind of future they wanted. In sessions and at home they focused on what drew them together and inspired them during their courtship: a passion for rock-and-roll, good literature, and social change.

Initially they had difficulty thinking about a life that wasn't filled with limitation and suffering. In truth, they were both disturbed by and addicted to the misery in which they felt enveloped. Because their own parents were so distant, they didn't know that anything else was really possible. But eventually they sensed that they could have a better relationship than their parents did, as they reconnected with long-buried personal passions for working with the elderly and helping at-risk teenagers. By following their inspirations and visions and living authentically, they enriched their relationship, which helped them flourish. They began talking about how to remake their own lives and their shared life in a way that reflected who they truly were. This included everything from what kind of work they did, to how they spent their leisure time, to where they lived and whom they socialized with. Over time, they were able to support each other in fulfilling lifelong dreams of creating a foundation for troubled adolescents and a community garden for the elderly. Something inspirational and unexpected occurred: their relationship became a place that cherished both of them and nourished their authenticity and autonomy while deepening their connectedness. Their relationship wasn't perfect—each had flaws and limitations that were obvious to the other—but it was "good enough" because it was emotionally satisfying, intellectually stimulating, able to accommodate their uniqueness, and fulfilling for each of them. They integrated friendship and love, emotional respect and physical passion. They each felt seen and valued and they trusted each other's integrity and reliability. When they confronted challenges, they kept their eyes on the big picture and worked together. Patience and humor were invaluable when they clashed or faced serious issues like the illness of a parent and potential job loss.

"We were at the precipice," Tim said.

"And now our relationship is like a flower garden that is thriving and blooming," added Lois, a gardener. "A riot of colors and scents that complement each other and make me smile whenever I see it . . . A rose garden with some thorns."

Epilogue:

Toward Flourishing

The phrase "Love is everything" came to mind as I sat down to write my concluding words. My thoughts immediately went in two directions:

- Love of others and ourselves is at the center of our lives—it is what makes us human
- Love contains the full range of emotions from ecstasy to agony.

When we are graced by love we feel immeasurably blessed, but when it is unrequited or falls apart we feel tormented and bereft. A wedding ring and a marriage ceremony don't offer genuine security or ensure an enduring union, as the epidemic of divorce illustrates. While each relationship is unique—and one-size-fits-all prescriptions don't really fit anyone—couples that flourish have several things in common: a willingness to search for and face the truth about themselves and their relationship; a reservoir of care and tenderness; and a commitment to take better care of themselves and their partners, which includes working on the obstacles to greater closeness.

Writing *The Art of Flourishing* has been a joyous journey of discovery. Chief among the many lessons I have learned is that self-care is the foundation of intimacy, and intimacy is the final stage and culmination of self-care. The actions of nurturing ourselves and deepening our connection with someone we cherish may seem at odds, but taking care of ourselves doesn't detract from devotion to others—they are actually two sides of the same coin. When we truly nourish ourselves we not only transform our lives, we create the cornerstone for intimacy.

A loving, intimate relationship is a work in progress that demands continual care and tending. I have given you as clear a map as I can of what that looks like and how to do it. Now you need to practice two steps: nurturing self-care and cultivating intimacy. The first involves building into your life what helps you flourish, from expanding inner space and appreciating beauty, to composting challenging feelings and harmonizing mind and body, to embodying your highest ideals and living authentically.

The second step is to nourish intimacy. Love is an environment that two people tend and sustain, or neglect and erode. We cultivate it by planting seeds of self-care and friendship, empathy and compassion. Trust and closeness grow immeasurably from the soil of empathic listening. Then we pull the weeds that arise, such as self-neglect, trying to win, and the expectation of mind reading. Next we compost the challenges that stand in our way including simmering resentments, poor boundaries, and abuse of power. Later we fertilize what we have sowed, from empathy and deepened understanding, to healthy boundaries and reinvigorated passion. Then we harvest what has grown, including expanded horizons and appreciation, which creates a garden of love.

A good union is transformative. Not only does it provide meaning and fulfillment, it challenges old and familiar ways of thinking and acting, expands how we feel about ourselves, and makes us significantly richer than if we were alone. A magnificent relationship widens our horizons of possibility and deepens our humanity.

But a great relationship is not simply the happy possession of a fortunate couple; it is a window into human beings at their best, offering hope and inspiration to other people, which is a priceless gift to the world.

Acknowledgments

Conversations over the years with friends, family, and colleagues helped me clarify and deepen my understanding of flourishing. Special thanks to Diana Alstad, George Atwood, Christine Bailey, Chip Brown, Erika and Jesse Cacsire, Aimee Dean, Kausthub and T. K. V. Desikachar, Doris Dlugacz, Marianne Horney Eckardt, Bettina Edelstein, Ben Holtzman, Carl Horowitz, Suzanne Ironbiter, Don Kalsched, David Kastan, Loch Kelly, Jesse Kornbluth, Joel Kramer, Sandi Mendelson, John Moody, Lou Mitsunen Nordstrom, Alice Peck, Johanna Pfenniger, Frank Richardson, Karl Roman, Elena Rover, Joyce and Harris Rubin, Bill Scott, Peter Shabad, Annalisa Traina, Mary Traina, Ann Ulanov, Dolphi Wertenbaker, Gail White, and Shinzen Young.

Discussions with George Atwood, Ben Holtzman, Joel Kramer, Lou Mitsunen Nordstrom, Alice Peck, Mary Traina, Dolphi Wertenbaker, and Shinzen Young were invaluable in formulating many of the central ideas and practices in this book.

Carl Horowitz, Alice Peck, Mary Traina, and Dolphi Wertenbaker generously and thoughtfully read the whole manuscript and offered invaluable feedback. The book has greater depth and is more accessible because of their insights and recommendations.

I owe a huge debt of gratitude to my patients for allowing me to accompany them in their journeys. This book and my life have been deeply enriched by our mutual efforts to understand the depths of their dreams and fears, potentials and conflicts.

The Random House team has been a joy to work with at every stage of the process. They demonstrated an exemplary level of engagement and flexibility, professionalism and talent. I want to thank Tina Constable, publisher of Crown Archetype, for her vision and stewardship of this project. Vanessa Mobley did a great job of editing the book, skillfully aiding me in articulating my vision. Jenna Ciongoli handled myriad tasks essential to the publication of *The Art of Flourishing* with impressive efficiency and good cheer. Faren Bachelis copyedited with a deft touch. Jean Traina created a beautiful and inspirational cover. Barbara Sturman fashioned an inviting interior design, Rachel Rokicki skillfully publicized the book, and Jen Robbins adeptly marketed it.

Institutions as well as individuals have been essential to the genesis and completion of this book, providing an opportunity to share and refine various concepts and practices. I am deeply grateful to the Esalen Institute, JCC of New York, the Ethical Culture Societies of Essex County and Northern Westchester, the Longboat Key Educational Center, New York Insight, The Open Center, Wainwright House, and Yoga Sutra for providing a forum for the presentation of my work.

I am deeply grateful to Flip Brophy for her faith in me and this book and her unflinching candor and support. Diane Salvatore's initial interest and belief in this project and vision of how to execute it were of inestimable importance in *The Art of Flourishing* seeing the light of day.

I owe a special debt of gratitude to Alice Peck, lover of all things literary and spiritual, who was a gifted midwife to the birth of this book.

The friendship and support of Mary were indispensable in the completion of this book. Sine qua non, again.

Notes

INTRODUCTION

p. 2 "living well and faring well": Aristotle, *Nicomachean Ethics,* trans. David Ross (New York: Oxford University Press, 1980), p. 5.

While the focus of this book and the title were inspired by Aristotle, my conception of flourishing differs from his in one crucial way. Aristotle assumed that humans at their best were self-contained and self-sufficient, as well as rational and virtuous. While he recognized the importance of friendship in the well-lived life, his conception of flourishing neglected the reality and power of human emotional and physical vulnerability and affliction and our consequent dependence on other people for protection and nurturance, validation and sustenance. This caused him to neglect emotional intimacy and love as crucial aspects of a well-lived life, as Alasdair MacIntyre suggests in *Dependent Rational Animals: Why Human Beings Need the Virtues* (Chicago: Open Court, 1999), pp. 1–9.

CHAPTER 1: EXPANDING INNER SPACE

p. 31 "timeless time": Joel Kramer and Diana Alstad, *The Passionate Mind Revisited: Expanding Personal and Social Awareness* (Berkeley, CA: North Atlantic Books, 2009), p. 201.

p. 32 "Clocks slay time": William Faulkner, *The Sound and the Fury* (New York: Random House, 1946), p. 105.

CHAPTER 2: THEY CAN'T STEAL THE MOON

p. 34 "hungry for beauty": John O'Donohue, *Beauty: The Invisible Embrace* (New York: HarperCollins, 2004), p. 2.

p. 35 "I return to thinking": Iris Murdoch, *The Sovereignty of Good* (New York: Schocken Books, 1971), p. 84.

p. 35 "We become absorbed": Hans Loewald, *Psychoanalysis and the History of the Individual* (New Haven: Yale University Press, 1978), p. 67.

p. 36 "architecture of the Parthenon": Crispin Sartwell, *Six Names of Beauty* (New York: Routledge, 2004), p. xiii.

p. 37 "healthy-minded" and "sick souled": William James, *The Varieties of Religious Experience* (New York: Longmans, Green and Company, 1902/1928), pp. 78–165.

p. 38 "pleasure far beyond what they give": R. M. Burke, in James, *Varieties,* p. 84.

p. 38 admirable deeds and moral beauty: My perspective on this topic was enriched by Peterson and Seligman's examination of appreciation. See Christopher Peterson and Martin Seligman, "Appreciation of Beauty and Excellence," in *Character Strengths and Virtues: A Handbook and Classification* (New York: Oxford University Press, 2004), pp. 537–51.

p. 38 "fated to extinction": Sigmund Freud, "On Transience," S.E.: 14: 303–7 (London: Hogarth Press, 1915), p. 303.

p. 39 he can't steal the moon: Raul Reps and Nyogen Senzaki, *Zen Flesh, Zen Bones: A Collection of Zen and Pre-Zen Writings* (Garden City, New York: Doubleday and Company, 1957), p. 12.

p. 39 "I ask not for the great": Quoted in Michael Kimmelman, *The Accidental Masterpiece: On the Art of Life and Vice Versa* (New York: Penguin Press, 2005), p. 212.

p. 40 "Boredom is lack of attention": Joseph Goldstein, *Insight Meditation: The Practice of Freedom* (Boston: Shambhala, 2003), p. 80.

CHAPTER 3: WHAT BRUCE LEE AND CARL JUNG CAN TEACH US ABOUT TRAINING FOR INTIMACY

p. 43 leads to improved mood: See Carlyle Folkins and Wesley Simes' "Physical Fitness Training and Mental Health," *American Psychologist* 36, no. 4 (April 1981): 373–89.

p. 45 "The relationship I had": Ram Dass, *Still Here* (New York: Riverhead Trade, 2001), p. 57.

p. 45 "That helped me avoid": ibid., pp. 187–88.

p. 45 "I also *am* my body": ibid., p. 188.

p. 45 "So then came the stroke": ibid., p. 186.

p. 49 "Artists are the antennae": Ezra Pound, *Literary Essays of Ezra Pound* (New York: New Directions Books, 1968). p. 297.

p. 56 "one man's food": Georg Feuerstein, *The Shambhala Guide to Yoga* (Boston: Shambhala, 1996), p. 66.

p. 56 health of the planet: Nina Planck's' *Real Food,* Michael Pollan's *In Defense of Food and Food Rules,* and Mark Bittmans's *Food Matters* provide constructive and concrete direction if you would like to read further on the subject.

p. 59 "Neurosis is self-division": C. G. Jung, "On the Psychology of the Unconscious," CW 7: *Two Essays on Analytical Psychology* (Princeton, NJ: Princeton University Press, 1917), p. 20.

p. 60 "recurrent, rhythmic wave": Tony Schwartz, *What Really Matters: Searching for Wisdom in America* (New York: Bantam, 1995), p. 231.

p. 63 "vinyāsa krama": T. K. V. Desikachar, *The Heart of Yoga: Developing A Personal Practice* (Rochester, VT: Inner Traditions International, 1995), p. 25.

p. 66 healing potential: See Henry Dreher's summary of this research in *The Immune Power Personality* (New York: Plume Books, 1995), p. 297.

p. 66 nurtures a strong body: Dreher provides a clear overview of this in *The Immune Power Personality*.

CHAPTER 4: BRINGING SPIRITUALITY DOWN TO EARTH

p. 70 Natural wakefulness is like a channel: My conception of this aspect of spirituality was deeply shaped by the psychotherapist and spiritual teacher Loch Kelly.

p. 70 "in my early thirties": Jane Kenyon, "Having It Out with Melancholy," in *Otherwise: New and Selected Poems* (Minneapolis, MN: Graywolf Press, 1996), pp. 190–91.

p. 71 **"Your love for our family":** "School Shooter's Wife Thanks Amish Community," Associated Press, October 15, 2006.

p. 71 **Just as we are what:** In the *Nicomachean Ethics,* Aristotle emphasizes the importance of habit in building character.

p. 72 **The tragedy "fine-tunes":** Sue Bender, *Everyday Sacred* (New York: HarperCollins, 1995), pp. 120, 124.

p. 73 **"She is one of a small":** Vince Beiser, "The Ultimate Forgiveness: To Err Is Human, to Forgive Divine—to Befriend Someone Who Took the Life of a Loved One Is Another Matter, What Motivates People Whose Empathy Seems to Know No Bounds?" *Los Angeles Times,* April 4, 2004.

p. 76 **denying signs of groupthink:** Daniel Goleman illuminates groupthink in *Vital Lies, Simple Truths: The Psychology of Self-Deception* (New York: Simon & Schuster, 1985), pp. 180–183.

p. 77 **"unforgiving attitude":** Elizabeth Lesser, *The New American Spirituality* (New York: Random House, 1999), pp. 20–21.

p. 79 **"I'm just trying to help":** David Chadwick, *To Shine One Corner of the World* (New York: Random House, 2001), p. 109.

p. 80 **the "point is to live":** Rainer Maria Rilke, *Letters to a Young Poet* (New York: Norton, 1954), p. 35.

p. 80 **creating a "bigger container":** Zen teacher Charlotte Joko Beck and psychoanalyst Ann Ulanov both use this metaphor. See Charlotte Joko Beck, *Everyday Zen* (New York: HarperCollins, 1989), pp. 49–52; and Ann Ulanov, *Spiritual Aspects of Clinical Work* (Canada: Daimon, 2004), p. 98.

p. 81 **"In the prison":** W. H. Auden, *Collected Shorter Poems* (New York: Random House, 1975), p. 143.

p. 81 **"Every day is a good day":** Katsuki Sekida, *Two Zen Classics: The Gateless Gate and The Blue Cliff Record* (Boston: Shambhala, 2005), p. 161.

p. 82 **if we don't share:** My formulation is indebted to Dolphi Wertenbaker's discussion of T. K. V. Desikachar's oral presentations on verse 3:12 of the *Bhagavad Gita:* "Only a thief would receive a gift and not try to share" (personal communication, 6/29/10).

CHAPTER 5: EMOTIONAL FLOURISHING: CULTIVATING SELF-AWARENESS, EMPATHY, AND WISE ACTION

p. 86 **Deepening our circle of empathy:** In Daniel Goleman's illuminating work on "emotional intelligence" he stresses self-awareness, managing emotions, motivating oneself, and recognizing emotions in others. See *Emotional Intelligence* (New York: Bantam, 1995).

p. 87 **feelings as if they are opponents:** George Lakoff, *Women, Fire, and Dangerous Things: What Categories Reveal about the Mind* (Chicago: University of Chicago Press, 1987), pp. 380–97.

CHAPTER 7: DISCOVERING OUR PURPOSE

p. 127 **"If you bring forth":** Elaine Pagels, *Beyond Belief: The Secret Gospel of Thomas* (New York: Random House, 2004), p. 53.

p. 137 **There are two main types of meditation:** There are many types of meditation including Christian, Catholic, Jewish, Sufi, Taoist, Hindu, and Buddhist versions. I shall be focusing on Buddhist meditation. Daniel Goleman's *The Meditative Mind* offers a clear and comprehensive overview of the main kinds of meditation. See

Goleman (Los Angeles: Jeremy Tarcher, 1988). Shinzen Young's "Five Ways to Know Yourself as a Spiritual Being" (2007) gives a suggestive flavor of five types within the Buddhist tradition. Retrieved on shinzen.org.

CHAPTER 8: EMBODYING OUR VALUES: CLOSING THE ETHICAL GAP

p. 149 a virus of immorality: My approach to the corrosion of character focuses on personal responsibility. There is a growing literature on the cultural forces that corrode trustworthiness and caring, accountability and empathy—including capitalism. See, for example, Richard Sennett's *The Corrosion of Character: The Personal Consequences of Work in the New Capitalism* (New York: W. W. Norton, 1998), Stephen Carter's *Civility* (New York: Basic Books, 1998), James Q. Wilson's *The Moral Sense* (New York: The Free Press, 1993), and Eva Bertram and Kenneth Sharpe's "Capitalism, Work, and Character."

p. 153 The Dalai Lama was teaching in L.A.: Joseph Goldstein, "Desire, Delusion, and DVD's," in *Hooked: Buddhist Writings on Greed, Desire, and the Urge to Consume*, ed. Stephanie Kaza (Boston: Shambhala, 2005), p. 17.

p. 155 "great [or universal] compassion": Dalai Lama, *Ethics for a New Millennium* (New York: Riverhead Books, 1999), p. 124.

p. 155 Jung's great insight: C. G. Jung, "The Transcendent Function," in *Jung on Active Imagination*, ed. J. Chodorow (Princeton, NJ: Princeton University Press, 1997), pp. 42–60; The Tavistock Lectures, pp. 143–53.

p. 156 Walt Whitman pointed toward: Walt Whitman, *Leaves of Grass* (New York: The Modern Library, 1993), p. 36.

p. 156 "If I am not for myself": R. Travers Herford, ed., *The Ethics of the Talmud: Sayings of the Fathers* (New York: Schocken, 1945), p. 34.

p. 159 Accountability to each other: Matthew Crawford, *Shoptalk as Soul Craft* (New York: Penguin, 2009), pp. 200–201. This book was instrumental in my reflections on human solidarity and ethics.

CHAPTER 9: THE SYMPHONY OF THE SELF

p. 162 a symphony of self: Erich Fromm, "Memories of D. T. Suzuki," in M. Abe, ed., *A Zen Life: D.T. Suzuki Remembered* (New York: John Weatherhill, 1986), pp. 127–30.

p. 165 a true self: I discuss the limitations of the idea of, and the search for, the true self in my book *A Psychoanalysis for Our Time: Exploring the Blindness of the Seeing I* (New York: New York University Press, 1998), pp. 99–113.

p. 169 A divided self: C. G. Jung mentions the divided self in various places including *The Undiscovered Self* (New York: Mentor Books, 1957), pp. 73 and 80. I explore the divided self from a different direction—the "good" and "bad" self. This formulation is heavily indebted to Joel Kramer and Diana Alstad's perspective in *The Guru Papers: Masks of Authoritarian Power* (Berkeley, CA: North Atlantic Books, 1993).

p. 170 We can become whole: Jung writes of the "undivided self" in "Marriage as a Psychological Relation," in V. Staub De Laszlo, ed., *The Basic Writings of C. G. Jung* (New York: The Modern Library, 1959), p. 539.

p. 175 the "virtuous circle" of discipline: Bill Bradley, *Values of the Game* (New York: Broadway Books, 2000), 24.

p. 178 a traditional Indian meditation: I learned this meditation from my yoga teacher, Dolphi Wertenbaker, who learned it from her teacher, T. K. V. Desikachar.

CHAPTER 10: A LIFE OF ONE'S OWN: AUTHENTICITY IN A WORLD OF SPAM

p. 186 **"tyranny of the shoulds":** Karen Horney, *Neurosis and Human Growth* (New York: Norton, 1950), pp. 64–85.

p. 187 **neurotic *solution*:** ibid., pp. 185–86.

p. 187 **"practice of self-cure":** Masud Khan, *The Privacy of Self* (New York: International Universities Press, 1974), p. 97.

p. 187 **arrested, damaged babies:** Stephen Mitchell, *Relational Concepts in Psychoanalysis* (Cambridge, MA: Harvard University Press, 1988), pp. 127–51.

p. 189 **Jiddu Krishnamurti:** "Truth Is a Pathless Land," talk on August 3, 1929, in Omnen, Holland.

p. 190 **"Someone once asked . . . Sasaki Roshi":** Joseph Goldstein, *A Heart Full of Peace* (Somerville, MA: Wisdom Publications, 2007), p. 91.

p. 190 **"focused lens of a microscope":** ibid., p. 93.

p. 191 **"option of *choosing wisely*":** ibid.

p. 193 **No one has the right:** Discussions with psychoanalyst Peter Shabad were instrumental in this formulation.

p. 193 **unconscious, self-centered bias:** I am indebted to Charles Guignon'a critical reflections on authenticity for this way of thinking about it. Charles Guignon, *On Being Authentic* (New York: Routledge, 2004).

p. 193 **"no such thing as an infant":** D. W. Winnicott, "The Theory of the Parent-Infant Relationship," in *The Maturational Processes and the Facilitating Environment: Studies in the Theory of Emotional Development* (New York: International Universities Press, 1960/1965), p. 39.

p. 193 **"i am through you so i":** e. e. cummings, "i am so glad and very," in *Complete Poems (1913–1962)* (New York: Harcourt Brace Jovanovich, 1972), p. 537.

p. 194 **"Men can starve":** Richard Wright, *Native Son* (New York: Harper and Brothers, 1940), p. 335.

CHAPTER 11: THE GARDEN OF LOVE

p. 198 **"Americans are asked":** Judith Wallerstein and Sandra Blakeslee, *The Good Marriage: How and Why Love Lasts* (New York: Warner Books, 1995), p. 5.

p. 198 **"Then you live in the everyday again": Willard Gaylin and Ethel Person, eds.,** *Passionate Attachments: Thinking about Love* **(New York: The Free Press, 1988), pp. 5–6.**

p. 199 **"Love is patient":** 1 Cor. 13:4–12.

p. 200 **What appears as love:** See, for example, Sigmund Freud, "On the Universal Tendency to Debasement in the Sphere of Love," S.E.: 11: 177–90 (London: Hogarth Press, 1957), and "Observations on Transference-Love," S.E.: 12: 157–73 (London: Hogarth Press, 1958); Sheldon Bach, *The Language of Perversion and the Language of Love* (Northvale, NJ: Jason Aronson, 1994); Jessica Benjamin, *The Bonds of Love: Psychoanalysis, Feminism, and the Problem of Domination* (New York: Pantheon Books, 1988), and *Like Subjects, Love Objects* (New Haven: Yale University Press, 1995); R. D. Fairbairn, "The Repression and the Return of Bad Objects (with special reference to the 'War Neuroses')," in *Psychoanalytic Studies of the Personality* (London: Routledge & Kegan Paul, 1943), pp. 59–81; Glen Gabbard, *Love and Hate in the Analytic Setting* (Northvale, NJ: Jason Aronson, 1996); Willard Gaylin and Ethel Person, eds., *Passionate Attachments: Thinking about Love* (New York: The Free Press, 1998); Otto Kernberg, "Between Conventionality and Aggression," in Gaylin and Person, *Passionate Attachments,* pp. 63–83, and *Love Relations: Normality and Pathology* (New Haven, CT: Yale University Press, 1995); and Stephen Mitchell, *Can Love Last? The Fate of Romance over Time* (New York: W. W. Norton and Company, 2002), and "Psychoanalysis and the Degradation of Romance," in *Psychoanalytic Dialogues, 1997,* 7, no. 1: pp. 23–41.

p. 201 **grandeur as well as by misery:** B. Pascal, *Pensées* (New York: Dutton, 1958), p. 110.

p. 201 **greatness as well as wretchedness:** Pascal, *Pensées,* p. 107.

p. 202 **"Love" is "said to be a child":** William Shakespeare, *A Midsummer Night's Dream* (London: Methuen & Co, 1595/1979), 1.1.239–40.

p. 203 **Is he honest and loyal:** See Blaine Fower's *Virtue and Psychology: Pursuing Excellences in Ordinary Practices* (Washington, D.C.: American Psychological Association, 2005), p. 4.

p. 204 **"But Love has pitched his mansion":** W. B Yeats, "Crazy Jane Talks with the Bishop," in *The Variorum Edition of the Poems of W. B. Yeats* (New York: The Macmillan Company, 1971), p. 513.

p. 204 **"an inevitable aspect of life":** Judith Wallerstein and Sandra Blakeslee, *The Good Marriage: How and Why Love Lasts* (New York: Warner Books, 1995), p. 329.

p. 206 **"My marriage was good":** Elizabeth Weil, "A More Perfect Union," *The New York Times Magazine,* December 6, 2009, p. 38.

p. 213 **people in the past:** Lawrence Stone, "Passionate Attachments in the West in Historical Perspective," in *Passionate Attachments: Thinking about Love,* W. Gaylin and E. Person, eds. (New York: The Free Press, 1988), p. 17.

p. 213 **"Public admiration for marriage-for-love":** Stone, p. 18.

p. 213 **"the main reason for marriage":** Stephanie Coontz, *Marriage, a History: How Love Conquered Marriage* (New York: Penguin, 2005), pp. 307–8.

p. 214 **"romantic space" in a relationship:** Wilkinson and Gabbard, "On Romantic Space," in *Psychoanalytic Psychology* 12, no. 2 (1995), pp. 201–19.

p. 214 **"a feeling of being in love":** Wilkinson and Gabbard, "On Romantic Space," p. 210.

p. 214 **conducive to imagination and creativity:** The following works contributed to my conception of potential space: D. W. Winnicott, *Playing and Reality* (London: Tavistock, 1971); Thomas Ogden, *The Matrix of Mind* (Northvale, NJ: Jason Aronson, 1986); Adam Phillips, *Winnicott* (Cambridge, MA: Harvard University Press, 1988); Christopher Bollas, *Being a Character* (New York: Hill & Wang, 1992); and Sheldon Bach, *The Language of Perversion and the Language of Love* (Northvale, NJ: Jason Aronson, 1994).

p. 215 **capacity to handle conflict:** Christine Bailey, personal communication, December 29, 2009.

p. 216 **a *philia* sort of love:** Aristotle, *Nicomachean Ethics.*

p. 218 **Experimenting with "disloyalty":** D. W. Winnicott, *Home Is Where We Start From: Essays by a Psychoanalyst* (New York: W. W. Norton and Company, 1986), p. 138.

p. 219 **Love is never a "final presence":** Ann and Barry Ulanov, *Transforming Sexuality: The Archetypal World of Anima and Animus* (Boston: Shambhala, 1994), p. 89.

p. 219 **"always being reshaped":** Judith Wallerstein and Sandra Blakeslee, *The Good Marriage: How and Why Love Lasts* (New York : Warner Books, 1995), p. 331.

p. 221 **"to create a religion that has a fallible":** Jorge Luis Borges, "The Meeting in a Dream," in *Other Inquisitions (1937–1952)* (Austin, TX: University of Texas Press, 1952), p. 99.

CHAPTER 12: NO WINNERS, NO LOSERS: EXPANDING INTERPERSONAL SPACE

p. 227 **empathized with his patient:** I do not practice client-centered therapy because I have discovered over the years that it may neglect hidden obstacles such as the client's incomplete knowledge of those forces from the past that sabotage his or her efforts to flourish in the present. Nonetheless, empathy is an incredibly powerful aspect of therapy and change.

CHAPTER 13: COMPOSTING INTERPERSONAL CONFLICT

p. 241 "I can observe when you hurt me": Jeanne Malmgren Cameron, "Mind in Asana: An Interview with Joel Kramer," *Yoga Journal* (July/August, 1986), p.2.

p. 244 "Sarcasm and cynicism": John Gottman and Nan Silver, *The Seven Principles for Making Marriage Work* (New York: Three Rivers Press, 1999), p. 29.

CHAPTER 16: THE YOGA OF SEXUALITY: REINVIGORATING PASSION

p. 270 "too busy, too stressed": Esther Perel, *Mating in Captivity* (New York: Harper-Collins, 2006), p. xiii.

p. 273 "alertness without tension": T. K. V. Desikachar, *Reflections on the Yoga Sutras* (Chennai, India: Quadra Press, 1987), p. 71.

p. 275 "Change base lust": John Stevens, *Lust for Enlightenment: Buddhism and Sex* (Boston: Shambhala, 1990), p. 101.

p. 276 hunt-and-chase game: "Transforming Sexuality: Changing the Context of Conquest: A Dialogue Between Joel Kramer and Diana Alstad," *New Age* (1978).

CHAPTER 17: AFTER THE BLISS, THE DISHES (AND ONLY I KNOW HOW TO LOAD THEM): NEGOTIATING POWER AND CONTROL

p. 278 "the morning after": James Ogilvy, *Living Without a Goal* (New York: Doubleday, 1995), p. 113. Jack Kornfield pinpoints the same truth when he reminds us that after the ecstasy of spiritual realization there is the laundry. See *After the Ecstasy, the Laundry* (New York: Bantam, 2000).

p. 278 "homicidal bitchin'": Leonard Cohen, "Democracy."

p. 279 "When one speaks of power": Michel Foucault, *Ethics, Subjectivity, and Truth: Essential Works of Foucault,* vol. 1, ed. Paul Rabinow (New York: The New Press, 1997), p. 291.

p. 281 "principle of perfect equality": John Stuart Mill, *The Subjection of Women* (Pennsylvania State University, Electronic Classics Series, 1869 [2006]), www .hn.psu.edu/faculty/jmanis/jsmill.htm.

p. 286 might tend to measure: Joel Kramer and Diana Alstad alerted me to this unconscious dynamic in human relationships.

p. 287 his own fullest humanity: Georg Hegel, *Phenomenology of Spirit* (Oxford: Clarendon Press, 1977), p. 111.

CHAPTER 19: SCORCHED-EARTH MOMENTS: SURVIVING HATEFUL FEELINGS

p. 300 "no love without hate": Judith S. Wallerstein and Sandra Blakeslee, *The Good Marriage* (New York: Houghton Mifflin, 1995), p. 187.

p. 300 "If way to the Better there be": Thomas Hardy, "In Tenebris – II." Accessed on The Poet's Corner//theotherpages.org/poems/hardy01.html.

p. 300 "good marriage is conflict-free": Wallerstein and Blakeslee, *The Good Marriage,* p. 143.

p. 301 "create a safe haven": ibid., p. 28.

p. 301 "Pain sure brings out": Bob Dylan, "She's Your Lover Now," *Basement Tapes.*

p. 302 "earliest function of rage": Otto Kernberg, *Aggressivity, Narcissism, and Self-Destructiveness in the Psychotherapeutic Relationship* (New Haven: Yale University Press, 2004), p. 32.

p. 303 Hate can also be triggered: Heinz Kohut, "Forms and Transformations of

Narcissism," in *The Search for the Self: Selected Writings of Heinz Kohut: 1950–1978*, ed. Paul Ornstein (New York: International Universities Press, 1971).

p. 303 **"identification with the aggressor"**: While this concept is usually associated with Anna Freud's 1936 *The Ego and the Mechanisms of Defense*, it was actually developed earlier by Sandor Ferenczi in *The Clinical Diaries of Sandor Ferenczi*, ed. Judith Dupont (Cambridge, MA: Harvard University Press, 1988).

p. 303 **Severe cases of hate**: Kohut, "Forms and Transformations," p. 657.

p. 304 **"all close relationships"**: Wallerstein and Blakeslee, *The Good Marriage*, p. 332.

p. 304 **doesn't have to be a deal-breaker**: John Gottman and Nan Silver, *The Seven Principles for Making Marriage Work* (New York: Three Rivers Press, 1999), pp. 26–34.

p. 305 **establish a "safety zone"**: Wallerstein and Blakeslee, *The Good Marriage*, p. 145.

p. 305 **a "Hate Club"**: I am indebted to Ann Ulanov, an eminent Jungian analyst and author, for the idea of creatively and protectively making space in a relationship for hate and other unsettling emotions.

CHAPTER 20: WHEN IT'S NOT REALLY OVER: RECOGNIZING THE GREEN SHOOTS IN A WITHERED GARDEN

p. 308 **"They never saw"**: Pablo Neruda, "The People," in *Fully Empowered*, trans. Alastair Reid (New York: Farrar, Straus & Giroux, 1975), p. 125.

p. 308 **"marriage has steadily become"**: Stephanie Coontz, *Marriage, A History: How Love Conquered Marriage* (New York: Penguin Books, 2005), p. 301.

p. 309 **John Gottman's research**: John Gottman and Nan Silver, *The Seven Principles for Making Marriage Work* (New York: Three Rivers Press, 1999), pp. 26–46.

p. 310 **"one partner withdraws"**: Gottman and Silver, *The Seven Principles*, p. 40.

p. 312 **a self-protective strategy**: Peter Shabad, *Despair and the Return of Hope* (Northvale, NJ: Jason Aronson, 2001), p. 70. The psychoanalyst Peter Shabad speaks here of "bracing for disappointment."

INDEX

About the Author

Jeffrey B. Rubin, PhD, is the creator of meditative psycho-therapy, a practice that he developed through insights gained from decades of study, teaching, and helping thousands of people flourish. The author of the critically acclaimed books *Psychotherapy and Buddhism, The Good Life,* and *A Psychoanalysis for Our Time,* Dr. Rubin is a practicing psychotherapist in New York and Bedford Hills, and has taught at various universities, psychoanalytic institutes, and Buddhist and yogic centers. He lectures around the country and has given workshops at the United Nations, the Esalen Institute, the Open Center, Yoga Sutra, and the 92nd Street Y. His pioneering approach to Buddhism and psychotherapy was recently featured in *The New York Times Magazine.*